UFO
REVELATION

UFO
REVELATION

The Secret Technology Exposed?

Tim Matthews

BLANDFORD

Acknowledgements

This book would not have been possible without the help of the following: my wife Lynda, Andy Roberts, David Windle, Gloria Dixon (BUFORA), John Locker, Eric Morris (BUFOSC), Chris Gibson, Philip Mantle, Jenny Randles, Brenda and Heather Wilkinson, Tony Gonsalves, James Diss, Kevin McClure, Dave Newton, Sandra Grundy, and all my other sources who wish to remain nameless. A special thanks to Bill Rose for his help and for allowing me to use rare photographs and images from his collection.

Thanks also to the witnesses – without you nothing would be possible!

Special thanks to US researchers Dan Zinngrabe, Steve Douglass and all the other stealthchasers out there.

TM

A BLANDFORD BOOK

First published in the UK 1999 by Blandford
A Cassell imprint

Cassell plc
Wellington House, 125 Strand, London WC2R 0BB
www.cassell.co.uk

Text copyright © 1999 Tim Matthews

The right of Tim Matthews to be identified as author of this work has been asserted by him in accordance with the provisions of the UK Copyright, Designs and Patents Act 1988.

Distributed in the United States by Sterling Publishing Co., Inc., 387 Park Avenue South, New York, NY 10016-8810

A Cataloguing-in-Publication Data entry for this title is available from the British Library

ISBN 0-7137-2733-0

Designed by Richard Carr
Edited by Pat Pierce
Printed and bound in Great Britain by Creative Print and Design Wales, Ebbw Vale

CONTENTS

FOREWORD

Unidentified *Lying* Objects

I WAS A TEENAGER when I first discovered the wonders of the UFO mystery. At that time the world was agog with the space race. Mankind was landing on another planet for the first time. It was all terribly exciting.

It was equally obvious to me what was going on. Although we had yet to be saturated by endless TV channels obsessed with the lure of alien conspiracies, the newspaper headlines screamed out loud, and all the books in the shops sang in one voice: UFOs were extraterrestrial spacecraft. All that mattered was proving this fact, echoing David Vincent in the then-popular TV series *The Invaders,* and demanding that the truth be told by our obsessively secret government.

To a Ufologist, the fact that the powers-that-be sometimes lied was beyond question. Indeed, in many places, little seems to have changed in 30 years. For today's popular tabloids, and the buzz about what is the second most popular subject on the Internet (sex is first), repeat all the inept nonsense.

The sad truth is that most of the UFO debate is like a central heating system. It circulates the same hot air round and round to keep couch potatoes happy as they doze in front of a TV. All stations are filled with popular programming about little grey men riding starships. It is soporific rot. Or, to put it another way, it is self-delusion like the myth of Santa Claus, invented to keep wide-eyed, unquestioning children happy.

Only when you dare to go out there in the field and investigate real cases, seeking answers, not mysteries, and letting the facts dictate the solution, does the fundamental realization hit you like a brick. It is not, in the main, the governments that lie to protect secrets about UFOs. The conspiracy is not some covert agency out to secrete crashed spaceships and pickled alien bodies. The real cover-up starts – and ends – much closer to home, with the UFO buffs. Too many fail to see the obvious and run from the truth because the answers that are revealed are less palatable than the ones they yearn to find. Ufologists conspire among themselves, both consciously and unconsciously, and willingly aided and abetted by a media that seems unable to treat these issues with the sobriety and objectivity they deserve.

There are not just UFOs out there but also ULOs – ULOs being Unidentified *Lying* Objects. These things deceive witnesses, and incite many who should know better than to deceive themselves.

It took me a long time to learn the home truths about the UFO world and even longer to appreciate just how few people actually want to hear them. I well recall an investigation mounted by the local group in Manchester, with whom I have worked for many years. It taught me much.

We had been getting reports of a strange orange object that was drifting silently through the air above the Rossendale Valley in Lancashire. Such was the excitement of these noctural encounters that the press dubbed the area 'UFO Alley'. It was tempting for me to jump to conclusions. I had been born in this mill-strewn valley, and grew up in the small hill village of Stacksteads, where some of these encounters were now happening. As a UFO writer I felt that it was almost as if 'they' were homing in on me.

Thankfully, our local team were a sensible bunch. We had a highly restricted membership, did not stage conferences and skywatches, but just set out to investigate sightings and tried to find the answer. We knew that more than nine out of ten UFO reports were resolved if you put enough effort into that task. We understood that potentially 100 per cent of them might be resolved one day. There was no desire to prove the impossible, just to learn what was really going on.

Of the Rossendale sightings, the clues were very evident. Undeniably, there was something there, because too many witnesses were seeing it on a regular basis. This included farmers tending flocks in the dead of night, and police patrols. This thing was described consistently.

It would have been simple to take the sightings at face value, put two and two together and make an alien starship. Then, of course, we could cash in on the hype and join in demands that the Ministry of Defence come clean and admit that ET had landed. But Ufology is not about wish fulfilment. It is about figuring out the options, eliminating one by one the possible answers and eventually deciding what has to be the truth. If that is an alien visitation – fine – our team were willing to embrace the prospect, but we had long since grown out of anticipation for that momentous discovery. We knew that the chances were very high that the answer would be from the earth, not off it.

So it proved to be. It took months of hard work – interviewing witnesses, checking with airports, weather centres, police records and so on. Once the pattern behind the reports fell into place, a possibility emerged as to what was happening. We set about trying to establish if this was the case. The behaviour of these sightings gave every indication that some kind of aircraft activity was involved. We also knew that the UFOs were appearing regularly, at around 2 am, heading in roughly the same direction and seeming to fly like aircraft. Yet they had no flashing navigation lights and (with minor exceptions) no engine noise either. How could they be aircraft?

There was only one way to unravel this confusion. Our cautious approach, and proof of our intent in past cases to find the truth (however mundane), gave us the edge. We persuaded sources that would normally not risk their credibility by dealing with a UFO group to help us try to crack this case. And crack it we did.

We set a trap — locating members of our team discreetly at different points along the flight path of the UFO in the middle of a selected night that research decreed fitted the pattern. These observers were well equipped to record what they saw.

The UFO returned, swooping through the air like a red ghost, then climbing slightly, to head off southwards with just the faintest hint of an engine. Back at a local airport's radar centre was a skilled group member, and the tracks of all air traffic across the North-West at the time were correlated with the sighting: we had our answer.

The UFO *was* an aircraft. It was on a commercial cargo flight. What was occurring, apparently, was that on fine winter's nights, the crew were enjoying their last few minutes as they descended towards Manchester Airport over an otherwise traffic-free region. So they switched off all the lights, throttled back the engine and virtually glided for a few miles over what seemed like barren, deserted Pennine hillsides. Once they got nearer to habitation, north of Bury, they throttled back and climbed a few hundred feet to resume their normal approach. The UFO being seen from below was simply the logo on the aircraft tail fin, illuminated by the one spotlight that had not been turned off.

All of this was quite illegal, of course, but — we were told — 'did happen'. This particular activity stopped after that night and so did the UFO sightings. Naturally, they returned soon enough, because many different things create UFO reports. We had won the battle, not the war.

Someone once calculated that over 250 different objects had been mistaken for a UFO at one time or another. So ridding the world, or at least Lancashire, of this spate of gliding cargo planes was but one footstep along the way.

I actually find this process of solving UFO mysteries to be the greatest fascination of the subject. To be sure, it is fun to speculate about alien invasions and creatures bent on genetic engineering, but there is only so much speculation you can do when faced with the significant lack of solid evidence to back you up. Of course, that is only a problem if you want it to be and most Ufologists do not.

One thing of which there is no shortage is the UFO sighting. They happen every day and hundreds are reported in Britain alone each year. Even if there is an intergalactic cavalry out there coming to our rescue (sadly, I doubt there is), then at the very most a tiny handful of the reported UFO cases are in any way evidence for that. The vast majority of UFO sightings have an explanation – sometimes simple and commonplace, now and then most intriguing and fascinating, and, once in a while, there is a real gem that requires skill and dedication to unravel. Once found, it may teach us something about the world around us.

Being a Ufologist is all about the variety of these encounters and the determination required. You are a detective out to solve the riddle of a seemingly intractable case. To find a logical answer is not – as many people think – a failure or even a minor irrelevance in the on-going quest to prove that the Martians have landed. It is a successful comple-tion of your job description, something offering true social lessons that people ought to heed when that answer points the finger in unexpected directions. Nor is it a disappointment, for there will always be another case, probably tomorrow, and who knows where that one will lead?

Unhappily, too few UFO enthusiasts seem to appreciate such matters. When the Manchester UFO Research Association (MUFORA, now NARO) endeavoured to tell the story of how we solved the Rossendale UFO sightings, the media were not interested. As it was put to me by one reporter: 'Mrs Jones sees a spaceship is news. We will happily print that – probably on page one. Mrs Jones sees an aircraft and thinks it's a spaceship. That's trivia. You'll be lucky to make page forty-one.'

I profoundly disagree. To me the reality of Ufology is the study of cases and the finding of answers. Many of those quests for truth are more fascinating than the repetitive twaddle churned out about aliens without an iota of evidence to back them up.

Not that you would ever know that there is another side to this UFO business, because it tends to be very effectively hidden from public view.

It is not being hidden any more. This book is long overdue and wonderfully welcome. Tim Matthews has cut through the clutter of nonsense that is so often the diet of UFO literature. Perhaps being a relative novice has helped, for he has not had so much baggage to sort through and discard. He has been able to see what is important, and point out far more likely explanations for some of the cases that the UFO world considers prime data.

I do not agree with all of the author's interpretations. For example, in the Belgian wave, I think it is important that just beforehand there were similar 'V-shaped UFOs the size of football fields' seen over eastern England. We traced them to a military exercise practising mid-air refuelling. The military were circumspect, as they so often are, not because these things were UFOs and they dare not say so, but because they had good reason to keep quiet about what they were doing. Long-range bombing missions to the Middle East were in prospect. Refuelling jet aircraft in mid-flight without landing is the quickest way to fly long distances, but it is difficult and dangerous and prohibited over populated areas.

Witnesses to these 'UFOs' in Staffordshire and Nottinghamshire did not want to know about what seemed to them to be dismissive answers. I was openly accused by angry callers on one radio programme of being a secret government agent because I was spouting this solution. They felt I was protecting the truth (which, I guess, they presumed was that they had seen ET). All I was doing was explaining where the evidence trail led – to me the most likely explanation.

Tim Matthews may face equally unjust condemnation. All I would ask is that you give this book a fair hearing and take it in the spirit with which it has been written. The author has done a magnificent job seeking evidence and marshalling a logical argument to make his main point. It deserves to be assessed free of the hysterical charges that there is some ulterior motive for such a worthy endeavour.

The only motive I see is the search for truth. You may not feel that truth is in this book, but I am sure you will applaud what is an excellent attempt to seek it out. You may suspect, as I do, that there is more to UFOs than the category of encounter skilfully dissected in this book, but the author seems well aware that he is telling only part of the story.

Personally, I do not need to be persuaded that some UFOs are the result of military technology. I doubt that anyone who has spent time chasing UFO reports can honestly say otherwise. But I was hugely impressed by Tim Matthews' cogent justification. In showing, as he has, why things are not as they seem behind so many UFO sightings, he has done a great service to legitimize an often misunderstood research field. Perhaps he will convince you, as he has convinced me, that the extent to which our own secret technology lies behind the cloak of UFO mystery is much greater than previously imagined.

I have no doubt that this is an important UFO book. It deserves to be read by far more people than most other titles that pepper the shelves. Ask yourself one simple question: am I interested in finding the truth about UFOs, or proof that aliens are visiting the earth? You will not find any spaceships among these pages. But if you are willing to be brave and true, then your answer should be that you seek the truth about UFOs, whatever it may be. In that case, you are in for an exciting time.

This book may be the one that you have been waiting for: the book that offers you a surprising revelation.

Jenny Randles
High Peak, Derbyshire

INTRODUCTION

25 January 1997 – 'A Day of Discovery' – UFO Conference, Southport, England

'Be careful Tim, the Americans won't take kindly to this kind of investigation.'

I'D JUST FINISHED giving a lecture to the Lancashire UFO Society, an organization I had helped to set up in 1995. The man who gave me the 'subtle warning' wasn't some pretender and it wasn't the first time that our paths had crossed. His business card said 'Military Aerospace Analyst' and I knew that he had worked in the aerospace industry for many years. I suspected that he had worked in 'black projects' – projects that utilize secret funds to develop secret technologies where those involved work on a compartmentalized or 'need to know' basis only.

Many people at the January conference had noticed that he and a couple of others took copious notes during my lecture. I had been talking about Britain's 'stealth' aircraft programme which involved test flights of unidentified triangular aircraft from a variety of locations including RAF Boscombe Down, Warton British Aerospace, DTEO (Defence Testing) West Freugh and HQ of the Fleet Air Arm at Yeovilton in the South-West.

I can hear some readers saying to themselves: 'We've heard this kind of thing before and it is frankly unbelievable. Where's the evidence?' I sympathize with this point of view. It is easy to pretend that you are more important than you really are in the world of UFO research or that you are being tracked by shadowy 'Men In Black'! The inevitable conclusion has to be, however, that UFO research is of the greatest interest to elements of the intelligence community and high-ranking personnel inside the military/industrial complex. The evidence is there for all to see: National Security Agency (NSA) personnel attending UFO conferences, and people from the aerospace industry ringing me up to bitterly denounce my work.

The first time I met the 'Aerospace Analyst' was at an event in Blackpool where I had been handing out a flyer about research into triangular UFOs. In the preceding months people had seen two different triangular UFOs operating along the Lancashire coast: a small 30- to 40-foot (9- to 12-m) unmanned aerial vehicle (UAV) and a much larger vehicle of approximately 100 feet (30 m) in length. A larger UFO had been filmed by a man in Morecambe earlier in the year. My leaflet mentioned these events and called for new witnesses to come forward. I had no idea that a couple of pieces of paper could cause such a storm.

That evening I received a phone call from the man. His brittle self-control was clear and he argued that no triangular UFOs existed because nobody had managed to take a photograph of one. He also took issue with one detail of my leaflet, but he did not take issue with the evidence that suggested that triangular UFOs were real, that they were neither 'visionary nor fictitious' and that they had been operating on occasions from the Special Projects Site at Warton in Lancashire. The caller admitted that he had knowledge of the site and had worked on a variety of projects there, 'but none involving triangles'.

I asked why he had attended the Blackpool UFO event in the first place, given his aggressive attitude. Had it been something to do with triangles perhaps? Oh no, just 'personal interest'. As if to disprove this, he went on to denounce the speakers at the event and the spurious nature of the evidence they presented. Although I agreed with him about some of the material presented (one of the speakers claimed to have possession of 'alien implants' removed from a variety of 'abductees'!), I still didn't understand why he had ruined his weekend by going to the event. Funnily enough, I remembered that he had made a beeline towards me as I was handing out my leaflets. Maybe he already knew who I was?

I got the impression that he had been relieved to discover that flying triangles were not high on the agenda whereas 'Conspiracies, Implants and Abductions' were. One speaker said that he didn't believe that triangles had ever flown from Warton (despite the fact that British Aerospace had previously admitted that they had!) and the 'CIA' paranoia of the event indicates just how far away from the cutting edge modern Ufology has actually moved in recent years; in fact the subject has become more like a New Age religion and not a movement for objective, detailed and cautious research.

Maybe the answer is right under our noses, and, to use an analogy, perhaps we cannot see the wood for the trees.

Reports of these triangular UFOs operating under escort by RAF Tornado aircraft, occasionally by military helicopters, have raised more than a few eyebrows. The information has been largely ignored by those who believe that UFOs are alien spacecraft and disbelieved by those who feel that it is operational suicide to fly these aircraft over the mainland. After all, 'they' would never do that, would 'they'?

Nevertheless, a covert agenda of secret test-flights of advanced prototype aircraft both in Britain and the United States has been established. It is the intention of this book to introduce the reader to some of the evidence relating to this agenda. *UFO Revelation* is also an attempt to explain how somebody who initially, perhaps unthinkingly, believed in stories of crash retrievals of alien spacecraft in the 1940s discovered a more shocking truth: that many UFOs are man-made and that the roots of modern UFO hysteria lie in the last days of the Second World War.

Tim Matthews
Southport

ONE

WARTIME GERMAN PROJECTS

T HE SEEDS OF this remarkable story were sown in the Germany of the 1930s. It was a crucial time in the development of military aircraft when the dream of flying beyond the speed of sound was becoming a reality. In fact, present-day military and stealth aircraft have their roots in the radical pioneering craft of Nazi Germany. The progeny of those early aircraft are vital to the truth behind the mystery of so-called 'UFOs'. Among the aircraft designers in Germany at the time, several were particularly outstanding.

Alexander Lippisch and Reimar and Walter Horten are not well-known names within the UFO research community, but they are of the greatest significance in our search for the origins of the modern-day 'flying triangle' or triangular UFO.

Alexander Lippisch

Lippisch (1893–1976) was a pioneering aircraft designer who was interested in tailless, delta-wing and all-wing aircraft designs (Schick and Meyer; Masters). This was no accident. He didn't prefer these designs for purely aesthetic reasons, but because they offered the possibility of stable flight, reduction of drag and the potential for great lift. He felt, like his predecessors Dr Edward von Prandtl and Dr Adolph Busemann, that the perfect aircraft would be one without surface protuberances. Busemann worked out mathematically that a swept-back wing design might prove the most effective (Bullard).

Dr Edward von Prandtl (1875–1953) was Professor of Applied Mechanics at the University of Göttingen from 1904 to 1953 where he set up a renowned school of aerodynamics. He discovered the 'boundary layer' in 1904. In simple terms the boundary layer is the layer of dead air that builds up in front of an aircraft as it moves along. The faster the aircraft goes, the greater the resistance. This resistance, or drag, could be reduced by the design of the aircraft. He subsequently developed a theory that suggested that a flat elliptical-shaped aircraft allowed for uniform air deflection along the entire wingspan. His wing theory led to an understanding of basic aerodynamics. It is no surprise that Lippisch became so interested in all-wing, tailless aircraft. From the late 1920s onwards he designed, step by step, a variety of glider aircraft or 'storch'.

The first of these to win international recognition was the Delta 1, a swept-back wing with a straight trailing edge. The triangular shape allowed, for the first time, the possibility that loads could be stored within the wing (Bullard). (Douglas Bullard runs the Nurflugel Flying Wing Internet web site – a major resource on German advanced aircraft technologies.)

The 1930s were a crucial time for the development of jet engines and the possibilities for high-speed flight. It was hoped that flight beyond the speed of sound could be achieved within a short time. In April 1937, after work undertaken in Britain and Germany, the first jet engines came into operation (Gunston, *Jane's*, 1989). Engines such as the Junkers Jumo 004 opened up many possibilities, and ideas for aerodynamics included crescent, delta and variable-sweep wings. No one was quite sure which type of aircraft to work on, and this is why so many different shapes and sizes of aircraft came to life on the drawing boards of the designers in the late 1930s and early 1940s.

In addition, designers and aerodynamicists were forced to turn their attention to the needs of war. From a purely practical point of view, the *Reichsluftfahrtministerium* (RLM), the body responsible for producing the most effective wartime aircraft, made life difficult for itself by undertaking too many differing projects and encouraging a plethora of radical designs. Nevertheless, it was these radical designs that were to prove so important in subsequent years.

Lippisch himself was employed by the Messerschmidt company in Augsburg during the early years of the war, where he worked upon the well-known Me163A and Me163B aircraft. He also worked on the Me262.

In 1943 he received a contract from the RLM to develop what was called a 'Very Fast Bomber'. He designed a pure delta-wing with a straight trailing edge. This was a radical design with a proposed top speed of 646 mph (1,040 kmph), a length of some 24 ¼ feet (7.4 m) and wingspan of some 33 feet (10 m). It became known as the 'Delta VI' (the original designation was 'P.11') and various different models were considered.

Unfortunate delays occurred because of differences between the Lippisch team in Vienna (where he had moved to in 1943 to head up the Aviation Research Institute) and the Henschel team in Berlin (where the chief designer of aircraft was Friedrich Nicolaus) who were tasked with actual production of the aircraft. However, some construction work did take place after Lippisch took the initiative in early 1945. The centre section of the Delta was built and, most importantly, the Americans managed to capture it. This was not the only Lippisch design to fall into the hands of the Americans immediately after capitulation.

His work with a group of students from the Universities of Darmstadt and Munich resulted in designs for a revolutionary series of aircraft designated 'DM' with the centres of learning in mind. What emerged was the DM-1, a small triangular aircraft. This was really a 'proof of concept' aircraft; it was to be carried piggy-back on the larger Siebel Si-204 to a height of 26,000 feet (8,000 m) before being released. The plane actually reached a speed of nearly 500 mph (800 kmph) in late 1944 propelled by a single rocket motor. The aircraft was effective at both high and low speeds and it was able to operate at speeds as low as 40 mph (65 kmph).

After the war, the DM-1 was shipped back to the United States in order to carry out further tests; the information gained from this was incorporated into various delta-wing aircraft projects in later years.

The concept closest to today's smaller triangular aircraft was undoubtedly the Lippisch Supersonic Flying Wing (Bullard). Not a great deal is known about this adventurous design but it seems to take much of his other work to its logical conclusions. This was a perfect delta-wing vehicle. It was to be powered by a single ramjet, and it was hoped that this would fly at twice the speed of sound. This, like many other similar all-wing designs, demanded that the pilot lie in a prone or semi-prone position. (Interestingly enough, this idea has been suggested as a possible solution to the problem of pilot 'blackout' resulting from sustained high-g flight.)

The allies were interested in more than just half-completed aircraft and recently completed prototypes. They also wanted to get their hands on technical information – plans and schematics – as well as scientists (McGovern). As we shall see later, many of these scientists were encouraged to work in the United States after the war.

The Hortens

Two men the Americans were particularly keen to contact were Reimar and Walter Horten. They came to prominence much later on in the war,

17

although their interest in all-wing aircraft started in the late 1920s (Dabrowski 1991; 1995). Like Lippisch, they had experimented initially with small gliders before moving on to design and build powered aircraft. They knew Lippisch well, although they had only a fraction of the government support. In fact it was only later in the war that their work was recognized at all, partly owing to Lippisch's support. The brothers had progressed through a series of glider designs on to jet-powered aircraft.

An experimental aircraft designated 'Parabola' deserves a mention because it was to become the focus for much concern in the immediate post-war period (AIR [US Air Intelligence Report] 100-203-79). This was a crescent-shaped experimental sailplane 40 feet (12 m) in length. However, despite the unusual shape, its use was to be strictly limited and it was never actually flown.

A sense of desperation affected German military chiefs from 1943–4 onwards. This set in after German reverses in the Soviet Union, and more particularly after the failure to protect German cities and civilians in the face of a thousand bomber raids by allied aircraft. As a result, Hermann Goering, First World War aviation ace and early supporter of Adolf Hitler, hoped to be able to develop a new range of 'superbombers' with the ability to fly over 600 miles (1,000 km) into enemy territory, to deliver a bomb weighing more than 2,200 pounds (1,000kg), and to fly at 600 mph (1,000 kmph). As part of his mission to deliver this 'Project 1,000/1,000/1,000' weapon, and in order to find out whether or not the flying wings were viable aircraft, Goering attended a demonstration of the HVII Horten wing aircraft at Oranienburg in 1944.

Scepticism about the flying wing was one of the reasons that the Hortens' work had received so little support (and perhaps why Lippisch was more successful in winning contracts for more conventional fighter aircraft) until 1944, but Goering was impressed enough to award a contract to the Hortens to produce a bomber to the new exacting standards (Späte).

HoIX

As Dabrowski notes in his *The Horten Flying Wing in World War II*:

> *New life was injected into the Horten firm when, in August [1944], Hermann Goering informed the company that work on the HIX turbojet fighter-bomber was to proceed with all urgency and that it was to construct a flyable, but unpowered, example as soon as possible.*

The new HoIX twin jet bomber was to be built within six months of receipt of contract and although this seemed an impossible task the Horten team had plenty of data from the HV and HVII aircraft. The plane was designated Ho229 by the government. In fact the HoIX could be used in a variety of roles and several versions of the aircraft had been suggested. The idea for the HoIX emerged in 1943 and an unpowered version of the HoIX made its first flight on 28 February 1944.

It was hoped that a powered version (V2; version 2 – not the V-2 rocket) could fly within three months but delays were caused by the intervention of the Air Ministry. To meet the deadline, and because of the growing shortage of materials and slave labour to produce them (it took 5,000 man hours to produce just 1 ton of aluminium), wood was used in construction. It was also easier to teach unskilled labourers to work with wood. Despite these problems what emerged was the first 'stealth' aircraft (Sweetman, 1989).

The word 'stealth' refers not to anything magical but to any vehicle with a very low Radar Cross Section (RCS). By reducing the RCS the vehicle is more difficult for enemy radar systems to detect (see J. Jones, 1989).

Although the HoIX would not have been 'invisible' to radar, the use of sheets of plywood with a sawdust/charcoal/glue composite sandwiched between them would have reduced the RCS. In addition, the construction process was simplified by the use of these composites built around a steel tube frame. The slender body might also have reduced the RCS.

We can still read books on the subject of UFOs that insist that stealth technologies were made available only after the US military recovered technologies from crashed alien spaceships (Hesemann and Mantle; Randle and Schmitt).

In actual fact, the HoIX was the first turbo-jet-powered flying-wing aircraft to fly in the world. The first test-flight took place on 2 February 1945. Jumo 004 engines were used and the pilot sat in an upright position. The aircraft itself fell slightly under the 'Project 1,000' standards – using two Jumo 004 engines allowed for a top speed of 607 mph (977 kmph) with a cruise speed of 430 mph (690 kmph). By this time, the Soviets had already reached the River Oder and Berlin was under serious threat. The third version of the HoIX was virtually complete by the time the Americans overran the construction yard at Friedrichsrode on 14 April 1945.

The aircraft was designated 'T-2-490' by the Americans (Dabrowski, 1991). T-2 appears to refer to the US foreign technology department responsible for collecting foreign technologies and equipment; the name 'T-2' figures in various intelligence documents written on the subject of UFOs in the immediate post-war period.

Other prototypes were recovered at the Gotha plant where the HoIX V-3 had been built and the aircraft was shipped back to the USA, destined for the H. H. Arnold collection at the Air Force Technical Museum.

At Gotha many technical documents were discovered as well. Bill Rose writes:

> *Many present-day military aircraft have their roots in Nazi Germany and one highly advanced prototype developed towards the end of WW2 was the Gotha Go-229 (also known as the Horten IX) jet-powered flying wing. This is now regarded as the first combat aircraft to feature a modern stealth capability. When the Gotha factory at Friedrichsrode was captured by the VIII Corps of the Third US Army on 14 April 1945 they discovered the finished Go-229, along with several other nearly completed prototypes and a large number of components for the first twenty production fighters. Almost immediately, US Intelligence moved in to seal-off the factory and virtually everything was shipped back to America for detailed evaluation under the highest possible security. Several experimental aircraft are thought to have emerged from studies of the Go-229 and the most successful of these may have been the subsonic Lockheed Gusto, which remain classified to this day (Rose, 1997).*

In addition a wooden glider prototype of the planned HoX aircraft was retrieved by the British who, it emerged, took the work of the Hortens and Lippisch very seriously. The HoX (given the cover name HoXIIIa/b) was intended to be a supersonic delta-wing aircraft and considerable work had already been done on this design which dated back, once again, to 1943.

It is not clear exactly what the HoX supersonic delta looked like, although a Royal Aeronautical Establishment report written in October 1945 stated:

> *In appearance the Horten X resembles the Lippisch designs for high speed and supersonic aircraft, especially the P.13. Horten declared that he had not known of anything of Lippisch's work until arriving in London [not true]. The major difference in the design lies in the fact that Horten regarded a special vertical surface as unnecessary, whereas Lippisch favoured a very large vertical rudder assembly [as for the DM-1].*

Other designs are worthy of note (Schick and Meyer). A proposal of interest was the Gotha P.60A heavy fighter, which was based on the work carried out by the Gotha company on the HoIX. The aircraft, with a wingspan of 40½ feet (12.4 m) and swept-back wing of 46 degrees, would have had a maximum speed of 569 mph (915 kmph). The aircraft would have been manned by a crew of two – one pilot and one radio operator – lying in a prone position. Again, the airframe was to consist of layers of wood surrounding a tubular steel centre structure. The Arado company, based at Landshut in Silesia, had also carried out development studies on triangular-planform aircraft with a view to constructing a high-speed fighter.

Although some technical information about the aircraft mentioned above has been made available, it is believed by modern-day researchers that much more was discovered by the allies and that there is more to be revealed about revolutionary German aircraft of the Second World War.

Nevertheless, we can cast some light on some incredible machines based upon the principles of Vertical-Take-Off and Landing (VTOL).

'Foo Fighters'

It had long been considered that the most effective aircraft would be one requiring the shortest runway. Shrouded in mystery, probably deliberately, are the circular-wing aircraft, or flying discs, developed and flown from secret facilities scattered throughout the Reich in the last two years of the conflict. It would appear that the most successful of these was the craft known as the '*Feuerball*' or fireball. It is my contention that this was, in part, responsible for reports of 'foo fighters'.

Foo fighters were reported in numbers by allied airmen participating in multiple bomber raids over enemy territory and by ground forces. The reports were not confined to Europe either: reports came in from the Far Eastern theatre as well, where Japan was fighting a rearguard action against allied forces. In recent years these accounts have been largely written off as unexplained natural phenomena or something known as 'St Elmo's Fire' (Durant). The facts indicate otherwise.

St Elmo's Fire is a bizarre phenomenon. It manifests itself as a glowing electrical halo that envelops the masts of ships, aeroplane wings and church steeples during stormy weather. It is said that air masses of different temperatures move against each other creating friction and then static electrical charges in the air. It is also the case that such phenomena may emerge in areas of tectonic (movements of the earth's crust) stress and perhaps this is why a variety of unusual aerial phenomena are seen during earthquakes.

On looking at details of foo fighter reports one can see a pattern. The first reports appeared in 1942. The following is fairly typical:

> *Royal Air Force pilot B. C. Lumsden observed two classic foos while flying a Hurricane interceptor over France in December 1942. Lumsden had taken off from England at 7 pm heading for the French Coast, using the Somme River as a navigation point. An hour later, while cruising at 7,000 ft over the mouth of the Somme, he discovered that he had company; two steadily climbing orange-coloured lights, with one slightly above the other. He thought it might be tracer flak but discarded the idea when he saw how slowly the objects were moving. He did a full turn and saw the lights astern and to port but now they were larger and brighter.*
>
> *At 7,000 ft they stopped climbing and stayed level with Lumsden's Hurricane. The frightened pilot executed a full turn again, only to discover that the objects had hung behind him on the turn.*
>
> *Lumsden had no idea what he was seeing. All he knew was that he didn't like it. He nose-dived down to 4,000 ft and the lights followed his every manoeuvre, keeping their same relative position. Finally they descended about 1,000 ft below him until he levelled out, at which point they climbed again and resumed pursuit. The two lights seemed to maintain an even distance from each other and varied only slightly in relative height from time to time. One always remained a bit lower than the other.*
>
> *At last, as Lumsden's speed reached 260 mph, he was gradually able to outdistance the foos.*

A report made by George Todt, columnist for the *Los Angeles Herald-Examiner*, stated that he had seen a typical foo fighter:

> *On one occasion a party of four of us – including a lieutenant-colonel – watched a pulsating red fireball sail up silently to a point directly over the American–German front lines in 1944 during the Battle of Normandy. It stopped completely before moving on.*

Todt was later to report that his, and other witness, sightings of these objects related neither to 'an hallucination' nor a 'temperature inversion'.

Carson Yorke recalled the following during an interview in 1958:

This occurred in September 1944, just outside Antwerp, Belgium, which the Germans were bombarding at the time with V2 rockets. At about 9 pm I stepped out of my vehicle and on looking upward saw a glowing globe travelling from the direction of the front line towards Antwerp. It seemed to be about three or four feet in diameter and looked as though it was cloudy glass with a light inside. It gave off a soft white glow. Its altitude seemed to be about 40 feet, speed about 30 miles per hour, and there was no sound of any sort.

I noted that the object was not simply drifting with the wind but was obviously powered and controlled. Immediately after it had gone out of view it was followed by another which in turn was followed by five others in all.

During this time I called some other men to see so the objects were observed by about five men. We weren't very impressed at the time because the Germans were using so many new weapons against us, such as the V1 and V2, so we assumed that these were simply some sort of new device of theirs. Also, remember that these objects were apparently following the same course [as] V2s which were falling on Antwerp regularly at the time, one every few minutes if I remember correctly.

Major William D. Leet reported the following fascinating events:

My B17 crew and I were kept company by a foo fighter, a small amber disc, all the way from Klagenfurt, Austria, to the Adriatic Sea. This occurred on a 'lone wolf' mission at night, as I recall, in December 1944 in the 15th Air Force, 5th Wing, 2nd Bomb Group. The intelligence officer who debriefed us stated that it was a new German fighter but could not explain why it did not fire at us or, if it was reporting our heading, altitude, and airspeed, why we did not receive anti-aircraft fire' (Clark and Farish; IUFOG [Internet UFO Group], 1947).

Interestingly, from the point of view of the geographical location, is this report involving a B-17 pilot flying near Neustadt, Germany. He saw a 'gold-coloured ball with a metallic finish' moving through the air but because of the position of the sun, low in the sky, could not tell whether the glow was internally or externally produced. A glowing golden sphere was seen in the same area by the pilot of a P.47. Various underground facilities were located nearby.

In December 1944 further evidence that the foos were intelligently controlled from the ground emerged when the pilot with the 415th Squadron came across two large orange glowing objects. The pilot reported that the objects ascended to his altitude, levelled off and stayed on a parallel course before peeling off and flying off 'under perfect control'. Crews with the 415th discounted the idea that what was being seen was a naturally occurring phenomenon.

Another sighting which might provide us with an answer as to the nature and origin of the elusive foo fighters came in March 1945 when American soldiers with the Sixth Armored Division saw several UFOs overhead. They were not in formation.

On the same evening a group of 30 men saw half a dozen bright orange objects approach the motorway at an altitude of 150 feet (46 m). Each object behaved in the same erratic way as if under individual control and the men could see that these UFOs were of approximately 3–4 feet (1–1.2 m) in diameter. They descended into a thickly wooded and dense forest before disappearing from sight.

Research at the Public Record Office at Kew, London, suggests that foo fighter reports were taken very seriously; in fact a special committee was set up in order to investigate these reports (AIR 14-2800 [UK]). It has been suggested that neither the Germans nor the British knew what these objects were, but the truth is somewhat different and perhaps suggested by the fact that many of the documents were classified.

Other reports surfaced in official US Air Force (USAF) archives relating to foo-fighter sightings. Again, they relate to late 1944:

December 18th – In Rastatt area sighted five or six red and green lights in a 'T' shape which followed A/C thru turns and closed to 1,000 ft. Lights followed for several miles and then went out. Our pilots have named these mysterious phenomena which they encounter over Germany at night 'Foo Fighters'.

December 23rd – More Foo-Fighters were in the air last night.... In the vicinity of Hagenau saw 2 lights coming toward the A/C from ground.

After reaching the altitude of the A/C they levelled off and flew on tail of Beau [Beaufighter – their aircraft] for 2 minutes and then peeled up and turned away. 8th mission – sighted 2 orange lights. One light sighted at 10,000 ft away, the other climbed until it disappeared.

December 28th – 1st patrol saw 2 sets of 3 red and white lights. One appeared on the port side, the other on starboard at 1,000 to

2,000 ft to rear and closing in. Beau peeled off and lights went out. Nothing on GCI scope at the time.

Observed lights suspended in air, moving slowly in no general direction and then disappeared. Lights were orange, and appeared singly and in pairs. These lights were observed 4 or 5 times throughout the period.

So the foo fighters seemed to have the following characteristics. They:

- often were orange in colour;

- often ascended vertically from behind German lines, or from German-held territory;

- often appeared to be under intelligent control, having the ability to change direction;

- were nearly always directed towards allied aircraft;

- were seen around underground Axis facilities.

The media had very definite opinions as to the foo-fighter phenomenon. *Time* magazine of 15 January 1945 (IUFOG) described the foos as 'the most puzzling secret weapon that the allies have encountered' and went on to suggest that some sort of psychological tool was being employed. Although scientists were baffled by the whole affair, front-line correspondents believed that a new secret weapon was being employed and that it must be operated by radio control.

A *Newsweek* report of the same date came to similar conclusions:

Apparently controlled by radio, the foo-fighters keep formation with planes, even when they dive, climb or take evasive action.... Possibly they are the results of a new anti-radar device which the Germans have developed.

The report also noted the existence of the Messerschmidt Me163, the radio-controlled rocket bomb which had an explosive charge in the nose and could be directed towards enemy aircraft. Interestingly, the Germans sent the Japanese various Me163 aircraft to use.

Although only a little research has been done on foo fighters, the 'debunking' CIA-organized Robertson Panel set up in 1952 officially described as a 'Scientific Advisory Panel on Unidentified Flying Objects' made comments about them, but concluded unanimously that there was 'no evidence of a direct threat to national security in the objects sighted'. Instances of 'foo fighters' were cited.

Unexplained phenomena sighted by aircraft pilots during the Second World War in both Europe and the Far Eastern theatres of war included 'balls of light' that would fly near or with the aircraft and manoeuvre rapidly. These were believed to be electrostatic (similar to St Elmo's Fire) or electromagnetic phenomena or possibly light reflections from ice crystals in the air (Durant).

Such comments make evident that there have been serious attempts to divert attention away from the truth about foo fighters. Obviously the panel chose to ignore the fact that US intelligence officers were saying that foos were enemy devices. The panel also chose to ignore the fact that the Germans had the technology to design, build and operate such devices.

German Anti-aircraft Devices

There are several particularly credible sources relating to revolutionary German anti-aircraft devices. The first is James McGovern. McGovern served with the US Army Signals Corps during the war and later he worked for the Office of Scientific Intelligence and the US High Commission. His book *Crossbow and Overcast* is a rare but important source of information about advanced German technologies, the allied responses to them, and the desire to get hold of as much of the technology, schematics and personnel relating to them as possible in the last months of the war. His book is mainly concerned with the V-2 rockets developed at Peenemünde on the Baltic coast and later at the Central Works (Mittelwerke) at Nordhausen in the Harz Mountains. He also mentions a device called the '*Wasserfall*':

> The Wasserfall *was developed at Peenemünde and was a ground-controlled anti-aircraft rocket. It had a remote-controlled guidance system and could be aimed at enemy aircraft by ground operators. The operator used a joystick-type device to control the weapon. The radio-controlled guidance system was later used in the A-4 [the original designation for the V-2] (Klee and Merk).*

A prototype A-4 with *Wasserfall* guidance system actually crashed in Kalmar, Sweden in 1944 and from the wreckage Anglo-American scientists were able to discern a little more about the secret weapons held in Hitler's arsenal.

Desperate Search

So, allied scientists and elements of the intelligence community knew that Germany was desperately trying to build the ultimate weapon with which to defeat the allies. As well as the V-2 there were other radio-controlled devices as noted in another important book – by Professor R. V. Jones of Aberdeen University and entitled *Reflections on Intelligence* (1989). Jones was hardly the dry and dusty academic type. During the war he had been involved in intelligence work and in 1946 became Director of Intelligence to the Air Staff and later Director of Scientific Intelligence at the Ministry of Defence. In his book Jones deals with various intelligence issues and provides fascinating insights into the state of knowledge in 1939 regarding German technological achievements.

In November 1939 Jones was passed a newly arrived document entitled *The Oslo Report* which had been spirited to England by naval attaché Hector Boyes. The report detailed various weapons, including the Junkers Ju88 dive-bomber, new rockets and explosive devices, new radar systems and also remote-controlled aircraft.

Jones was called on to report on these systems to the Defence Committee of the War Cabinet. It seems both that they were taken very seriously and that the allies had detailed knowledge of them. Churchill himself noted in *The Gathering War* that the British had made 'contacts of a most secret character' with some of the important German generals.

On remote-controlled aircraft *The Oslo Report* made the following points:

> The German Navy has developed remote-controlled gliders, that is, small aircraft of about three metres span and three metres long. They carry a large explosive charge. They are not powered by an engine and are launched at great height from an aircraft.
>
> These used remote-control by means of 'ultra short waves in the form of telegraph signals'. This enabled the craft to fly left, right or straight from a ship or aircraft. The glider could be used against enemy shipping.
>
> Under the secret code number FZ10 an autopilot (remote-controlled aircraft) is being developed. This is to be controlled from a manned aircraft and is to be used, for instance, to destroy barrage balloons.

Section 5 of the report made the following disclosure:

> *The Army Ordnance Office (HWA) is the development centre for*
> *the Army.... Rocket propulsion is employed and the stabilization*
> *is brought about by an installed gyro.*

There is little doubt, then, that Germany had some very intriguing technologies that the allies wished to get hold of.

One important point to make here is that it is not the case that the new generation of man-made flying saucer advocates are 'apologists' for Nazism, as is suggested by the sceptics who claim that because some 'Nazi' saucer researchers are of dubious political persuasion then *all* subsequent research is invalid (Sivier; McClure, 'Yesterday belongs to Me', *Abduction Watch*, 1998). This type of guilt by association is an ineffective way of disputing the evidence.

Secondly, debunkers argue that because some supposed sightings of flying saucers have been explained, or are explainable, then *all* sightings should be called into question. The reader will see that there are impressive UFO sightings that clearly relate to structured circular craft and that these have been reported from around the world with a concentration on the USA – a fact which surprises few researchers.

Despite the argument that German scientists had no more advanced technology than the allies, one American was very clear as to the technical achievements of Nazi scientists. Major-General Hugh Knerr, Deputy Commanding General for Administration of US Strategic Forces in Europe, wrote to Lieutenant-General Carl Spatz in March 1945:

> *Occupation of German scientific and industrial establishments*
> *has revealed the fact that we have been alarmingly backward in*
> *many fields of research; if we do not take this opportunity to*
> *seize the apparatus and the brains that developed it and put this*
> *combination back to work promptly, we will remain several*
> *years behind while we attempt to cover a field already exploited*
> *(quoted in McGovern).*

It is possible to look into the area of German flying saucers without reference to so-called 'established' sources. These authors are often targeted for attack by sceptics, and include Allen Harbinson, who has contributed to the subject through his exciting series of *Project Saucer* novels and the more recent non-fiction paperback *Projekt UFO,* and Renate Vesco, whose research appeared in the late 1960s as a paperback with the title *Intercept but Don't Shoot* and later as *Intercept UFO*. Vesco appears to have cooperated with 'hidden knowledge' writer David Hatcher Childress in the production of *Man-Made UFOs – 50 Years of Suppression.*

The final point to bear in mind regarding this subject is that the victors of any conflict have a head start in writing the history books and, in the case of the immediate aftermath of the Second World War, burying or spiriting away evidence, documents, plans and blueprints, actual technology and a variety of other materials that the allies did not, and do not, want the public to know about – for a variety of reasons that may become apparent.

Despite the fact that the man-made origins of flying saucers are of the greatest implications in terms of our understanding of post-war history, 'man-made UFO' researchers have to some extent been deliberately ostracized and smeared.

Nevertheless, a great deal of new information *has* emerged in recent years and there is still more to come. The suggestion that 50 years after the end of the Second World War new information *cannot* emerge, because this period has been the subject of the most intense scrutiny, is an illogical one.

For any number of reasons information can stay buried and, beyond mere speculation, we know that files relating to the Second World War remain locked in the deep, dark vaults of the Public Record Office in Kew, London. Remember this – records are routinely held for 30 years and can be held for 50, 75 and 100 years after the event (Redfern). By the time they emerge they may have been altered, edited or sanitized to 'protect' the identity of those responsible for the implementation of policy.

One simple example that comes to mind is the emergence in recent years of new and credible information about the German nuclear research programme under way during the Second World War. Much of this has been the result of research undertaken by Philip Henshall, who has also contributed a great deal to our understanding of advanced German weapons projects through his books on the rocket research facilities at Peenemünde on the Baltic coast (Henshall, 1985; 1995).

Other sources are equally intriguing. One of these indicates that from the mid-1930s there was significant interest in both Vertical-Take-Off and Landing (VTOL) and circular-wing aircraft. This led to a number of designs one of which was the Focke-Wulf VTOL.

Circular-wing Aircraft

Professor Heinrich Focke was particularly interested in emerging helicopter and autogyro technologies and was involved in the design and production of the FW-6, Fa-223, Fa-226, Fa-283 and Fa-284 models during the war. The creation of the jet engine encouraged him to design a propulsion system known as the 'turbo-shaft' still used in most helicopters today. In 1939 he patented a saucer-type aircraft with enclosed twin rotors. This was a revolutionary development described as follows:

> *The exhaust nozzle forked in two at the end of the engine and ended in two auxiliary combustion chambers located on the trailing edge of the wing. When fuel was added to these combustion chambers they would act as afterburners to provide horizontal propulsion to Focke's design. The control at low speed was achieved by alternately varying the power from each auxiliary combustion chamber (Miranda and Mercado).*

This was by no means the only circular aircraft. There was a circular wing known as the AS6 (V-1) and the information about this emerged in an article written by Hans Ebert and Hans Meier based to a certain extent upon information and a photograph provided by German aviation expert Wolfgang Späte. (Späte was the former commander of Operational Test Unit 16 during the war and more recently recognized as a leading aviation expert. He served in the refounded post-war Luftwaffe.) The article, entitled '*Prototypen – Einselschicksale deutscher Flugzeuge, Der Kreisflügler AS6 V1*', was included in the respected *Luftfahrt International* in 1980.

In certain respects the AS6, built by Messerschmidt, was based on much the same thinking as the Zimmerman V-173 'flying flapjack' – designed for use by the US Navy from 1942. The 'flying flapjack' was far more successful and developed at the Chance-Vought works in Connecticut, and despite its supposed limitations was a propeller-driven aircraft designed to be flown from an aircraft carrier, hence the need for Short-Take-Off and Landing (STOL) capability. The flapjack was able to fly at low speeds of approximately 40 mph (65 kmph). The flight envelope was between 40 and 425 mph (65 and 684 kmph) and a more advanced version, the XF-5U1, was also tested (Angelucci and Bowers).

One other important feature of these circular wings was an early 'stealth' capability. ('Stealth' means that the shape was excellent in terms of reducing the Radar Cross Section. Most aviation writers are agreed on this point and it is interesting to note in *Skunk Works* by Rich and Janos that in their view a flying saucer would be 'the ultimate in low observability'.)

The Horten brothers, Reimar and Walter, known for their many successful flying-wing prototypes, had developed a composite wing made of plywood held together by sawdust, charcoal and glue intended to absorb radar waves for use in their HoIX model.

While it is likely that any information relating to the limited AS6 would have been taken by the allies for examination at a later date, it would seem that there is some evidence to suggest that a more advanced jet-powered flying saucer was at least designed, if not built, from around 1943 onwards.

The Schriever Story

The first source is Flight Captain Rudolph Schriever, who came forward in 1950 and claimed that he had worked with a small team at facilities near Prague with a view to developing a flying saucer-type vehicle. The Schriever story first emerged in *Der Spiegel* magazine dated 30 March 1950 entitled '*Untertassen-Flieger Kombination*':

> *A former Luftwaffe captain and aircraft designer, Rudolph Schriever, who says engineers throughout the world experimented in the early 1940s with 'flying saucers', is willing to build one for the United States in six to nine months. The 40-year-old Prague University graduate said he made blueprints for such a machine, which he calls a 'flying top', before Germany's collapse and that the blueprints were stolen from his laboratory. He says the machine would be capable of 2,600 mph with a radius of 4,000 miles. Schriever is a US Army driver at Bremerhaven.*

This is a most intriguing story. Schriever claimed that the model built for testing was completed in 1944 with a view to flying it in 1945. Nevertheless, the Russian advance ended any hopes of a test-flight. (Prague was the last area of the crumbling Reich to fall, on 10–11 May 1945.)

A *Luftfahrt International* report (May/June 1975) took these claims seriously and noted that after Schriever's death in the late 1950s papers found among his belongings included technical drawings of a flying saucer. Schriever seemed to argue that, although a saucer had existed, it had not flown. This is contradicted by a possible eyewitness, George Klein (Harbinson, 1994; Vesco). After the war, he claimed in an interview given on 18 November 1954 to the Zurich-based *Tages Anzeiger* that he had actually seen a flying saucer test on 14 February 1945 and that the craft had performed remarkably well, reaching an altitude of 30,000 feet (9,150 m) in three minutes, as well as a high speed of hundreds of miles an hour. Despite the fact that subsequent information leads us to conclude that a primitive jet-powered flying disc was developed at the end of the war Klein spoke of a 'ray-guided disc'.

In Sayer and Botting's *America's Secret Army*, which gives a detailed account of the activities of the US Counter Intelligence Corps, we hear the story of CIC agents:

> *Scientific and technological know-how was also a prime CIC target.... Another weapons specialist who fell into CIC hands was Werner Piel, described as a special air courier of secret technical devices for the Luftwaffe. During his interrogation Piel claimed that the same laboratories that had devised the V-1 and V-2 had also devised an array of diabolic weapons, including a so-called 'secret ray' produced from a device known as...Eagle Apparatus. This device, according to Piel, was capable of knocking out the engine of a tank, truck or plane by firing a ray at it.*

This seems a little fanciful, and maybe Piel wanted to curry favour with his interrogators. Nevertheless, the post-war UFO literature includes many reports of 'car-stop' or vehicle interference cases (Rodeghier).

Some things Klein said made more sense. For instance, he claimed that some of the work on the flying saucers had taken place at Peenemünde. Peenemünde was of course the focal point for the development of the A-4/V-2 rocket.

Interestingly, Klein also claimed that the necessary stability for the saucer had been attained through the use of a gyroscope. This is exactly the method used in German rockets developed by the rocket enthusiasts in the 1930s. This was perfected with the V-2 rockets towards the end of the war (R. F. Pocock).

Philip Henshall's research was predicted to a certain extent by the controversial Major Rudolph Lusar, whose *German Secret Weapons of World War II* (1959) attempted, according to the author at least, to set the record straight regarding the technical achievements made by German scientists and which were the cause for allied concern. On pp. 166–7 Lusar notes the existence of a flying disc. He seemed to have developed the theme of Schriever, but also mentioned that flying saucers had been developed by the Americans, that this had involved 'the former designer Miethe' and that the reason the US Air Force had given the order not to shoot at UFOs (this is covered later on) in the post-war period was that they were of terrestrial origin. Kevin McClure ('Yesterday Belongs to Me' and *Secrets or Lies*, both 1998) has been very critical of Lusar and has accused him of being an 'unreconstructed Nazi', although there is not a great deal of evidence to support this claim. Lusar's book is very intriguing in certain respects including his knowledge of the German nuclear programme covered by Henshall in his 1995 book entitled *Vengeance: Hitler's Nuclear Weapon — Fact or Fiction?*. Clearly Lusar had some good information.

The evidence presented above seems to have been taken seriously not only by mainstream magazines and national newspapers in the 1950s, but also by the author of *Brighter Than a Thousand Suns*, Robert Jungk. This is an authoritative and historical account of the development of the atomic bomb written by a respected author. The book itself, still available and published by Harcourt Brace, received critical acclaim from Bertrand Russell, among others. A section of text on p. 87 of the paperback edition states:

> *The indifference of Hitler and those about him to research in natural sciences amounted to positive hostility.*

The accompanying footnote reads as follows:

> *The only exception to the lack of interest shown by authority was constituted by the Air Ministry [Reichsluftfahrtministerium or RLM]. The Air Force research workers were in a peculiar position. They produced interesting new types such as the Delta [Lippisch and Horten]...and flying discs. The first of these 'flying saucers', as they were later called — circular in shape, with a diameter of some 45 yards — were built by the specialists Schriever, Habermohl and Miethe. They were first airborne on February 14th 1945, over Prague and reached in three minutes a height of nearly eight miles. They had a speed of 1250 mph which was doubled in subsequent tests. It is believed that Habermohl fell into the hands of the Russians. Miethe developed at a later date similar 'flying saucers' at A. V. Roe and Company for the United States.*

This use of the original Schriever story is interesting if only because the author felt that the information was good and warranted exposure. Given the nature of the book, we might well ask whether the author had any other information that supported the claims made as to the characteristics of the circular aircraft. It is up to the reader to decide whether these claims make any sense and, more importantly, how this might affect our understanding of flying saucer history.

Saucers *Were* Tested

Until recently, it would have been rather safer and more prudent to argue that although various prototype saucers existed in whatever form, they were never tested. However, thanks to three years of painstaking research by UK astronomy, aviation and photographic specialist Bill Rose which included on-site research in Germany, Canada and the USA, we now know a great deal more. Initially Rose felt, like many sceptics, that the evidence for German flying saucer (and UFO) reality was very shaky.

Nevertheless, and without reference to the UFO community in his personal quest for the truth, he was able to use his expert technical knowledge to follow up leads and to make significant progress.

First of all, he was able to discover that Dr Walter (?) Miethe (*see* illustration no. 2), who all sources agree was involved with Schriever, Klaus Habermohl and Giuseppe Belluzzo (an Italian engineer), had been the director of the saucer programme at two facilities located outside Prague. In May 1945, after testing of the prototype had taken place, both Miethe and Schriever were able to flee in the direction of allied forces. Habermohl was captured by Soviet forces and spirited east where he ended up working on various aviation projects quite probably at facilities located outside Moscow.

It would seem that Klaus Habermohl was the man who developed the radial-flow jet engine, described in various articles as a system of 'adjustable' nozzles, of great significance just ten years later. (Radial flow allowed for VTOL performance and used the little-known 'Coanda' effect.)

The Coanda effect is mentioned in post-war documents relating to man-made flying saucers and can be described as 'the tendency of a fluid to follow the wall contour of a curved surface' or by the statement 'Coanda jets are generated by blowing a moderate- to high-pressure gas (such as air) or liquid through a narrow slot over a surface which in some cases might be convexly curved'.

Rose learned not only that test-flights had taken place but that there was film footage of them. This had always been rumoured and makes perfect sense given the Nazi obsession with keeping records on everything. The footage, of good quality, has subsequently been stored in a secure location and shown only to a handful of people. Rose was shown some stills taken from the original 16mm film and, given his expert photo-technical background, concluded, after careful consideration, that this was probably real and historical footage.

He calculated that the craft was around half the size claimed in Klein's report. The saucer, rather less contoured and sleek than post-war artists' impressions might suggest (and unlike Bob Lazar's S4 'Sports Model'!), was perhaps 75 feet (23 m) in diameter. The saucer was shown in flight above the runway over the heads of a couple of observers.

Although this is in itself of the greatest significance, other, more contradictory evidence has emerged. One of the people that Rose met had good information about the February test-flight and was able to confirm that several people had seen the flight – as we might expect. It was said that Schriever himself had piloted the test-craft.

This does seems sensible (and logical) given Schriever's background in the Luftwaffe – although it is at variance with his own account. One can only speculate as to why this might be.

It should be pointed out that the performance characteristics of this jet-powered aircraft have probably been exaggerated and, although it might have been technically possible given further research and development to approach supersonic speeds, this was almost certainly not achieved in February 1945. Finally, it seems as if Klein himself was centrally involved in the saucer project and may indeed have had responsibilities for procurement.

We know a little more about Dr Miethe. One of the important pieces of information came in the form of a rare group photograph showing various young German scientists in 1933. The photograph shows Werner von Braun and Walter Miethe (or Richard Miethe – different sources mention different first names). It would seem that these two knew each other well. During the war various lists of 'wanted' German scientists were drawn up. One of these was the 'Black List' used by Counter Intelligence Corps and Combined Allied Field Teams (CAFT) as they moved through Germany from 1944 in order to help them find the important scientific personnel.

Dr von Braun was certainly at the top of the list and if Miethe and he were old friends and had cooperated on early rocket projects, there is little doubt that Miethe would have been a target too. Nevertheless, his work near Prague put him out of reach and only through Miethe's own efforts did the allied teams get their hands on him. (In a US television interview, Dr Alexander Flax, former Secretary to the US Air Force, admitted that Miethe had indeed worked in the USA after the war.)

One thing is for sure: hundreds of Nazi scientists *as well as* intelligence personnel (Simpson), many of whom had been involved in the abuse of thousands of slave labourers, were transported via 'Operation Paperclip' (so named after the original designation 'Overcast' had been compromised). Many of these technical personnel were sent initially to Fort Bliss in Texas. From here they were farmed out, according to their ability and expertise, to the many advanced scientific facilities dotted throughout the USA and Canada (McGovern).

Interestingly, Chance-Vought, builder of both the V-173 and the XF-5U1 prototypes, moved their base of operations to Texas in early

1947 or 1948. The company seems to have been less than candid at this early stage about the true nature and extent of its involvement in flying saucers. The official story of the demise of the XF-5U1 – that there was no interest in developing a propeller-driven aircraft from 1948 after the advent of jets – is now in question. It would seem that a jet-powered version using Allison J33 engines was actually test-flown at Muroc Field in 1947. The history books tell us that the propeller-driven version was to be tested here before the programme was cancelled (Angelucci and Bowers). Nevertheless, our understanding of the situation is that technical drawings of the jet-powered version have now surfaced through a series of Freedom of Information Act requests.

Given the overall design of this craft and the many sightings of flying saucers in New Mexico and along the Western seaboard in the late 1940s, it is safe to conclude that the sightings related to a saucer of terrestrial origin with limited performance characteristics (see Hall, 1964).

There is a final twist to this most unique story. I regularly receive information from a range of contacts. One is Maurizio Verga, an Italian UFO and secret-weapons researcher. It would seem that just a few days before the Schriever story broke in the German and Italian press in March 1950, Giuseppe Belluzzo, an Italian engineer on the Miethe team, claimed in several Italian newspapers that he had worked on a flying saucer of the type being reported in such numbers at the time. This is further corroboration that the men worked on a flying disc and that advanced technologies were fact, not fiction.

As time goes by it seems more and more likely that after 50 years the truth is starting to emerge about the German–American origins of the 'flying saucer' – by any standards a tremendous human technical achievement. Now we turn our attention to the immediate post-war period, a time that is critical to the understanding of both the myth and the reality of flying saucers or UFOs.

THE POST-WAR
UFO PANIC

TO FIND OUT what might have happened both during and after the
Second World War, we first need to turn our attention to the
flying-saucer sightings of 1946–7. The fundamental misunder-
standing about the nature and origin of UFOs seems to have started in
June 1947 when the apparent reality of structured-flying-saucer
reports became entangled with the myth of extraterrestrial contact
(*Fortean Times*, Evans and Stacy, 1997).

Efforts to research this basic flaw in our approach to flying saucers
are now being addressed beyond the usual debunking and scepticism
of, for instance, Philip Klass. What a small number of researchers – for
example, Maurizio Verga and Bill Rose – are now saying is that some of
the objects reported as disc- or crescent shaped aircraft in the early
post-war period were unconventional aircraft that combined the most
interesting of captured German and cutting-edge American technologies (Verga, UFO Online Internet site, 1997; Rose, 1997).

Scepticism about flying saucers has thrown up a number of fantastic
'solutions' whereby researchers pretend to put themselves in the shoes
of witnesses to the unfolding events of June 1947. We need to go back
to basics and listen to what the witnesses to the 'start of the modern
UFO wave' actually described seeing, and to see if we can provide any
sensible suggestions as to what might have been going on (Aldrich).

The Arnold Sighting

The most famous witness is, of course, Kenneth Arnold. Arnold made
many attempts to explain what he saw on 24 June 1947. A detailed
account, in his own words, was published in the excellent *UFO*

1947–1997, Fifty Years of Flying Saucers edited by Hilary Evans and Denis Stacy (Arnold).

In a private plane which he used for business trips, Arnold was travelling through the Cascade Mountains of Washington State in the north-western United States. He decided to look for the wreckage of a C-46 marine transport aircraft that had crashed on the slopes of Mount Rainier.

Arnold stated that:

> *I hadn't flown more than two or three minutes on my course when a bright flash reflected on my airplane. It startled me as I thought I was too close to some other aircraft. I looked every place in the sky and couldn't find where the reflection had come from until I looked to the left and to the North of Mount Rainier where I observed a chain of nine peculiar looking aircraft flying from North to South at approximately 9,500 ft elevation and going, seemingly, in a definite direction of about 170 degrees.*

He went on to say that 'I merely assumed they were jet planes'. But these were no regular jet planes and they flew in an unusual manner, dipping and making slight alterations to their course. The objects were strung out in a line stretching some 5 miles (8 km), although their speed did not seem particularly fast. Arnold observed the objects through the open window of his plane and noted that the aircraft were smaller than a DC-4. They had unusual tails and appeared to be more crescent-shaped than anything else.

Arnold himself did not believe that he had seen 'extraterrestrial' spacecraft. That is a fundamentally important point to make. Hear the words of Kenneth Arnold writing to military authorities at Wright-Patterson airfield on 12 July 1947:

> *It is with considerable disappointment you cannot give the explanation of these aircraft as I felt certain they belonged to our government.*

He went on to say in a longer statement regarding his sighting that other people he had talked to suggested that the objects might have been prototype missiles or aircraft of some sort. A former Army Air Force pilot suggested that Arnold had seen 'some sort of jet or rocket propelled ship that is in the process of being tested by our government or possibly by some foreign government'.

At this early stage it appears that hardly anyone believed that these objects were alien craft on scouting missions, a myth that was to become ingrained in popular consciousness as a result of wild reporting and the machinations of the press. Before June 1947 extremely powerful imagery had been presented to millions of listeners in the form of Orson Welles' *War of the Worlds* radio broadcast in 1938. There can be little doubt that his idea of an alien civilization watching and waiting had a deep psychological effect on even the most rational person.

It is clear that Arnold's sighting was treated in a hysterical way by the media, who claimed that the object was travelling at 'terrific speed across the face of Mount Rainier', which, in Arnold's own account, was not the case.

In addition to this, the groundwork had effectively been laid for the confusion of saucers and aliens through various statements by people like Dr Layman Spitzer, Associate Professor of Astrophysics at Yale University, who left objective and scientific methodology out of the equation when making comments about the possibility that 'Martians' may have already visited Planet Earth (Aldrich).

His words had been to some extent been predicted and preceded by Charles Fort years earlier when he claimed that 'Visitors from a multitude of worlds have come to earth over the centuries' and that they might have altered our evolutionary development. Meanwhile, essays and articles with a similar theme emerged in the pages of two pulp fiction magazines called *Amazing Stories* and *Fantastic Adventures* edited by Ray Palmer. Nevertheless, a Gallup poll on the subject of mystery aircraft indicated that the public were perhaps a little more sensible: 33 per cent didn't know what these objects were while 29 per cent, unsurprisingly, attributed sightings to 'imagination, optical illusion, mirage etc.'.

However, 15 per cent of respondents opted for the possibility that a 'U.S. secret weapon, part of atomic bomb' (the bomb was very much in the public's mind just two years after its first use and the subsequent developments in nuclear technology) had been responsible. (*Fortean Times*, Evans and Stacy). It now seems as if they were right.

'Operation Paperclip'

The allies were desperate to get their hands on the various advanced German technologies. This was done through a variety of means including the targetting of valuable human assets through the 'Black List'. Werner von Braun is the best known of these scientists. One of the popular myths surrounding the targeting of scientists and technologies is that this was done under the banner of 'Operation Paperclip'.

'Paperclip' was merely an extension of 'Operation Overcast' described in a memorandum of 21 May 1945 sent by Major L. F. Cranford (Chief of Interrogation Branch, Office of the Assistant Chief of Air Staff) to the Assistant Chief of Air Staff, Intelligence. It described the scientists as 'German Civilian Technicians' and said that the Material Branch MIS (Military Intelligence Staff) had been charged with the responsibility of 'implementing and setting up an organiza- tion that will cover the handling of subject personnel' from Europe to the USA. On arrival the personnel were to be interrogated and moved to other parts of the country for 'further exploitation'. This was 'Operation Overcast': a limited and short-term plan mainly conceived to enable German scientists to help win the war against Japan in the East. This related to just 350 specialists who would be offered six- month contracts. That is the official story.

The truth is that Overcast was also created in order to stop German scientists falling into the hands of the Russians and to stop them being used to rebuild German might (McGovern; Simpson).

Paperclip came into being on 13 March 1946 when the secretary to the Joint Chiefs of Staff sent out the following memorandum:

SUBJECT; Substitution of Code Word

1 – Effective this date, the word PAPERCLIP has been substi- tuted for the word OVERCAST, due to the compromise of the latter word.

2 – The meaning previously attached to OVERCAST was not compromised and will now attach to PAPERCLIP.

In addition, there was a realization that the German scientists were too valuable to simply release after a short-term contract and Paperclip enabled longer-term exploitation and granting of full immigrant status to the scientists, who would also be able to bring their families to the USA. More scientists and technical experts were involved too: by May 1948 there were 1,136 German and Austrian nationals in the USA, 492 being specialists and 644 dependants. The largest single group were rocket scientists but Paperclip scientists worked for a variety of other agencies. For instance, Major-General Walter Dornberger (Braun's superior at Peenemünde and Nordhausen) worked for the Air Force before joining Bell Aircraft Company. He went on to work on the Bell X-1 and 'Dyna-Soar' hypersonic aircraft and became Vice- President of Bell Aerospace Corporation (McGovern). Phil Butler's War Prizes details allied recovery of German aircraft.

Smith's Story

The majority of German scientists did, however, end up at Fort Bliss in Texas where they had state-of-the-art equipment at their disposal. Did they only work on rockets? Until recently it was assumed that they did, but in July 1997 during the hysteria surrounding the 50 years 'celebration' of the 'Roswell UFO crash retrieval' one man came out with a remarkable story that added weight to suspicions that, after all, flying saucers were man-made, and were being tested before 1947. The following story provides a potentially fatal blow to standard UFO histories (Good, 1987), and more particularly to the theory that saucers are of extraterrestrial origin.

Thomas C. Smith graduated from Penn State University in mechanical engineering and went to work for Chance-Vought Aircraft in Stratford, Connecticut (see Gunston, Jane's, 1989) after the war. I spoke to him at length in early 1998. Smith was working on new composites involving the high-altitude bonding of layers of wood and metal. He wanted to know a little more about the uses of this material and claims to have been taken to a guarded hangar by a supervisor and shown a new jet aircraft that the company was developing. He also saw a flying saucer made of the composite. This was a streamlined, khaki-coloured craft with a bubble window in the centre which gave a pilot a good all-round view. Smith also saw this craft undergo tests and he testifies that the pilot lay in a prone position. We already know that the Hortens used a wood/glue/sawdust composite and would have used metal had it been more readily available. In addition, many designs of delta-wing and tailless aircraft required the pilot(s) to lie in a prone position (Schick and Meyer).

The Chance-Vought saucer was powered by a fairly conventional propeller engine. Nevertheless, there were rudders for added control and stability and the saucer was a Vertical-Take-Off and Landing (VTOL) vehicle. Smith said that 'they'd get it off the ground and it would disappear' and went on to say that local people reported seeing this unidentified craft. Was this the more advanced XF 5U1?

The Chance-Vought company moved to Dallas, Texas in 1947 or 1948 (Smith says 1947, but see Gunston, 1993) – just down the road from Fort Bliss where hundreds of German scientists, some of whom will have worked upon anti-aircraft devices and associated technologies, were stationed. Not only that; the new base of operations was not too far from New Mexico – where the many stories about UFO crash retrievals were born (Scully; Steinman and Stevens; Randles, 1995). Coincidence?

In later years Smith worked for the Hamilton Watch Company and Woodstream Corporation. He is a retired vice-president of marketing with the Woodstream Corporation, as stated in the *Lancaster New Era* report. Smith seems to be a reliable and objective witness (Lindemann).

As regards the excitement of 1947, it has become customary for some researchers to focus on Kenneth Arnold's sighting. There were many other sightings of equal merit which shed light on the possible reality behind flying saucers.

Natural Phenomena or Remote-controlled Devices?

It has been suggested in more recent times by supporters of the 'earth lights' theory (under these proposals UFO sightings are the result of energy forced up through gaps in the earth's crust at times of greater tectonic stress) that Arnold's sighting was in fact the result of natural phenomena (Devereux and Brookesmith).

Although there is much to commend the earth lights evidence, particularly in that a great deal of the work has been undertaken by respected scientists, other witnesses reported similar sightings in different areas. Richard Rankin of Palm Springs said that he saw a formation of ten flying saucers over Bakersfield, California on 23 June 1947 – a day before Arnold.

Rankin told the *Las Vegas Review-Journal* (2 July 1947 issue) that the planes were travelling 'maybe 9,000 feet up and fairly fast, maybe 300 or 400 miles an hour'. He initially saw ten 'planes' flying north. only to see seven returning on a reverse course at 2.15 pm the same afternoon. These were 'almost round' as Rankin described, and looked most like the US Navy's 'Flying Flapjack' aircraft developed, coincidentally, by the Chance-Vought company in Connecticut. The Navy denied that the 'Flapjack' had ever left its eastern-seaboard home (Angelucci and Bowers). Rankin, like Arnold, was a pilot with several thousands of hours of flying time under his belt. His report seems honest and used the word 'planes' to describe what he saw. Once again witnesses were arguing that these were mechanical aircraft under intelligent control.

There were many other similar reports and what is most interesting is the percentage of early saucer sightings that related to the Pacific North-West of the USA (Hall). More importantly, these were good sightings made by apparently credible witnesses. Take for instance the following selection:

• 4 July 1947 – Portland, Oregon. Policemen and other witnesses see UFOs in formation from around 1.05 pm.

- 4 July 1947 – Boise, Idaho. United Airlines pilot and crew *en route* to Portland, Oregon see nine disc-shaped UFOs.

- 4 July 1947 – Redmond, Oregon. Occupants of car see four disc-shaped objects passing Mount Jefferson.

- 6 July 1947 – South Central Wyoming. Aviation engineer sees oval UFO.

On 8 July 1947 a famous sighting takes place further south at the secret test-site then known as Muroc Air Force Base, now as Edwards. In the morning two spherical, disc-like UFOs were joined by a third object. A crew of technicians saw a white-aluminium UFO with a distinct oval outline descending and moving against the wind. Later on the same day a thin metallic UFO ascended, descended and hovered over the field. This was seen by a test-pilot in the vicinity.

The next day, back in the North-West, an aviation reporter saw a flat, circular UFO manoeuvre in front of clouds. In fact over two-thirds of 91 sightings collated and investigated by the National Investigating Committee on Aerial Phenomena (NICAP) from June–July 1947 came from the five north-western states: Washington (38), Idaho (11), Utah (8), Oregon (6) and Wyoming (2) (Hall).

In July 1948 near Pasco, Washington State, a private pilot saw a disc diving and climbing away at high speed, while the following year, on 3 July, at Longview, Washington a Navy commander and others watched a disc pass above an air show. The year 1950 was an especially important one because good photographic evidence was forthcoming relating to these sightings. Paul Trent, a farmer living in McMinnville, Oregon, took two photographs of a metallic disc on 11 May (*see* illustration no. 5). These photographs have caused a storm in UFO circles with many sceptics suggesting that they were hoaxes.

Nevertheless, extensive analysis of the images has suggested that they provide some of the best evidence for flying-saucer reality (Maccabee). The photographs are clear and show a structured object. They were initially reproduced by *Life* magazine ('Farmer Trent's Flying Saucer') on 26 June 1950, and the comment was made that the negatives did not appear to have been tampered with in any way.

The question is simple: were these unidentified flying objects of terrestrial or extraterrestrial origin? Perhaps the US intelligence community knew something. It is to their manipulation of information and output of black propaganda that we turn next.

THREE

THE OFFICIAL RESPONSE

THE US INTELLIGENCE community appears to have been actively involved in UFO investigations from August 1947, when attempts to discover the truth behind the Muroc Field (now Edwards Air Force Base) sightings of 8 July were begun. Some of the authorities made serious attempts to evaluate the reports of UFO sightings. It is within these reports that researchers can find fascinating clues that may point towards the truth.

The Muroc Sightings

Several military and civilian personnel stationed at the facility reported their sightings in the form of sworn affidavits. They all agreed that the objects they had seen were not birds, conventional aircraft, an optical illusion, weather balloons or anything similar. Their statements are remarkably similar in that they agreed that the objects seen were oval-shaped, made of a metallic material, possibly aluminium, with the ability to fly against the wind. The speeds demonstrated by the craft were, once again, unremarkable. In a statement given on 11 July, First Lieutenant Joseph McHenry, who was based at Muroc Army Air Field, said:

(It should be noted here that *all* the intelligence documents mentioned from here on in this chapter are *fully referenced* in the Bibliography under 'IUFOG' [Internet UFO Group]. The group's 'Project 1947' has an extensive library of similar material available to the public.)

Looking up, as I always do, I observed the aircraft, and looked slightly to the left, whereupon I observed two silver objects of either a spherical or disc-like shape, moving about three hundred miles an hour, or perhaps less, at approximately eight thousand feet, heading at about three hundred twenty degrees due north.

He asked two sergeants, Gerald E. Nauman and Joseph Ruvolo, to come over and have a look at the object. All three agreed that these were flying discs, and that they could not be weather balloons as they were flying against the wind! Nauman was particularly interested in the tight circular manoeuvres performed by one of the discs he saw.

Mr Lenz, a civilian working on the base at the time, made an interesting speculation when he said that in his view this was 'a man-made object, as evidenced distinctly by the outline and functional appearance'.

Efforts to get more information on the discs continued and on 20 July Lieutenant-Colonel Donald L. Springer received a letter from a Fred Johnson that appeared to add further weight to the suggestion that flying saucers were real. Johnson stated that he was prospecting up in the Mount Adams area on 24 June. He had the use of a telescope and was able to discern a number of oval-shaped objects of around 30 feet (9 m) in diameter travelling at an altitude of 1,000 feet (3,000 m).

Writing from Headquarters Fourth Air Force at Hamilton Field, California on 25 August, Springer suggested, in a letter to the Special Agent in Charge at FBI regional headquarters in San Francisco, that Johnson's report may have been based on newspaper reports relating to the Arnold sighting. There were definite similarities between the two reports, although of course Arnold stated that the objects were at a much higher altitude. Oddly enough, in this case no action was taken and it was stated that 'this headquarters does not intend to investigate this incident'. It was left to the FBI to conduct an investigation if it saw fit. This was an interesting departure because clearly there was enough official interest to warrant investigation of the Muroc sightings. Although no further action was deemed necessary after the statements from military personnel were taken, serious efforts were under way to 'evaluate' the sightings.

Hidden Clues

The information was passed on to Intelligence Branch A2. A month later on 23 September a (now famous) document, written by Lieutenant-General Nathan Twining, was circulated by Headquarters, Air Material Command (AMC) based at Wright Field, Ohio (latterly

Wright-Patterson Air Force Base). It presented a 'considered opinion' on flying discs. AMC believed that 'the phenomenon is something real and not visionary or fictitious'. The document went on to make, not unlike the majority of official (intelligence) documents relating to these early sightings, a number of fascinating comments:

...

b. *There are objects probably approximating the shape of a disc, of such appreciable size as to appear to be as large as man-made aircraft.*

...

d. *The reported operating characteristics such as extreme rates of climb, maneuverability (particularly in roll), and action which must be considered evasive when sighted or contacted by friendly aircraft and radar, lend belief to the possibility that some of the objects are controlled either manually, automatically or remotely.*

This tends to indicate to the reader that some kind of man-made craft might have been seen.

These documents have been used by proponents of the extraterrestrial hypothesis to suggest that they indicate technology beyond the cutting edge of late 1940s technology. In addition, the ETHers (Extraterrestrial Hypothesis supporters) suggest that the documents indicate that the craft seen could not have been of domestic origin. Again, they are wrong. Paragraph (f) of the document quoted above states clearly that:

It is possible within the present US knowledge – provided extensive detailed development is undertaken – to construct a piloted aircraft which has the general description of the object in subparagraph (e) above which would be capable of an approximate range of 7000 miles at subsonic speeds *[TM's emphasis]. (See also Brookesmith, 1996.)*

But how could this be achieved? Many possibilities existed and other declassified documents give us a good idea.

Schulgen Memo

The seven-page report entitled 'Intelligence Requirements on Flying Saucer Type Aircraft' dated 30 October 1947, known in UFO circles as the 'Schulgen Memo', adds further weight to the claim that flying saucers were not the product of some extraterrestrial intelligence. Claims made by sceptics that witness credibility was in question are not supported here. The memo notes that reports had been made by 'many competent observers, including USAF rated officers'. Significant features common to many reports were the general absence of sound, an oval or disc shape, and absence of exhaust trail except an occasional blue or brown diesel-like exhaust.

It was speculated that this might relate to the use of a special catalyst or chemical agent for extra power. The suggestion that a chemical agent or catalyst might be used under certain conditions seems to have been ignored by researchers for 50 years. Frank Whittle, designer of the British jet engine, had developed a device called an 'augmenter' which was actually a reheat system whereby the addition of extra fuel into the engine allowed for a significant (and immediate) increase in aircraft speed (Gunston, *Jane's Aerospace Dictionary*, 1986). The Horten brothers had also toyed with similar systems. It is possible that the use of such a device would have led to an unusual contrail.

Other features noted were the relatively small size of the objects seen (the same as a C-54 Constellation); the ability to operate in tight formation; and the ability to take evasive action, indicating the 'possibility of being manually operated, or possibly by electronic or remote control devices'.

The most intriguing comments made in the document do in fact relate to 'recovered' technologies but not from some alien spacecraft: 'For the purpose of analysis and evaluation of the so-called flying saucer phenomenon, the object sighted is being assumed to be a manned aircraft, of Russian origin, and based on the perspective thinking of the *actual* accomplishments of the Germans' [TM's italics]. The author of the report went on to mention the experimental and failed crescent-shaped Horten Brothers design known as the 'Parabola'.

Many researchers have noted Kenneth Arnold's description and drawing of a crescent-shaped object (Clark, p. 60; *Fortean Times*, Evans and Stacy, p. 28) and concluded that the 24 June sighting was *dissimilar* to other UFO sightings of June–July 1947. (Note that the Muroc event of 8 July related to disc-shaped objects.)

Russian Craft?

There were possibly two (maybe more) separate types of aircraft operating from 1946 onwards: a flying wing very similar to the Horten designs, and a flying disc, possibly based on a combination of German-recovered and pre-existing American technologies.

One of the major concerns reflected in the Schulgen Memo and similar declassified intelligence documents was that the Russians might have had access to similar technologies and that they were flying unidentified craft, with impunity, through US airspace. A possible reason for such concern was that the Russians had gained control of various research and development facilities in Germany including the Gotha plant where the Horten HoIX had been developed. Bill Rose states:

> At the end of the Second World War, Russian forces stumbled across four largely completed examples of the German DFS [Deutsches Forschungsinstitut für Segelflug – German Research Institute for Sailplanes] 346 high altitude supersonic rocketplane at the Siebel factory in Halle. Securing advanced Nazi technology was a priority for all the major powers and these DFS aircraft, along with most of the technicians who had worked on them, were shipped back to Podberezhye in the USSR (Rose, 'The Hidden Aurora', UFO Magazine, 1996).

In order to determine the true nature and extent of Russian developments the memo suggested that former German scientists with a 'better than average' understanding of flying-wing technologies should be 'located and interrogated'.

In addition, further intelligence was required relating to possible construction of Russian flying wings. Finally, in another eye-opening remark, the memo asked: 'What is the Horten perspective thinking on internal controls or controls that are effective mainly by streams of air or gas originating from within the aircraft to supplant conventional external surface controls?'

This is where those researchers with a knowledge of German flying-saucer technologies start to smell a rat. It seems that the intelligence community was more knowledgeable than it pretended. Talk of 'interrogating' people concerned with flying-wing developments would seem to indicate a desire to control the release and availability of information relating to these craft.

Detailed knowledge of German developments in flying-saucer research is also hinted at. Section 2(a) of the memo states that information concerning disc or saucer-shaped craft using 'Boundary layer control method by suction, blowing, or a combination of both', 'Special controls for effective maneuverability at very low speeds or extremely high altitudes' and 'openings either in the leading edge top and bottom surfaces that are employed chiefly to accomplish boundary layer control or for the purpose of reducing induced drag' should be sought. It should be pointed out that the German saucers reportedly used similar methods of control: a craft that sucked in the 'dead' air of the boundary layer and expelled it, thus increasing speed.

In the few books dealing with German developments concerning the 'suction' method the authors of the report conclude that this method was used from 1942 onwards (Harbinson, *Projekt UFO*, 1995). Under this system the engines would be an integral part of an all-wing or elliptical aircraft with directional jets used to create the necessary thrust.

According to reports, Dr Walter Miethe, one of the men involved in the German saucer project (and who was transported to the United States in the immediate post-war period), had been able to develop a disc powered by an early version of vectored thrust (a propulsive thrust whose axis can be rotated to control vehicle trajectory; term normally applied to swivelling-nozzle jet engine of plane). Under these circumstances paragraph 6(b) takes on added significance:

> *The power plant would likely be an integral part of the aircraft and could possibly not be distinguished as an item separate from the aircraft. If jet propulsion is used, large air handling capacity, characterized by a large air inlet and large exhaust nozzle, should be evident.... It is possible that the propulsive jet is governed or influenced for control of the aircraft. The presence of methods of changing the direction of the object should be observed.*

The final comment in the memo can be regarded as the icing on the cake. Again, inside knowledge of advanced hidden technologies is evident: 'catalytic agents for super-performance or normal cruising power'.

The Schulgen Memo hints at German technological achievements made in the Second World War and parallel developments made in Britain, but not generally known or discussed – certainly not in UFO circles. These included disc-shaped aircraft, flying wings, new propulsion systems and special fuel mixtures for extra performance. Most importantly, the memo makes it clear that flying-saucer sightings could well be the product of terrestrial technology.

Wind-tunnel Tests

Just two weeks after the emergence of the Schulgen document, Headquarters Counter Intelligence Corps Region VI (for information on the role and activities of CIC, *see* Sayer and Botting) released a report on flying saucers rated 'Secret'. The document was released to CIC Regional Commanding Officers throughout Bavaria, and it answered various questions and concerns raised by Air Material Command. Clearly intelligence agencies believed that flying saucers existed. In fact the following statement should raise a few eyebrows: 'At the present time, construction models are being built for wind tunnel tests. It is further suspected that the flying objects may have been developed from the original plans and experiments conducted by the Germans prior to capitulation.'

Construction models built for wind tunnel tests? Models of flying saucers? It is not made at all clear where or who is involved in the supposed tests and the sentence is just dropped into the larger paragraph. Although this is a shocking admission, the document appears never to have been used by the many published UFO researchers. Why not?

The CIC also requested information about German aircraft specialists and test pilots who might have some knowledge of similar aircraft. The veil of secrecy is once more apparent where the author – Special Agent William E. Lahned Jr – requested that 'This canvass is to be made discreetly and to conceal our interest in the subject.'

The date for final submission from regional intelligence and technical specialists was 12 December. On 16 December the Office of Military Command for Germany got in on the act. The letter, written by Lieutenant-Colonel Harold H. Pretty to the Deputy Director of Intelligence European Command – Frankfurt, concerned the 'Horten Brothers (Flying Saucers)'.

As well as mentioning the peculiarities of Reimar and Walter Horten and their early technical advances in terms of flying-wing design and construction, the letter noted that the HoIX was tested in the supersonic wind tunnel at the Aerodynamic Research Institute in Göttingen under the supervision of Professor Betz. It went on to detail the tortured wheeling and dealing relating to the HoIX, which never got beyond the prototype stage. It seems that both Walter and Reimar had been interrogated by British authorities and had spent three months in England ending in April 1946. However, and somewhat true to form, the British had messed things up by not offering either brother a contract. (Walter Horten wrote to Jack Northrop in 1947 about the possibility of his going to America to work. Unfortunately, Northrop did not have the clout to be able to effect such a move.)

On the central question of flying saucers, none of those questioned were, if the author of the report is to be believed, able to provide any leads about them, although it was generally agreed that such an aircraft would be 'highly practical and desirable'.

Of course, this particular authority had interviewed only a limited number of people regarding saucers and it is quite possible that other undisclosed authorities had learned about similar technologies in the immediate post-war trawl. The highly compartmentalized nature of intelligence activity means that it is perfectly believable that Headquarters Berlin Command of the Office of Military Government for Germany did *not* know about flying saucers. In any case, it seems that by December 1947 some of the men really involved in the German saucer projects were long gone and had in fact been spirited over to Fort Bliss in Texas, where they were subsequently split up and farmed out to facilities in New Mexico, California and Canada.

The role of the CIA in one of the biggest cover-ups of all time was to befuddle researchers for decades. Their success was based on information management, and ranged from no response or flat denial to tarring the reputations of those who observed, passionately believed in or researched UFOs, as we will see.

FOUR

THE CIA AND UFOS

ALTHOUGH THE LANGUAGE of officialdom has convinced some commentators that there was no US interest in (German-derived) aircraft that might be mistaken for UFOs, intelligence documents and pronouncements by Jack Northrop suggested otherwise.

Meanwhile, Air Material Command continued to look into flying-saucer sightings. A letter written by Major-General C. P. Cabell from Headquarters, US Air Force on 3 November 1948 is typical of declassified documents on the subject (IUFOG). Despite the fact that intelligence documents had already talked about 'flying saucers', Cabell wrote to the Commanding General, Air Material Command at Wright-Patterson Air Force Base. Cabell stated that 'Identification and the origin of these objects is not discernible to this Headquarters.' It becomes clear that either the right connections had not been made, the document was simply a cover, or that someone who did know about these sightings was keeping quiet about a domestic saucer programme or programmes. Under the circumstances the latter seems sensible. Just because 'this Headquarters' did 'not know' the origin or nature of flying saucers does not mean that another agency or headquarters did not know. This simple fact has been ignored by the vast majority of UFO researchers.

Gerald K. Haines' (Haines) piece of black propaganda makes a number of important points and we shall examine these in detail later on (see pp. 71–2).

The CIA and the USAF appear to have disagreed on the methods to be employed in dealing with an inquisitive press and public (soon the reports themselves became a focus for concern).

Paragraph (3) of the Air Force document mentioned above entitled

'Flying Object Incidents in the United States' noted 'the necessity of informing the public as to the status of the problem. To date there has been too little data to present to the public.'

This seemed fair enough, but then Cabell went on to say that the press was going to 'take it into its own hands and demand to be told what we do or do not know about the situation. Silence on our part will not long be acceptable.' While the Air Force saw a need to appease an influential press, in most cases the CIA preferred to rely on 'plausible deniability' or just *plain silence*. It would appear that there was an increasing focus upon information management.

In reply to the 3 November letter, latterly known as the 'McCoy memo', Headquarters Air Material Command stated that it had studied approximately 180 incidents. It was clear at this early stage in proceedings that there were several different UFO phenomena: discs or flying saucers, cigars, balloon-shaped objects and balls of light. Paragraph (7) gives further evidence of the misleading language of the intelligence document that the UFO research community appears to have been unable to penetrate. Regarding the comment that 'All information that has been made available to this Headquarters indicates that the discs, the cigar shaped objects and the balls of light are not of domestic origin' might lead to the conclusion that not all the information had been made available to Air Material Command. Continuing, the paragraph hints at a man-made solution to some sightings. 'Engineering investigations indicates that disc or wingless aircraft could support themselves in flight by aerodynamic means. It is probable that the problems of stability and control could also be solved for such an aircraft.'

This much had already been demonstrated by the Hortens, Northrop, Zimmerman (*see* p. 70), and a team of German flying-saucer engineers working near Prague. The art of deception is soon apparent, however, and is a stunning example of 'Intelspeak'.

Having told the reader that wingless or spherical craft were possible technologically, the letter turns the known facts on their head by concluding that 'according to current aerodynamic theory in this country, aircraft with such configurations would have relatively poor climb, altitude and range characteristics with power plants now in use'. Not true!

The Northrop Lecture

In the 35th Wilbur Wright Memorial Lecture held in the Lecture Hall of the Institution of Civil Engineers, Great George Street, London, on

29 May 1947, Jack Northrop, father of the American B-35 and YB-49 flying-wing aircraft, spoke on 'The Development of All-Wing Aircraft' to a packed auditorium (Northrop). Northrop made it clear that he was fully aware of the work of the Horten brothers and that their conclusions 'were surprisingly similar to our own' – namely that the all-wing aircraft was superior to other forms in many respects including:

- a major reduction in drag, up to 20 per cent;

- gains in aerodynamic and structural efficiency;

- use in military or commercial applications;

- up to 40 per cent less power needed to power a flying wing at the same speed as a more conventional aircraft;

- better fuel efficiency (up to 30 per cent) for heavy loads.

Northrop went on to recount a little of the history of his various Second World War aircraft designs, including the N-1M and the N-9M, which acted as a successful testbed in over 200 flights. By September 1942 Northrop's team was working with rocket motors in combination with a flying-wing design in order to build a 'highly maneuverable fighter'.

The XB-79 turbo-jet aircraft was not dissimilar to the Messerschmidt ME163 although the US programme fell behind as a result of problems with the rocket engine. Northrop realized that the Germans had forged ahead and that their work had resulted in the many radical designs noted above. Improved materials and more effective rockets or jet engines, possibly based on German technology, may have helped to solve the teething troubles experienced by the Northrop team. Northrop concluded that despite the conservatism of the aviation industry the gains resulting from the employment of the all-wing configuration would by far outweigh any problems associated with his work.

Perhaps the most important part of the Northrop lecture came towards the end when he speculated on the aircraft of the future. These could be seen as a natural progression from the work of the Northrop, Horten and Lippisch teams: 'If a sufficiently high altitude is chosen it seems quite possible that adequate volume can be secured in the wing, in spite of its thickness ratio, by using low aspect ratio planforms approaching the triangular.' Oh yes, Northrop mentioned in the lecture that some of his flying wings had been tested at – Muroc Air Field.

Amusingly, from the point of view of the supposed Roswell UFO 'crash retrieval', the McCoy memo argues that the idea that the objects came from another planet had 'not been ignored'. It later stated that 'although it is obvious that some types of flying objects have been sighted, the exact nature of those objects cannot be established until physical evidence, such as that which would result from a crash, has been obtained'. So, according to Air Material Command, are we to infer that no ET craft crashed near Roswell? It is difficult to say. Nevertheless, the kind of doublespeak that emerges in these and similar documents hardly fills us with confidence on such important points. The bottom line is that intelligence documents sometimes *attempt to deceive*. Only in the light of new information can we make an informed judgement about the veracity of the claims of Air Material Command.

Researcher and former Roswell crash retrieval advocate Kent Jeffrey has made much of this and similar documentary material. He claims that this, as well as personal conversations he has had with high-ranking personnel stationed at Wright-Patterson Air Force Base, is enough to 'disprove' that any crash took place in July 1947. Perhaps rather naively, Jeffrey believes that people would never lie to him (Jeffrey).

A Flawed Approach

Perhaps it is sensible to approach the conclusion of this chapter by highlighting the typical, though flawed, approach to intelligence documents.

This particular case is taken from *Beyond Top Secret* by popular UFO writer Timothy Good (Good, 1996). A US Army report dated 13 January 1949 is headed 'Unconventional Aircraft'. Good highlights paragraph (5):

> *It is felt that these incidents are of such great importance, espe-cially as they are occurring in the vicinity of sensitive installa-tions, that a scientific board be sent to this locality to study the situation with a view to arriving at a solution of this extraordi-nary phenomena [sic] with the least practical delay.*

This is typical of the many documents reviewed. They were basically saying: 'We haven't got a clue what these objects are and somebody ought to look into them.'

And yet, paragraph (4) states that: 'Still another belief that is advanced is that, it is highly probable that the United States may be carrying on some top-secret experiments.'

Colonel Eustis Poland, author of the document in question, was suggesting that it was *highly probable* that something of a top-secret nature was going on. We have already seen that this might well have been the case. Given that Headquarters Fourth Army was based in Houston, Texas, we might conclude that there was a link between the 'unconventional aircraft' reported and the activities of German scientists based at nearby Fort Bliss. Link or no link, paragraph (4) is overlooked by Good – no surprise given his convictions regarding aliens and crashed saucers.

In any case, Colonel Poland had no 'need to know' about top-secret experiments, and could only pass on his concerns in the hope that some factual information might emerge in time.

Air Force Office of Investigation report (AIR 100-203-79), written in 1948, and rated 'Top Secret', made it quite clear that the objects seen 'most closely resembled' Horten flying-wing aircraft. It was also made quite clear that witness reports were credible and that their reports should be taken seriously:

> A number of reports on unidentified flying objects come from observers who, because of their technical background and experience do not appear to be influenced by unfounded sensationalism not inclined to report explainable phenomena as new types of airborne devices.

The report mentioned some of the better sightings including one captured by cinetheodolite during April 1947 – before the saucer panic began. Two employees of the Weather Bureau Station near Richmond, Virginia saw a metallic disc on three occasions. The disc was described as 'shaped something like an ellipse with a flat bottom and a round top'. Details were also given of the William Rhoads Arizona photographs. These are of significance because they show a sort of hybrid design – part disc, part crescent with a square tail (Randle and Schmitt, 1994). Most importantly, the photographs were examined by experts who concluded that these were 'true photographic images and do not appear to be an imperfection in the emulsion or imperfections in the lens'.

Importantly, none of the reports relate to objects travelling at speeds beyond those possible using jet engines. A number of actual sightings were dealt with in Appendix 'C': 'Selected Reports of Flying Object Incidents'. In chronological order, the facts are clear:

- Section 2c details an incident reported by a pilot flying at 10,000 feet (3,000 m) over Nevada. He estimated the speed of the object as 285 mph (460 kmph).

- Section 21 relates to a sighting by pilots on board a DC-3. Flying at 170 mph (275 kmph), a flying disc crossed their path and they turned to give chase. After four minutes the disc moved out of sight.

- A 12 November 1947 report estimated a speed of between 700 and 900 mph (1,120–1,500 kmph).

- On 30 April 1948 a pilot saw a 'light coloured sphere' travelling at 100 mph (160 kmph).

- Section 2t reports an incident that took place near Andrew Field, Maryland where two pilots attempted to intercept a UFO. On this occasion the object flew off at an estimated speed of 500–600 mph (800–970 kmph).

I have mentioned these particular sightings because they were all reported by pilots in the air who would have had a much better chance of making a reasonable estimate of speeds.

Undoubtedly these reports were taken very seriously. Although it was made clear that the reports varied in terms of credibility and detail the impression was given that these were terrestrial aircraft:

> The above tends to indicate that some type of object has been seen and the possibility exists that the object or objects seen are conventional domestic devices, such as weather balloons, test rockets, **or jet-equipped aircraft with pancake or flying wing configurations** (TM's emphasis).

Referring to the early April 1947 case noted above, the authors of the report wrote that:

> ...on the basis of this one report it appears that the discs are not balloons. It would appear that this sighting was not influenced by the reports of foreign incidents, the newspaper accounts of domestic incidents, nor by misidentification of a conventional object.

Later documents relating to the involvement of the CIA in these matters indicate a change of attitude. It became clear that an attempt to question and undermine even the most credible sightings made by trained military personnel was under way. Not only that, 'Project Sign', initially set up to investigate UFO reports and to collect detailed evidence relating to them, had been redesignated 'Project Grudge'. It has been suggested that there was a desire to downgrade the whole subject of UFO reports.

While in 1947 and 1948 intelligence documents we find suggestions that UFOs might be a combination of misidentifications, natural phenomena or unconventional aircraft, the suggestion that domestic secret aircraft projects might be responsible was not popular with certain agencies. In subsequent reports an emphasis was placed on doubting the credibility of witnesses, debunking tactics and anti-Soviet paranoia.

CIA Involvement

The newly formed Central Intelligence Agency (CIA) was interested in UFO sightings; we have a reasonable selection of material to draw upon including some 50 pages made available in 1992 to Computer UFO Network researchers based in Seattle, Washington following Freedom of Information Act requests (CUFON).

A letter written by Edward Tauss on 1 August 1952 came at a time when increased numbers of UFO sightings, including many over Washington, DC, were again causing concern. Tauss argued that the vast majority of sightings could be explained, although a number of 'unexplainable' sightings required continued vigilance. There was also the suggestion that not enough information had been collected and that was why some cases remained unexplainable. (Nevertheless 'Project Blue Book' reports were later to suggest that a significant number of cases, 701 out of a total of over 12,618, remained unexplained.)

There is little doubt that the CIA handled their UFO investigations badly, although this was not to emerge until much later. Researchers who argue that there was (and is) a cover-up of information on the subject of UFOs would enjoy reading the following from the Tauss letter:

> It is strongly urged, however, that no indication of CIA interest or concern reach the press or public, in view of their probable alarmist tendencies to accept such interest as 'confirmatory' of the soundness of 'unpublished facts' in the hands of the U.S.

So why the attempts to hide CIA interest? It would seem sensible to suggest that this had nothing to do with supposed extraterrestrial spacecraft and a great deal to do with programmes involving advanced aircraft that the CIA did know about. One thing that becomes increasingly clear from CIA documents is that the Agency had a close working relationship with the Air Technical Intelligence Centre (ATIC) at Wright-Patterson Air Force Base, and that it passed on all official enquiries to it.

Minutes of the Branch Chief's Meeting of 11 August 1952 made this clear:

> *Mr. Steele wanted to know if P&E [Physics and Electronics Division/CIA] should be in a position to answer requests coming to us. Since ATIC has a standard form for reference purposes, requests would be answered through contact with them.*

On 14 August another report noted a press conference held by General Samford, who claimed that 'no pattern of anything remotely consistent with any menace to the United States' was apparent from on-going investigations into UFO sightings. He went on to argue that 'unexplained sightings could not have resulted from any experiments or tests conducted by the United States'. This is the misleading language of officialdom.

Firstly, we are told that the objects are *not* a menace to the United States at the same time that other intelligence agencies are pontificating about a possible Soviet threat (AIR 100-203-79, written just a month earlier, goes into some detail on this matter).

Secondly, Samford mentioned experimental or test vehicles. What about the possibility, as stated although denied in other CIA documents on the subject, that the unexplained craft of the flying wing or disc varieties were not experimental but *operational* craft? It is clear that the question of experimental or test vehicles was a difficult one.

The document again stated the need to play down the subject of UFO sightings. Both ATIC and CIA were concerned to keep a lid on any possible 'hysteria' surrounding them. It seems that the main concern was the reports themselves.

On the question of saucers being US secret weapons the report noted that it had been denied officially at the highest level of government that this was the case. The cynic might well suggest that such a denial could be taken as an admission of guilt!

Nevertheless, Samford's statement was a rather meaningless one even in light of the CIA's supposed contact with a Dr Whitman, chairman of the Research and Development Board. Whitman apparently denied the existence of a domestic saucer programme. As supporting 'evidence' the author of the report tends to lend credence to this denial by noting that Air Force commanders had issued an order to 'intercept but not shoot down' unidentified flying objects! Now this is very important. At the height of anti-Soviet paranoia at the highest levels of government a CIA document was arguing that UFOs, even if they might be of Soviet origin, should not be intercepted! This is quite incredible and frankly unbelievable.

The military would not want to shoot down *domestic* flying saucers although they would have to try to bring down any foreign aircraft not cleared to fly through US airspace.

Remember that we have other intelligence documents noting an average speed of some 300 mph (483 kmph) for most sightings and how these could relate to aircraft constructed within the present US technical know-how.

There are many contradictions in declassified intelligence documents. Certainly the CIA and the Air Force could not initially agree on a common position on UFO sightings despite their desire to explain away as many of them as possible.

As we have seen, the CIA insisted that a majority of sightings took place over atomic installations while the 1948 Air Force Office of Investigation (AFOIN) document AIR 100-203-79 suggested that:

> There is a large concentration of sightings along the Eastern Seaboard; another large concentration throughout the Western coastal states, and a few sightings in the Middle West.

As if to further suggest that a domestic terrestrial solution for some sightings was in order, Appendix 'D' of the 1948 report presented some basic facts about the Horten Flying Wing, the Northrop YB-49, the V-173 Flying Flapjack and an intriguing home-made circular-wing aircraft built in 1935 called the Arup Tailless Monoplane which had a top speed of 86 mph (139 kmph). It was speculated that other similar US home-made aircraft may have built although it is unlikely that these could have been responsible for more than a tiny fraction of UFO reports.

The masks of deception employed so far were merely leading up to an even better way to discredit researchers – psychological warfare, in which the mental state of whoever was rocking the boat was questioned.

FIVE

PSYCHOLOGICAL
WARFARE

T HE CIA HAD a cornucopia of oft-repeated tricks to debunk, confuse and obscure credible and detailed reports of UFOs. These have ranged from attributing sightings to little-understood natural phenomena, publicity seekers and the Soviet threat, to a new attack. This was to question the psychological state of the observer, coming to the conclusion that the sightings were 'internally generated'.

Ominously perhaps, it was at this stage, mid-1952, that the CIA started talking about the psychological-warfare implications of UFO reports. Initially, this concern was directed towards possible Soviet efforts in this area (despite the CIA's having previously argued that UFOs were of no potential threat to the USA!). The interest in this area was summed up in points 1 and 3 of a 1952 memorandum circulated by CIA Director Smith:

> *I am today transmitting to the National Security Council a proposal in which it is concluded that the problems connected with unidentified flying objects appear to have implications for intelligence and operations.*
>
> *I suggest that we discuss at an early board meeting the possible offensive or defensive utilization of these phenomena for psychological warfare purposes.*

The more one looks at the *language* used in intelligence documents released by any of the agencies, especially by the CIA, the more one notices the increasing attempts to mislead or deceive. Take this example from a draft CIA document dated 15 August 1952 (CUFON): 'Finally, no debris of material evidence has ever been recovered following an unexplained sighting.'

CENTRAL INTELLIGENCE AGENCY
WASHINGTON 25, D. C.

195

OFFICE OF THE DIRECTOR

MEMORANDUM TO: Director, Psychological Strategy Board

SUBJECT: Flying Saucers

1. I am today transmitting to the National Security Council a proposal (TAB A) in which it is concluded that the problems connected with unidentified flying objects appear to have implications for psychological warfare as well as for intelligence and operations.

2. The background for this view is presented in some detail in TAB B.

3. I suggest that we discuss at an early board meeting the possible offensive or defensive utilization of these phenomena for psychological warfare purposes.

                                        Walter B. Smith
Enclosure   Director

Was the document dating from the early 1950s the start of a programme that has carried on for 40 years? Was the Hudson Valley 'flap' of the 1980s an example of 'psywar' in action?

Maybe to the average researcher this sentence is unworthy of examination. In actual fact it is vital. The CIA were talking about an unexplained sighting.

What about the crash of an unconventional aircraft which they knew about: a 'known' and not an 'unknown'? This was not dealt with, even though there was evidence to suggest that craft did crash in the New Mexico/White Sands Proving Ground area in 1947 and 1948. Discussion of psychological warfare and other 'psychological factors' is a cause for deep concern in relation to the wider study and understanding of UFO phenomena. Nobody doubts that a majority of the 1,500 cases investigated by ATIC could be explained as elusive natural phenomena, misidentifications and so forth, but the fact is that some 20 per cent remained unidentified, not only through lack of information. This fact was made clear on several occasions.

Examination of supposed 'psychological factors' comes across as an attempt to explain away credible and detailed reports. Such factors were said to be personal, emotional, to do with publicity seeking, the physical and mental condition of the witness in question and possible eye strain (!).

What concerns me is that there is little middle ground in UFO research. On the one hand we have believers who insist that the unexplained percentage of reports indicate an extraterrestrial explanation and these people might advocate general support for the witness. This could be summed up in the statement 'witnesses know what they are seeing'.

On the other hand we have the sceptics who tend to argue exactly the same case as the CIA psychologists. The sceptic might argue that UFO sightings are reliant upon the witnesses' mental state, belief systems ('the need to believe'), possibly understanding of aircraft lighting arrangements and so on. In other words, UFOs are explained as 'psycho-social' or 'geo-physical' in nature. This is the belief that UFOs are 'internally generated'. Of course, these explanations are possible, maybe even probable for some cases. But neither camp can explain away sightings of structured aircraft: the flying-disc or flying-wing aircraft.

The Psycho-social Hypothesis

The psycho-social hypothesis is one which 'hold[s] that UFO experiences are largely psychological in nature' (Clark). The theory was developed by Jung in his *Flying Saucers: A Modern Myth* (1991) and taken on board by Jacques Vallee in his *Passport to Magonia* (1970). John Keel also suggested that psychological explanations may be important and that 'ultraterrestrial' and 'non-human' intelligences were interacting with people who explained these events in terms of certain UFO sightings and related paranormal phenomena (Keel).

I find it difficult to see how these researchers could arrive at such conclusions in relation to sightings of clearly structured aircraft, sometimes with unusual contrails (suggesting a jet engine)! Nevertheless, the CIA appear to have developed the psychological explanation for UFOs in advance of the UFO researchers. Perhaps the latter did so because they confused sightings of structured craft with encounters of a more paranormal nature.

Having suggested that numerous factors came into play before, during and after a UFO sighting, the CIA appears to have concluded that many difficult cases could now be effectively dealt with and debunked. As a result, declassified information tended to concentrate on easily identifiable objects misperceived by witnesses as UFOs: for instance, weather balloons (some 4,000 were launched daily in the late 1940s and early 1950s – CIA briefing, 22 August 1952) or the reflection of sunlight off an 'unpainted aircraft':

> In the daytime, aircraft, particularly those that are unpainted, can give extremely brilliant reflections of sunlight. An interesting case under known conditions is one which occurred last year in Maryland. A group of aircraft design engineers went into the country to witness tests of their own jet airplane. The three test aircraft, with unpainted wings and fuselages, passed directly overhead. All engineers agreed that if they had not known what the objects were, and since they could not observe the silver wings against the sky, they would have reported the red fuselages as flaming tails and they would have imagined objects emitting them.

Many of the good 'daylight disc' reports do not mention flaming trails shooting out of the back of the craft. This example is one where a spurious comparison is made in order to knock it down – an old debunking trick. In any case, how can we use this as evidence of misinterpretation? We cannot know what the design team would have reported under different conditions!

Similar example of this play on words surfaces in the 15 August CIA draft document:

> [ATIC] feel that the remaining 20% might be reducible to 10% were it not for these reasons:
>
> • insufficient information reported;
>
> • incorrect information unwittingly or purposely reported;
>
> • insufficient or total lack of subsequent investigation of details.

So, in what appears to be a somewhat desperate attempt to explain away the reports, we are left with 10 per cent – or approximately 150 reports. It is later argued that these 'might have been caused' by little-understood natural phenomena including 'little known clouds of ice crystals which exist at an altitude of 60,000 feet'. But how many reports of disc-like craft relate to objects at 60,000 feet (19,000 m)? Under the terms of the draft it would be possible to explain away any report by suggesting that there were not enough details, that the witnesses were hoaxers, that the investigation was flawed.

Soviet Threat

Reports emerging from inside the Soviet Union suggested that US panic about flying saucers was an attempt to 'fan war hysteria'! What is known, however, about intelligence is that the majority of information received comes via HUMINT – human intelligence. That means operatives on the ground, spies in place inside the military/industrial complex, or personnel tasked with keeping an eye on high-security facilities. In other words, if the USSR wanted to know about the state of war readiness it might be far more sensible to place operatives in position to keep an eye on US military bases. This would have been a relatively easy task and much simpler than attempting to penetrate US airspace with advanced flying-saucer aircraft! Perhaps the suggestion that the Soviets were penetrating US airspace was a deliberate lie intended to deflect researchers away from the origin of many saucer sightings – the United States and Canada themselves.

Nevertheless, it is only fair to point out that the Soviets may have had their saucers too and undoubtedly more is to emerge from the Russian archives. As a result the USA would undoubtedly have been concerned to build competing and similar aircraft. Once again, such Soviet work would have been based on recovered German, not alien, technologies and there has been some suggestion that the Soviets did indeed develop flying saucers. Jan Aldrich's Project 1947 (*Fortean Times*, Evans and Stacey) has sought to collate information about early flying-saucer sightings and media reports.

One of these reports may have originated via 'Project Wringer', a post-war effort directed to interview military, industrial and other personnel of former Axis countries, prisoners-of-war held in the Soviet Union and other Eastern Bloc nations or displaced persons with intelligence or military information. Jan Aldrich found the following report while undertaking research at the US National Archives:

10. SOURCE: EP 134892, Rpt. No. 5418–47758 dated 19th January 1954. Date of Observation: May 1953.

Preamble: During his internment in PW camp #1 in STALIN-GRAD (48/42N 44/30E) SOURCE ????? some ???? of general interest and ??? allegedly observed a couple of flying saucers. SOURCE was always interned in the camp. He understood a little Russian.

Flying saucers: SOURCE emphasized that he had never seen or heard anything of flying saucers before he observed two of them on a dusty morning over Stalingrad in May 1953 when he was on guard within the camp. He observed them in a rather high altitude flying fast in one direction, one following the other.

Thinking they had something to do with scientific research of Russia he forgot about his observation until he came back home in Oct. 1953 and saw designs of flying saucers in West European magazines. He could not provide further details.

In a conversation with Bill Rose in December 1997 he suggested that much of the evidence for flying-saucer reality had effectively been buried. He added that saucer technologies had been captured by both the Americans and the Russians. Certainly, Habermohl was spirited east, as we have seen (*see* p. 34), and it is more than likely that other information from Reinhard Gehlen's network of spies in Russia (Simpson) relating to Soviet saucers would have been passed on to US intelligence agencies.

The growing Soviet threat which led to Air Force Regulation 200-2 (August 1954) was very real. My latest research indicates that Soviet disc planes were probing the North American Distant Early Warning radar system as early as 1949. Hence the interest in UFO reports, foreign technology and in fully controlling the flow of information relating to these.

Until 1952–3 it had been suggested in a variety of intelligence documents that UFO sightings were on the one hand totally explainable given enough information, or on the other hand they were Soviet unknowns operating over US airspace. It had even been suggested that extraterrestrial vehicles were responsible. Despite the multifaceted nature of UFO phenomena the most obvious solution, and one admitted to be feasible under a variety of circumstances, was that some UFOs were of domestic origin. This explanation was, for obvious reasons, not popular with the military or with UFO enthusiasts emotionally attached to a belief in 'Flying Saucers from Outer Space'.

CIA Response

The CIA position on flying saucers was made clearer in a briefing presented on 22 August 1952 (CUFON). It once again laid the primary responsibility for investigating sightings on the shoulders of ATIC personnel and also the Air Force Office of Special Investigations (AFOSI). AFOSI has been rumoured to be involved in the UFO cover-up. One of its operatives, now retired, Richard Doty, was heavily involved with UFO researchers William Moore and Linda Moulton-Howe during the 1980s; the intention appeared to be to spread disinformation (Friedman; Good, 1992).

It was argued that sightings of flying saucers were more frequent in the vicinity of atomic-energy facilities and that these might be 'by-products' of atomic fission. This nonsense might have seemed believable back in 1952 but cannot be taken seriously in 1998. Any apparent link had 'not been disproved'. This kind of flawed logic is similar to the oft-repeated maxim of a modern-day Ufologist: 'The photograph/film has not been proved to be a hoax.' *Neither has it proved to be the case!*

Importantly, and perhaps without regard for the consequences, paragraph (IV) suggested that 'the greatest number of sightings has been made at or near Dayton, Ohio where the investigations are going on'. This was a marvellous example of black propaganda. On the one hand, the CIA denied that flying saucers were any threat to national security and claimed that they were, in fact, most likely to be a variety of 'as yet unexplained' natural phenomena. It also seemed to work into the mindset of the 'believer' Ufologist by suggesting that UFOs take an overt interest in high-security military facilities! I have no doubt that these words were intended to resonate inside the minds of UFO researchers. Psychological warfare indeed.

In fact, this much is admitted in the 22 August briefing (para. VI): 'The Air Force is mostly interested in the "saucer" problem because of its psychological warfare implications.'

As an afterthought it was suggested by the CIA that several flying-saucer societies had been investigated and a conclusion had been reached that these were of 'doubtful loyalty'. It was further suggested that the funding of these groups was 'unknown'. The reader would do well to realize that these comments were made at a time of anti-Soviet paranoia and the beginnings of 'McCarthyism' and the anti-Communist witch hunts of the 1950s.

Under these circumstances it was deemed to be perfectly justifiable for the CIA or other intelligence organizations like J. Edgar Hoover's FBI to infiltrate these groups. In addition, and perhaps more significantly, it would be possible to use these groups to put out a

certain message about UFO sightings through the release of information and stories about sightings. Most importantly, many military and
intelligence personnel ended up in control of the National
Investigations Committee on Aerial Phenomena (NICAP). These
included the first Director of the CIA, Roscoe H. Hillenkoetter (Clark,
1998). Many of the saucer societies lent themselves to this process of
disinformation but perhaps they were encouraged – an operative
within a group would hardly be likely to point the other members and
investigators in the right direction. Perhaps that is why all the major
organizations concluded that UFOs were of extraterrestrial origin?

The Computer UFO Network (CUFON) collection of declassified CIA
documents indicates that the psychological implications were of great
concern and the Air Force apparently believed that 'a public made
jumpy by the flying saucer scare would be a serious liability in the
event of air attacks by an enemy'.

However, according to the Air Force this scenario was most unlikely.
In any case the vast majority of the American public supported moves
to hound potential and actual Communist subversives in the 1950s. It is
not likely that they would panic as a result of saucer sightings. They
had not done so in Washington, DC in 1952 when unidentified objects
appeared over the capital. In fact, it had been radar operators and a
variety of military personnel who had panicked (Ruppelt)! If anything,
the wild stories that appeared in the press relating to UFOs served only
to discredit the subject in the eyes of the public.

In fact, it seemed as if the intention was to control the UFO phenomenon entirely. The CIA recommended that procedures for the identification of aircraft both visually and by electronic means should be
implemented while improving the defensive capabilities of US forces.
The CIA also hoped to be able to control and predict UFO sightings as
part of an overall strategy of psychological warfare.

Both the CIA and the Air Force were interested in these possibilities.
The fact that the CIA and the Air Technical Intelligence Center (ATIC)
worked closely together on the question on UFOs belies the suggestion
that there was conflict and confusion between the different agencies
relating to this 'problem'.

On 13 October 1952 in a letter written by James Q. Reber, Assistant
Director of Intelligence Coordination, more information emerged.
Again, a detailed examination of the wording is necessary. Reber wrote:

> c. It is far too early in view of the present state of our knowledge
> regarding Flying Saucers for psychological warfare planners to
> start planning how the United States might use US Flying
> Saucers against the enemy.

That is exactly what he wrote: how the United States might use US flying saucers against the enemy. US flying saucers? We were led to believe that the CIA did not know of their origin. Or is this perhaps a simple mistake, a typographical error perhaps? Maybe, but probably not.

In fact, research into official attitudes regarding UFO sightings is revealing. In his *The UFO Controversy in America* David Jacobs (1975) traces attempts by scientists to get to grips with seemingly elusive UFO phenomena against the background of an emerging Air Force/CIA position by noting that '1952 marked the highpoint of the Air Force's UFO investigation'.

These efforts, undertaken in conjunction with a team of scientists from the Battelle Memorial Institute, appear to have been seriously hampered after the Washington, DC sightings of July 1952.

From then on, and demonstrated by the debunking Robertson Panel (Durant), the reports were to be actively discouraged and 'explanations' were to be found at all costs. Air Force Regulation 200-2 (February 1953) instructed airbase officers to discuss reports only if they had been solved. Unsolved cases were to be immediately classified.

The most important point to make is that while moves to play down the significance of UFO reports were set in motion, the US was developing flying-saucer-type aircraft. 'Project Blue Book' was headquartered at Wright-Patterson Air Force Base, its personnel were involved in the cover-up of U-2 spyplane flights (Haines); in February 1955 the technical report for Project Silver Bug (*see* p.74), a joint US–Canadian–British flying saucer, was released to the intelligence community.

Military personnel involved in 'Operation Mainbrace' in 1952 had witnessed several UFO sightings that appeared to relate to structured aircraft (Redfern). From then on, given that further test or operational flights were to be carried out, a veil of secrecy needed to be put in place – 'Project Blue Book' was the mask behind which a covert agenda of secret aircraft development was well hidden for 40 years.

SIX

US AND CANADIAN
FLYING SAUCERS

INTRIGUING INFORMATION has occasionally been revealed since 1953–4 regarding the development in the 1950s of advanced aircraft such as 'Silver Bug' (*see* p. 73). Such details tend to confirm the true source of many 'UFO' sightings, in which government involvement had been denied vigorously for decades.

But we should step back ten years before examining the possible links between German flying saucers and subsequent US–Canadian designs. In 1942 the United States Navy was concerned to develop a VTOL aircraft for use on board aircraft carriers.

In 1941 a circular-wing aircraft of unusual capability was designed by Charles Zimmerman (*see* illustration no. 7). This was the V-173 and was first flown on 23 November 1942 by Chance-Vought test pilot Boone Guyton. In fact the famous Charles Lindbergh also flew the prototype, which underwent some 200 tests. Known also as the XF-5U, the craft was able to fly at remarkably low speeds, almost approaching hover, thus allowing effective use from a carrier platform. Short-Take-Off and Landing (STOL) was possible and the lack of fuselage and low aspect ratio led to decreased drag – a major problem for designers on both the allied and the Axis sides. The aircraft was also able to perform well at high speed and manoeuvrability could be greatly improved through the use of its reduced wing loading.

Zimmerman had hoped that the aircraft would be a good performer under the most difficult conditions. The test-flights indicated that it was virtually impossible to stall it or put it into a spin (Angelucci and Bowers, 1987).

In 1944 the US Navy was sufficiently impressed to order two proto-types and the airframes were completed in August 1945. This may well be the same or a similar craft to that seen by Thomas C. Smith in

1946, although his testimony suggests that the aircraft was often tested at the time, whereas contemporary reports claim that testing was limited owing to the non-arrival of specially prepared articulated propellers.

The aircraft was also revolutionary in its use of 'metalite' material; this would seem to be the same as that described by Thomas C. Smith – a sandwich of balsa between two layers of aluminium. Smith suggests that extensive tests were carried out while the official history states that only tethered tests were undertaken. Plans to test the XF-5U1 at Edwards Air Force Base (Muroc Field) were also apparently cancelled. The Navy had, we are told, lost interest in propeller-driven aircraft – perhaps unsurprising given the new and developing jet engines that were the white heat of technological progress in the immediate post war years. Given the Muroc sightings of 1947, it seems almost impossible to believe that flying discs were not tested there.

Jet-powered Circular-wing Craft?

What about a jet-powered version of the XF-5U1? Until recently we had no information on this, but aviation researcher and photographic expert Bill Rose tracked down line drawings and diagrams for a jet-powered circular-wing aircraft through Freedom of Information Act requests. Rose believes that the McMinnville, Oregon, photograph taken by farmer Paul Trent may show one of these aircraft in flight; this could be possible, if the craft had flown from a facility either in the North-West or from a test facility at Muroc Field.

UFO researchers tend to view places like Muroc/Edwards as open sites where everybody knows exactly what is going on. The area in question is huge, however, and there have been persistent rumours linking the northern part of the base with secret or 'black' programmes (Patton, 1997). The CIA's admission in late 1997 (Haines) that they had used the flying-saucer reports as a cover for the test and operational flights of the 'Top Secret' U-2 spyplane caused a great deal of controversy within the UFO movement and in the press. It seemed that the admission could only lead to allegations that other truths were to emerge relating to 'Top Secret' projects.

At the time numerous UFO researchers, including myself, were contacted and asked to give a view on this revelation contained within a report written by CIA historian Gerald K. Haines. Most of us expressed a certain amazement at some of the things that Haines had admitted to; for instance:

Air Force BLUE BOOK investigators aware of the secret U-2 flights tried to explain away such sightings by linking them to natural phenomena such as ice crystals and temperature inversions. By checking with the Agency's U-2 Project Staff in Washington, BLUE BOOK investigators were able to attribute many UFO sightings to U-2 flights. They were careful, however, not to reveal the true cause of the sighting to the public.

Under these circumstances can we believe the following story included in Haines' report relating to a flying saucer sighting?

Adding to the concern was a flying saucer sighting by US Senator Richard Russell and his party while travelling on a train in the USSR in October 1955. After extensive interviews of Russell and his group, however, CIA officials concluded that Russell's sighting did not support the theory that the Soviets had developed saucerlike or unconventional craft. Herbert Scoville, Jr, the Assistant Director of OSI, wrote that the objects were probably normal jet aircraft in a steep climb.

This sounds rather like an attempt to explain away a sighting. After all, the ground had been laid for this in both CIA reports from 1952 and the Robertson Panel report of 1953. In fact, the incident seemed staged.

We have already seen that in a variety of intelligence documents there was a great deal of concern about possible Soviet developments in this field. Are we to assume that US concern was unfounded? There was also a suggestion that if the Soviets were developing a flying saucer then it made no sense for them to be developing conventional aircraft as well. This is an illogical point of view, to say the least. Conventional aircraft manufacture kept large numbers of skilled people working. Neither the USA nor the Soviets could halt production of conventional aircraft simply because an unconventional design was being developed and tested.

Further revelations are contained in the Haines report including the admission that:

CIA officials knew that the British and Canadians were already experimenting with 'flying saucers'. Project Y was a Canadian–British–US developmental operation to produce a nonconventional flying-saucer-type aircraft, and Agency officials feared the Soviets were testing similar devices.

Do not expect to hear a great deal about 'Project Y' beyond the pages of this book. It presents a unique problem for both UFO 'believers' and 'sceptics'. My mention of Project Y in the UK UFO magazine *Sightings* (Matthews, 'The New Ufology', 1997) has highlighted this problem.

On the one hand the believers cannot admit that flying saucers can be anything other than vehicles for the carriage of interplanetary visitors while the sceptics either have to play down the significance of such a development or suggest that it was interesting, though seemingly hypothetical.

If UFO sightings relate in part to the operation of real flying saucers, then all-encompassing, tremendously fashionable and sceptical theories about the internally generated, 'psycho-social' or 'geo-physical' explanations seem less solid, to say the least.

Silver Bug

What was Project Y? I suggest that it could be the key to solving an important part of the UFO 'mystery'. There were actually *two* unconventional flying saucer aircraft – Project Y and Project Y2. Haines mentions only Project Y, the less advanced of the two, and this might be an indication of attempts to play down the significance of flying-saucer programmes. What is most important about these aircraft is that their development ties in many theories about flying saucers that had previously been typically anecdotal and lacking in substance.

The information about Project Y and Project Y2 relates to an overall programme known as 'Silver Bug'. The information was declassified on 29 March 1995, and its release has been all but ignored by the mainstream UFO community for perhaps obvious reasons already noted. What is even more unfortunate is that information about the project had appeared in press reports ('The Flying Disc', *Air Intelligence Digest*, December 1954 [available only in Project Silver Bug report]).

Silver Bug was a project coordinated under the direction of the Air Technical Intelligence Center (ATIC). *So much for the constant ATIC denials of knowledge relating to flying saucers!*

The document is headed *Technical Report TR-AC-47 Joint ATIC-WADC Report on Project Silver Bug, Project No. 9961, 15th February 1955* and was published by ATIC at Wright-Patterson Air Force Base. It might not have escaped the reader's notice that this was the place tasked with UFO investigations – headquarters for Blue Book from 1952.

The report lays to rest much of the misinformation contained in the many intelligence documents. It now seems likely that the trend was towards openly hostile treatment of both UFO reports and organizations related to the development of a number of 'Top Secret' advanced aircraft projects from 1953–4 onwards.

This much is clear in the Silver Bug report: it states on p. iii that 'Two versions of small research VTO aircraft have been designed by the contractor, which by company designation, are Project Y (Secret)...and Project Y2 (Secret)'. In Section A we are told that 'Numerous schemes have been proposed' relating to an immediate need for dispersed bases using Vertical-Take-Off and Landing aircraft within the US Air Force. This was because the US Air Force considered that the increasing concentration on aircraft requiring longer runways (owing to increased speeds) made for greater vulnerability to Soviet air attack. What was proposed was a new type of aircraft based on the concept of the 'flat-riser' like the Bell VTO aircraft or the aptly named 'Flying Bedstead'.

This was a concept in which a large radial-flow engine was built into a circular-wing aircraft. A much larger multi-engine version was planned. One feature of the radial-flow engine was that it would allow the craft to fly edge-on, not unlike today's triangular 'UFOs', said to be able to operate in the same way.

One reason for producing the report in 1955 was, according to the anonymous authors, to address the intelligence community and

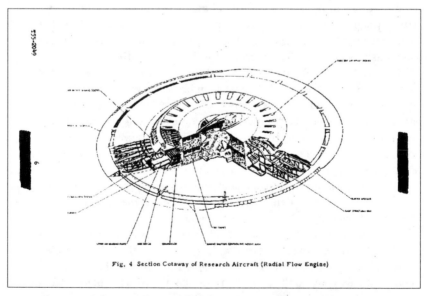

Fig. 4 Section Cutaway of Research Aircraft (Radial Flow Engine)

Technical Report: 'Project Silver Bug', a secret supersonic flying-saucer aircraft. The technical documents relating to this are not widely known. One page is reproduced here. Complete report available from the author at matthews@zetnet.co.uk present it with the 'current state-of-the-art *facts* [my italics] thereby alerting them to intelligence information which may become available indicating Soviet interest in this specialized field'. In addition, an emphasis was placed on the fact that the project was 'in no way associated with any science fiction or Flying Saucer stories because of external appearance'. Although Silver Bug was the result of 'an engineering investigation into the solution of a particular problem', it is impossible to see how flying-saucer sightings, in Canada at least, can have been unrelated.

The Silver Bug project was an ambitious one: the intention was to build a supersonic research aircraft with VTOL characteristics. Perhaps the most unusual feature was the proposed use of directional exhaust gases to control the aircraft. This would mean that conventional control surfaces would not be required.

Although it is not seen as 'politically correct' to mention the German saucer projects, it cannot be a coincidence that according to some sources, the German craft had used a similar system. The Information, as we have already seen, does not come from supposed 'Nazi pseudo-history', but from fairly credible sources like David Masters (Lusar; Masters). Masters' Jane's publication entitled *German Jet Genesis* says that:

> *The Schriever and Habermohl design comprised a large-area disc rotating around a central cupola-like cockpit. The disc was made up of adjustable wing surfaces which could be positioned for take off or level flight. Dr. Miethe also developed a 138 ft (42 m) diameter flying disc powered by vectorable jets.*

There seem to have been certain similarities between the two designs. More specifically they might have shared the same designer – Miethe.

Canadian 'Flying Saucers'

There were rumours that AVRO Canada had been developing a radically advanced aircraft since the early 1950s. For instance, *The Toronto Star* announced on 11 February 1953 that flying saucers were being developed at the Malton airfield while government experts were reported to have declared that 'The Defence authorities are examining all ideas, even revolutionary ones, that have been suggested for the development of new types of supersonic aircraft, also including flying discs.'

On 16 February the *Star* reported that the Minister for Defence production, C. D. Howe, had said that 'the government was constantly studying new concepts and fighters and designs for fighters...adding weight to reports that Avro is even now working on a mock-up model of a "flying saucer" capable of flying 1,500 miles per hour and climbing straight in the air'. Despite the apparent confirmation of the existence of Silver Bug prototypes, there was still confusion.

In Britain, Air Vice-Marshal D. M. Smith was reported as having stated that the craft in question was a gyroscopic fighter with VTOL capability and a speed of 1,500 mph (2,415 kmph) (something that all the reports seem to have in common); a gas turbine would revolve around the pilot, who would be positioned at the centre of the disc. This, of course, was not what was proposed in the ATIC technical report.

Nevertheless, there seems to be good evidence to suggest that from 1954 a prototype had been tested:

> CIA officials knew that the British and Canadian governments were already experimenting with 'flying saucers'. Project Y was a Canadian–British–US developmental operation to produce a nonconventional flying-saucer-type aircraft (Haines).

Possible confirmation of the advanced nature of certain Canadian projects came in the well-known (or notorious, depending on your point of view) book by Donald Keyhoe. *Flying Saucers from Outer Space* (1953) was obviously written by a excitable man passionate in his beliefs that extraterrestrials were visiting earth and that this fact had been covered up. Nevertheless, there are many intriguing comments woven into the fabric of the story about Keyhoe's attempts to prove the case for extraterrestrial reality. In reports of a conversation held between Keyhoe and W. B. Smith, head of the first Canadian government investigation into UFOs – 'Project Magnet' – Smith is reported to have said the following:

> My government is now taking the saucers seriously. The Defence Research project is in secret, but I can tell you this. They're analyzing reports very carefully, and so is RCAF [Royal Canadian Air Force] Intelligence. Several of our best scientists are helping on the technical aspects – they stopped scoffing after the sightings early in 1952.... Since the newspapers have the story, I can tell you it's true. AVRO is building a new type of plane – revolutionary, in fact. I think it will make present types obsolete, but that's all I can say.... It hasn't anything to do with our rotating disc experiments. It doesn't use electromagnetic propulsion.

Which would seem to be a reasonably truthful presentation of the known facts. Silver Bug was a flat riser, not a rotating disc. We shall see later that there was a great deal of interest in the mid-1950s into electromagnetic and exotic propulsion systems.

Keyhoe also states earlier in the book that:

> Later in '51, Smith told me that they had made laboratory tests with a rotating disc, but by then Project Magnet had been classified.

There are many gems in the Keyhoe book. What becomes clear is the way in which he was able to influence subsequent generations of UFO researchers through his singular interpretation of saucer sightings. Take for instance this reported conversation between the author and a fellow investigator:

> Most of the cities where they've hovered or circled have defence industries, a big airport, or defence bases, so it's hard to tell what they're looking at.

The assumption here is that 'they', the aliens, are watching our defences. This kind of thing can be heard over and over within the UFO community. I venture to suggest that what is actually happening is that in some cases the UFOs are operating from the bases themselves and that they are a product of terrestrial technology. The Muroc sightings of 1947 might well have been the result of secret tests undertaken from a secure part of the base. Even Keyhoe's book quotes an episode where a suggestion printed in *US News and World Report* that the saucers were jet-powered versions of the XF-5U1 Flying Flapjack was met with derision and subsequently denied by an Admiral Cal Bolster:

> I'm afraid somebody has sold them a joke.... We had one model, as you know, without jets. But it was never produced. We're denying the Taylor and US News reports.

Such denials leave us a with a great deal of open territory. Keyhoe and his supporters would, no doubt, have taken US government denials of the sort put out by Major-General John Samford as evidence of a cover-up, so why should denials of domestic technological progress of a fairly unremarkable nature not be treated as a similar diversion?

After all, did it not make perfect sense to suggest that the next logical step was to develop a jet-powered circular-wing aircraft with VTOL characteristics?

The Turner Disc

It certainly did make sense, and the recent re-emergence of an article on the subject of flying saucers has confirmed that we are on the right track. The article in question was featured in *Look* magazine, 14 June 1955 (Vol. 19) and included an article written by Thomas Turner, 'a 30 year old British Aeronautical engineer working for Republic Aviation Corporation'.

The article included some fascinating insights into possible saucer designs and Turner seemed to have some inside knowledge – his proposal for a VTOL circular-wing aircraft was very similar to Silver Bug. His saucer relied upon a system of 'deflected jets' and would eliminate the need for conventional runways.

An accompanying illustration indicated that saucers could operate from dispersed and camouflaged facilities. Perhaps this is where authors like Vesco got their idea about flying-saucer bases in the wilds of Canada (Vesco). In fact this type of operation was highly desirable:

> *Brigadier-General James Kelsey was reported to have said that modern fighters and the need for longer and longer runways made for vulnerability and that a single A-bomb might be able to take out a base in one go. Use of underground facilities, of the kind said to be popular in defence circles [Sauder], would allow for safe operation and might actually cost less.*

In the Turner disc, the pilot would lie in a prone position. This hinted at an understanding of advanced German projects (Schick and Meyer). In a prone position the pilot would be able to withstand high-*g* turns, and the craft would have much greater manoeuvrability and faster acceleration than a conventional counterpart. Other advanced features were said to include the use of titanium to enhance the inherent strength of the saucer design and a large gas-turbine engine that 'acts as a stabilizing gyroscope keeping the plane level even when it is hovering'.

The article described the use of directional jets by which lift was attained:

> *When the lower [adjustable] flap is deflected, the jet blast is diverted downward. Air above the saucer then flows down with the jet stream. This reduces pressure on the top surface and the pressure difference between the upper and lower surfaces causes the saucer to rise. Deflected jets provide additional lift.*

Avrocar

There seems little doubt that a great deal of effort was put into the development of advanced flying saucer designs well beyond Avrocar. In fact, the failure of Avrocar is often used by proponents of the extraterrestrial hypothesis to 'prove' that man-made flying saucers were a failure (Good, 1992, pp. 135–7).

I suggest that the existence of Avrocar was almost as perfectly engineered as the cover up of flying-saucer reports: the public was encouraged to believe that Avrocar was the only man-made flying saucer, and hence to infer that flying saucers must be of extraterrestrial origin.

Let us be clear on this point: Avrocar was totally separate from Projects Y/Y2. It was not the same project, as the Silver Bug document made clear. In fact there were several AVRO projects involving the development of unconventional aircraft: Avrocar itself, Project Y2, and P724 (possible alternative to Project Y), noted in several official histories of the A. V. Roe Company (Jackson) and in *The UFO Files: The Canadian Connection Exposed* by Palmiro Campagna.

It is a little odd that the UFO community is not more aware of these projects because it would seem that they had a great deal to do with UFO sightings. This evidence has largely been ignored – until now.

SEVEN

THE FEDERAL HYPOTHESIS

A S UFO SIGHTINGS – and the testing of stealth aircraft – increased, the various intelligence agencies honed their skills in the art of black propaganda. Such propaganda was not limited to simply being 'economical with the truth' in public pronouncements. Covert activity had many dimensions in light of the complex network of relationships between and among different sections of the US military and the intelligence community.

More evidence of serious and sinister involvement in UFO research began to emerge, leading a small number of researchers to conclude that any withholding of information (dare one suggest a 'cover-up'?) has been related to the development of a range of very advanced aircraft. These are the flying disc and the flying triangle.

We are talking about the Federal Hypothesis. In simple terms the Federal Hypothesis states that the UFO phenomenon has been used and controlled by government intelligence agencies since the days of the post-war UFO flap, and that this may relate to clandestine warfare operations. Like the extraterrestrial hypothesis, it is not as developed as we might like and in fact this particular school of thought within the UFO research community is very much the poor relation.

It tends to exclude those who believe that 'contact' has been made and also those who believe that a variety of strange (natural) phenomena can account for the multiplicity of unexplained UFO phenomena. Thus the Federal Hypothesis attracts those unhappy with the popular explanations for UFO sightings. Its supporters prefer to concentrate on misleading information put out by intelligence agencies, the many attempts to lead the UFO community 'up the garden path', and the development of secret aircraft for secret missions.

To my knowledge the Federal Hypothesis was developed in the 1970s by William Spaulding, a well-known Ufologist associated with the Ground Saucer Watch organization, and Todd Zechel, a former intelligence operative (Spaulding, 'Agents of Confusion', 1981). Their considered opinion was that not only had official interest in the UFO subject continued after the much-publicized closure of Project Blue Book in 1969, but the CIA was behind attempts to cover up some of the best evidence relating to UFO sightings. Indeed, the evidence appeared to indicate that in a few cases witnesses had been actively discouraged from coming forward.

Zechel believed in a pro-active approach to the problem. This involved directly approaching government agencies. Responses to requests for information were very similar to those contained within the handful of intelligence documents we examined earlier in the book. One reported reply from the US Air Force to an enquiry stated that 'the phenomenon does not represent any advanced technology beyond our present capability and...poses no direct threat to the United States'. It added that 'there is no evidence indicating that sightings categorized as "unidentified" are extra-terrestrial vehicles'. In a way there was, as in all intelligence documents, more than an element of truth in this. Yes, there were 'unidentified' craft, but they were no threat to the USA.

In which case, the craft must have been of domestic origin, given that we have already seen how illogical, questionable and unreliable stories of crashed extraterrestrial vehicles really were (Randles, 1995). On the other hand, the Robertson Panel had concluded in January 1953 that, although there was no threat posed by UFOs in terms of national security or from a scientific point of view, the sightings should still be investigated because reports might lead to 'the orderly functioning of the protective organs of the body politic' (Durant).

People were already used to the idea of flying discs. A small percentage of the population claimed to have seen one and an even smaller percentage probably *had* seen one. Under these circumstances, and given the great interest in saucer-shaped aircraft shown by ATIC and companies like A. V. Roe, what were agencies like the CIA to do?

As has been pointed out, the Silver Bug vehicle was a state-of-the-art craft intended to be used as a weapons platform, probably to be utilized for covert operations only. It was highly advanced and beyond highly speculative stories in newspapers or 'Scullyesque' ravings about crashed spaceships (Scully; Steinman and Stevens). Its actual existence and capabilities were known to only a very limited number of people either within the military/industrial complex or in the intelligence community. As a result, it was possibly the perfect craft for psychological warfare or reconnaissance missions.

Flying saucers, it was generally believed by the public, were the weapons of mysterious and possibly dangerous 'extraterrestrial beings'. They had no reason to disbelieve this, if only in terms of the powerful imagery created by a plethora of alien and flying-saucer films so popular in the 1950s (Randles, 1997). It had been made quite clear in public statements made by high-ranking CIA and USAF spokesmen that these craft were not to be shot down. The Robertson panel had concluded that even though UFOs represented no threat to national security sightings had to be debunked and the public 'educated' (Durant).

It was a matter of great concern to Zechel and Spaulding that the few intelligence documents released as a result of their Freedom of Information Act (FOIA) requests were sanitized and often censored. How could this be if UFOs were not a threat to national security?

Evidence of Covert Agenda?

More specific evidence of a covert agenda emerged after an extensive analysis undertaken by Ground Saucer Watch of one of the films presented to the Robertson Panel. The film in question was a contro-versial 'UFO Classic' taken by US Navy Warrant Officer Delbert Newhouse in July 1952 near Tremonton, Utah. Newhouse was in fact a trained Navy photographer. The film was analysed by the Naval Photographic Interpretation Center (NAVPIC). Over 1,000 hours of analysis was undertaken but the results were inconclusive: the objects may have been self-luminous spheres travelling at high speed. Despite this in-depth examination, the Robertson Panel concluded that the film showed birds! This convenient conclusion was reached after film footage of seagulls reflecting sunlight was shown to the panel.

Nevertheless, NAVPIC was closed down in 1953, when the CIA took the programme under its control, no doubt hoping to ensure that similar convenient conclusions would be reached in future should some unfortunate government-trained photographer happen to film saucer-shaped objects at a distance of 10 miles (16 km)!

Was 'Blue Book' a Front?

Another part of the hypothesis put forward by Zechel and Spaulding was that 'Project Blue Book' had been nothing more than a front for a more serious and sinister involvement in UFO research. To some extent, this was the view reached by David Jacobs (Jacobs) and also the late and lamented Dr J. Allen Hynek, possibly the best-known advocate for UFO reality and the extraterrestrial hypothesis, who argued that Blue Book was a cover and that the best cases were 'sent upstairs' (Hynek, 1972; 1977). FOIA requests indicated that the CIA still received intelligence reports relating to UFO sightings and that other agencies received them too, including the Defence Intelligence Agency (DIA) and the National Security Council (NSC). Examples were the Spanish UFO flap of 1973–4 and cases from Tunisia in 1976 (*see also* Good, 1996; Fawcett and Greenwood).

'Men in Black'

Even more sinister perhaps were the activities of shadowy figures often described as 'Men In Black' (MIB). These 'Walter Mitty' charac- ters had been known to visit witnesses' houses after exceptional UFO events. It is nearly always suggested that these MIB were either aliens themselves (!) or government agents sent to cover up evidence of ET visitation.

Like many UFO stories, both extremes seem to miss the point. Why should MIB be aliens trying to cover up an 'alien agenda'? And why should UFO sightings relate only to a series of bizarre natural phenomena, misidentifications of so-called conventional aircraft or spacecraft? What about a different solution, a new way of looking at UFOs that suggested that the government knew about a significant percentage of UFO sightings and that they did keep a close eye on them because they involved terrestrial technologies?

Jenny Randles and William Moore (Randles, 1997) argue that MIB offer a 'perfect deception'. Both researchers put the searchlight on the activities of a highly dubious organization known as the Air Force Special Activities Center (AFSAC). William Moore described it as the real 'Men In Black': 'really government people in disguise...[who are] members of a rather bizarre unit of the Air Force Special Activities Center' headquartered at Fort Belvoir, Virginia (Clark, p. 383). AFSAC describes its work as devoted to 'the collection of intelligence obtained by covert means directly from human sources'.

One thing is clear: witnesses who claim to have suffered an MIB visitation recall the probing nature of many of the questions asked and the unusual behaviour of their interrogators. Given that AFSAC draws its operatives from prisons and appears to seek out confidence tricksters to undertake activities on its behalf, we might well ask what their *modus operandi* really is. How many members of the general public are going to take a UFO sighting seriously if it involves Men In Black?

Manipulating the Evidence

The Ground Saucer Watch (GSW) researchers also noted the existence of similar shady organizations including the CIA's Director of Operations (Clandestine Section) and the Domestic Operations Division (Spaulding, 'Agents of Confusion', 1981).

In the 1970s the GSW team argued that various intelligence agencies had been manipulating the UFO evidence in a callous though effective manner for three decades. They even believed that certain civilian UFO groups had been penetrated by agents with a view to spreading disinformation. This seems a distinct possibility given the CIA's opinion that these groups were of questionable loyalty.

Latterly the number of 'former' CIA and intelligence operatives becoming active within American Ufologists has grown considerably, raising eyebrows among both UFO investigators and conspiracy researchers.

In addition, the spreading of false information might prove worthwhile from the point of view of a psychological study into why people believe what they believe and why. Using friendly reporters in the press to put out a limited number of false stories or points of view might also help any deception. Of course, these kinds of argument sound to some like the birth of a rather paranoid conspiracy theory although there have been a number of fascinating studies into press manipulation.

American libertarian intellectual Professor Noam Chomsky has commented on this in his many thought-provoking books (Chomsky, 1992; 1997). He notes the ease with which the media has been able to 'manufacture consent' in which the mass media reflects the economic system in that it is controlled by a tiny elite. It reduces all threats to the military/industrial system. This might allow the press to treat the UFO subject, though important given its potential national security and political impact, with ridicule and to portray its adherents as harmless cranks and lunatics. Perhaps that is why UFO researchers are written off in so many cases as 'buffs' or 'enthusiasts' rather than people dedicated to discovering certain vital truths about the relationship between a government and its people.

When one starts looking at the Federal Hypothesis in the light of historical or more recent attempts to encourage the general public to think about the UFO subject in a certain way in combination with the test-flight of numerous secret aircraft (either as prototypes or in operational mode), then it seems more attractive. The question is this: have the intelligence agencies been pursuing a policy regarding UFOs for 50 years or have the intelligence agencies handled UFO reports in a certain way only on occasions? The former would seem to be the case.

Disinformation and the 'UFO' Community

The focal point for much disinformation has been the UFO community itself. This is not to suggest that there are no government 'agents' working under deep cover within the UFO research community. In many cases, the disinformation is limited and may be spread by only a couple of people. Its effect on an investigation can be devastating, while its effect on a researcher can be equally jarring.

The intention is to ensure that information about any classified activity is distorted before it reaches the public (Strieber). Perhaps the best way to do this would be to encourage UFO researchers to believe that, for instance, flying saucers are 'extraterrestrial spacecraft' and that several different alien races are visiting the earth. This could create a whole realm of speculation, pseudo-science and pseudo-religion with adherents so convinced of alien reality as to shut out all other possible solutions.

Under these circumstances, every time a UFO report is made and publicized an automatic cover-up is set in motion. UFO sightings, even those occurring over and around military facilities, are said by the vast majority of researchers to be alien visitations and headlines will appear in the local press: 'Close Encounters Of The Anytown Kind — Local Enthusiasts To Investigate!' Or maybe: 'Have you seen an alien space-craft?' The latter is an actual example of a headline printed in response to a letter I wrote to the editor of a local newspaper in June 1997 asking for information on sightings of triangular aircraft.

All this, and much more, leads to an inevitable conclusion about some UFO reports. To paraphrase Peter Brookesmith (1981): 'UFOs are controlled not so much by an intelligence as by an intelligence agency!'

EIGHT

THE UK-US RELATIONSHIP

BRITAIN AND THE USA have been enthusiastic allies since 1945, through the North Atlantic Treaty Organization (NATO) and the perceived need for Western allies to unite against Soviet aggression (Urban; Burrows and Windrem; Bissell). There have been disagreements throughout the post-war period between the governments of the two countries, but the general mood has been one of close cooperation especially in military affairs. An historical perspective suggests that the two countries were bound to cooperate closely given cultural and language ties, a view held by Winston Churchill.

The Special Relationship

The 'special relationship' between these countries has operated on a number of levels. An excellent example of close cooperation could be said to be the Falklands War of 1982, when the Americans made certain advanced weapons available to the UK and produced vital intelligence relating to Argentinian troop strengths and locations.

It would appear, however, that in other areas the relationship has not so much been strained, as one-sided. In terms of electronic intelligence (ELINT) and signals intelligence gathering (SIGINT) facilities operated under the terms of the UK–US Treaty of 1947, the Americans have been able to use stations at Menwith Hill, North Yorkshire (operated by the National Security Agency [NSA]), Chicksands in Bedfordshire, and Morwenstow in Cornwall (from 1972–3) to gain vital intelligence information via a host of sources (Urban). Meanwhile, the UK government's Communications Headquarters (GCHQ) facility at Cheltenham has been involved with the NSA in the collection and handling of vast amounts of information received via the many US satellites (Urban).

A Partnership of Equals?

The UK was supposedly an equal partner, although it is suggested that the USA was the main beneficiary of the material and that the UK could benefit from its own projects – hence the ZIRCON satellite debacle. Nevertheless, the relationship is clearly of more benefit to the USA:

> *The requirements from our friends across the water often had to be met first under the special relationship. They were quite clearly the Big Brother. If a suitably worded request came in and the only way was to divert resources from a low-priority target to a 'flash' US one, then it was pretty obvious what would happen. The special relationship was regarded in the highest possible esteem (Urban).*

Although Britain has considered 'going it alone' in terms of intelligence-gathering, this has been actively discouraged by the Americans. Britain has chosen, by and large, to invest money in American systems and, according to Mark Urban, special agreements beyond those made via treaty have been used to hammer out the details of the continued relationship:

> *The complex arrangements were agreed in a super-secret memorandum of understanding between the US and UK governments which I believe was signed in the latter part of 1988. One of the satellites would...have a Union Jack on the side, but Britain could also consider itself part-owner of all of them, sharing the take of the entire constellation.*

Of course, the technology used within the satellite systems remained firmly under North American control.

The problem remained that by then the UK was a literal 'client' of the USA, dependent in terms of intelligence and with no guarantee that the agreement would last for ever. I believe that a similar arrangement exists between the two countries in the matter of advanced aircraft technologies. As we have seen, from 1943 there were plans set in motion to acquire, by all means at their disposal, all the technological hardware, plans, documents and so forth relating to German advanced technologies. In the 1950s, we have evidence that the UK and USA were involved in the flying saucer 'Project Silver Bug' – A. V. Roe, a subsidiary of Hawker-Siddeley, being the company most closely associated with this.

The main difficulty for the researcher is attempting to work out the exact nature of the relationship at a given time. It is, however, unlikely that the UK has developed any black-project aircraft without American knowledge and support (Cook, *Interavia*, 1995).

UFO Crash Retrieval: The Evidence

It is now possible for us to throw a large spanner into the accepted timeline regarding triangular aircraft development. We now have evidence of a 'UFO crash retrieval' from 1967.

Late in 1997, during a conversation with the highly respected West Yorkshire UFO researcher and *Fortean Times* contributor Andy Roberts (the man who solved the notorious 1980s Cracoe Fell UFO case (Roberts and Clarke), a new case emerged. Andy had been contacted by a man who claimed to have been involved in a recovery operation involving an unidentified flying triangle. What follows is the transcript of a conversation between Roberts and the witness. I have added the odd comment in brackets.

> AR: OK. You tell me what happened first and I'll ask questions afterwards.

> Source: I can't remember when it was, it was back before I was married and I got married in 1967, so it could have been early 1967 I think, but I'm not entirely certain.
> I was in the Air Force and I used to be attached to the Air Salvage and Transportation. Very often we'd go out and pick up bits of aircraft that had crashed, and being one of the electricians I used to go along in case there was any electrical work to be done, disarming batteries and systems or whatever.
> This thing had either crashed or been brought down, and it was near Heyford [RAF Upper Heyford], and on a map I'll show you exactly where we picked it up. We got there fairly late in the operation, and there were cranes of all sorts, civilian police, Military Police, and the surrounding area was cordoned off. I was sent out there to see if there was anything I could do electrical wise, and I didn't know what we were going to.
> Anyway this flying machine, I'll put it, had crashed, you could see where it had gone in, there was a big scar mark across the fields, as if it had come down and bounced a bit, as they do. To describe it, it was like polished aluminium is the best way to describe it. You know when you've got aluminium cooking pans

and you rub a bit of Scotch Brite or something, and they come right up, and they've got like a bluish sheen, and this had a bluish sheen on it. It was twenty five foot in length, roughly estimated, I couldn't be absolutely certain, but roughly twenty five foot in length. It was about fifteen foot wide, roughly. I'm five foot six, so I can relate it to my height so it's about two and a half times as tall as me, so that would make it about twelve foot, something like that, three times my height wide, and sort of about five times my height long, roughly. I'll tell you what, I saw a programme the other night and it just looked like the front end of a stealth bomber, it was like that but the short version. It was just like the nose cone or the front end of a stealth bomber. There were no marking as far as I can remember, but I didn't really take any notice.

We picked it up, put it on the back of a low loader and it was brought from where it landed or crashed to RAF Bicester, because that was a salvage flight, so it had all bits of crashed aircraft down the hangars. This was taken, instead of a hangar, it was taken straight down the bomber dump. I didn't really think much of it at the time. It was taken straight down to the bomber dump and I had occasion to go down there a few days later and the doors had steel bars welded across, and the whole place was sealed. So I can draw you a rough sketch of it, and that's about the tale.

AR: Can you be more specific as to what time of year it was?

Source: Early part of 1967, it wasn't cold enough to be winter, it was sort of like spring. It was early 1967, about March/April. We got married July 1967, and it was two or three months before that. Yes, it would have been March or April time.

AR: What time of day was it?

Source: Well, we went out about mid-morning.

AR: Was it a weekday or weekend?

Source: It was a weekday. I can't remember whether it was a Tuesday or a Wednesday.

AR: Do you know when the actual crash had taken place?

Source: No.

AR: Who gave you the order to go to the site?

Source: Flight-Lieutenant V, who was in charge of our section at the time.

AR: As closely as possible, what did he say and how did he refer to it?

Source: He said that there was a salvage. He didn't really refer to it as anything, so I just assumed that it was an aircraft that had gone down, as they do.

AR: How many of you were there?

Source: There was me, Chunky P, I can't remember his real name, we just called him Chunky. He used to live across the road, lived next door but two. What was his name...Sergeant P, little fellow he was. Wilf O, and then Jerry B, that ginger-haired Corporal, Doug E, Fritz was there, a Welsh lad. There was some from the ???? flight. I can't remember their names [surnames omitted].

AR: What was your mission, what were you told you were going to do?

Source: Salvage, that's all we were told.

AR: You mentioned a low-loader. Did you go in this?

Source: Well I didn't go in the low-loader, but there was a low-loader and the forerunner of the Transit van, used to be called a J-4, a military version of a Transit van.

AR: Where was the object, where had it landed?

[The source pointed to an open area (on an Ordnance Survey map) half-way between the town of Bicester and the base at Upper Heyford.]

AR: Was it a straightforward drive back or did you cover it up with anything?

Source: We probably slung a sheet over it, as you do when picking wrecked aircraft up.

AR: What was there when you got to the object?

Source: There was other bits of wreckage, but I didn't really bother with them, I looked but didn't notice much.

AR: Was there anyone else there when you arrived?

Source: Yes, there were Military and civilian Police. Some personnel from Heyford, certainly looked like Yanks anyway.

AR: Did you overhear any comments as to what it may have been?

Source: No.

AR: Did they appear to be excited or agitated about the event?

Source: Well, we were all excited and agitated because it was a crash. Everyone was sort of milling around, and the usual confused behaviour.

AR: Did you know how long it had been down for at that time?

Source: I haven't a clue.

AR: Was the area cordoned off?

Source: Yes.

AR: Just the field, or the road adjacent to it?

Source: If we refer back to the map again, that road there. Just out of this Upper Heyford village, just there was stopped. I don't know about the railway. That's as far as I know.

AR: What did you do when you got there?

Source: Loaded it on to the low-loader, with a crane.

AR: Was it heavy?

Source: You can usually tell if a crane was lifting something excessively heavy, but I wouldn't say this was. The crane could handle it easily. It was a normal load, a twenty tonner or something like that.

AR: Was there anything about it like lumps, propulsion systems etc.?

Source: No, as far as I can remember it was totally smooth. Mind you I didn't really take much notice. You're not really looking around for lumps and bumps and things like that.

AR: Any sign of landing gear?

Source: No, not that I can recall. It's not the sort of thing you bother taking any notice of.

AR: Were you told where to take it when you were at the site or after you'd set off?

Source: We just jumped back in the vehicle and followed the low loader.

AR: Did anyone tell you to keep quiet about it, or not to mention it?

Source: No, because we were already under the Official Secrets Act and all that, we already knew not so say anything about it anyway.

AR: Once you'd delivered it to the bomb dump, did you hear any rumours about it?

Source: No.

AR: And were there any media reports locally?

Source: No.

AR: That's surprising, that something would have come down and not been in the local paper?

Source: No, there wasn't anything in the local paper.

AR: What is the local paper for that area?

Source: Bicester Advertiser.

AR: I'll have to check because sometimes things get mentioned, or I might put a letter in to see if anyone else remembers it. So what did you think it was?

Source: At the time I just thought it was some sort of experimental aircraft.

AR: Had you seen any other experimental aircraft, or heard about them?

Source: Loads of them. DS2, that was at Bicester, I worked on that. I went on the crash investigation when the prototype crashed and exploded.

AR: So, as you were saying what do you think it was?

Source: At the time I did think it was an experimental aircraft of some description, something akin to the TSR2 or maybe a fore-runner of the stealth bomber when you come to think of it.

AR: Have you changed your mind on that then?

Source: Well, I've never seen anything developed from it.

AR: You don't think that the Stealth as we know it developed from it?

Source: It is maybe an extension or development from it.

Source: But looking back, it puzzles me as to why this object was like it was, it was like an aircraft but wasn't like an aircraft, like the front end of an aircraft but it wasn't.

AR: It's bizarre, especially as you say you can't recall seeing any kind of aircraft like it.

Source: No, I can't. There's nothing there, as far as I can recall. When you're working like that, you've got things to do, you've got cranes slinging stuff around, you're hanging on to a rope and all you want is to go off for a cup of tea, you don't take it in.

AR: Are you still in contact with any of the people who were with you on that day?

Source: No, I've lost contact with everybody. I came out of the Air Force in 1969, so it's thirty years ago. If I got in contact with Russell, he might recall something, although I don't know whether he does or not.

AR: Do you have any objection to your name being used anywhere?

Source: Well, I'm not still sworn to the RAF, because I came out in 1969.

AR: You said you could do a drawing of it, could you do that now?

Source: I wonder if it was part of an experimental aircraft. It makes you wonder. I remember exactly what shape it was. That's a side view and a plan view would be like that. Looking at the back, would be like that. I'm not very good at sketching. I could draw you a circuit diagram of a Vulcan bomber if you want, I could draw you a full diagram of a nuclear bomb if you wanted. I could make you one, they're easiest enough to make.

Just a few days after interviewing the former Air Force witness, Andy Roberts phoned me. I said that I would see if there was any substantiating evidence to back up the important parts of the story.

I made contact with several people associated with my research, and they were able to provide bits of information that confirmed several things. One person I spoke to had a relative who had been stationed at RAF Bicester in 1967. In a private letter to me he said:

During the late 1960s we were stationed at 71 M.U. [Maintenance Unit] RAF Bicester. One of the wide variety of tasks was the transportation and storage of the abandoned project the TSR2. The new Wilson government cancelled it after discovering that Britain was broke and the cost of the project, already enormous, would increase further. Only the US could afford this kind of money [TM's emphasis]. One or more of the aircraft were transported to Bicester and stored in one of the hangars kept closed to most station personnel.

Certain details of the crash retrieval are therefore confirmed: the fact that RAF Bicester was the place where 'hush-hush' (a term popular at the time) aircraft were sent, and the fact that this was a Maintenance Unit.

In addition, and importantly, American personnel were on hand to see the clean-up operations taking place. This was not the only time that a possible UK–US link can be established.

There are probably many other cases to come to light but bearing in mind our exploration of the events surrounding the Belgian flying-triangle flap of March 1990 and the flight of a UFO in the South-West, it appears that similar covert activities can be traced back to the beginning of the 1960s.

Super-secret Agreements

Jane's Defence Weekly correspondent Nick Cook, an authority on certain classified programmes, believes that in the 1960s a secret formal agreement was reached between the Kennedy and Macmillan governments regarding stealth materials and aircraft testing (Cook, *Interavia*, 1995). He argues that this arrangement was initially made in order that the Americans could use various Radar Absorbent Materials captured by the UK from the Germans at the end of the war for their new reconnaissance aircraft.

Whether or not the arrangement was made at this point or not – and we may not know for some time – American personnel seem to appear in many stories relating to secret aircraft and UFO sightings.

More vitally important information on the nature of the UK–US agreement is reported in Richard Bissell's *Reflections of a Cold Warrior* (Yale, 1996) in which he gives details of the arrangement between the two countries during the early days of the U-2 spyplane and its covert operation over the USSR. Britain was the most supportive country in this endeavour.

Bissell is a very important figure in the history of secret military aircraft development. Several books (for instance Ranelagh; Patton, 1997) describe him as an influential man with powerful allies, including Allen Dulles, head of CIA Clandestine Services from 1948 and later the agency's director (1953) (Marchetti and Marks).

Not only did Bissell initiate an agreement with Dick White of MI6 involving use of RAF Lakenheath in East Anglia as a base for U-2 operations in 1956 (Bowyer, 1994), but he also allowed the highest levels of access to British personnel. 'British involvement was implemented and three or four RAF pilots were brought to Groom Lake, where they received the same training as US pilots and freely associated with members of our detachments' (Bissell).

The relationship was central to this: 'The CIA worked closely with MI6 and regarded its people as close allies.'

The U-2 aircraft at Lakenheath were housed during 1956 'in a segregated hangar and workspace', not unlike the SR-71 some 17 years later (Graham).

Advanced Technology and US Personnel

The UK–US relationship involved the stationing of large numbers of US personnel in the UK, and also work on advanced aircraft technologies.

The evidence is especially clear on this point, making it much more likely that I am right in my assertion that other agreements of a highly secret nature have been signed between UK and US agencies. The CIA–MI6 relationship was particularly valued. It is the clandestine agencies – the CIA and National Reconnaissance Office – that have operated not only satellites like the KH-11/KH-12 but also a number of spyplanes: U-2, A-12/SR-71, the original 'mystery aircraft' and their futuristic counterparts, so often reported as UFOs (Federation of American Scientists [FAS]).

Bissell's mention of Groom Lake (*see* p. 200) is noteworthy especially given that we believe that flying discs were operated there in the 1950s. Future man-made UFO research will focus upon this period. It should be remembered that it has been admitted already that the UK, US and Canada have cooperated on advanced flying-saucer development programmes, as well as SIGINT/ELINT gathering. It is quite likely that RAF personnel have been involved in many secret programmes at Groom Lake, including test flights of the F-117A.

We can see that the groundwork for future operations of advanced secret US military aircraft was laid back in the 1950s. Through each decade there are sightings of 'UFOs' that strongly indicate that this analysis is correct.

An Unusual Night Operation

A second report involving American personnel is included here for its potential significance. The story is much less easy to check than the 1967 crash retrieval although I have been able to confirm some of the details through a confidential report made to the British UFO Research Association (BUFORA).

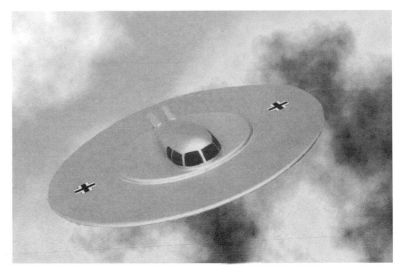

1. Simulation of a Heinkel/BMW flying disc, designed by Dr Miethe, in flight. This design was allegedly nearing completion at the end of the Second World War and may have fallen into Soviet hands. (Photography by Bill Rose)

2. This photograph of the German saucer designer, Dr (Walter/Richard) Miethe (exact name unknown), was allegedly taken at Kummersdorf in about 1933. Dr Miethe worked on the von Braun rocket programme and eventually headed the flying-disc programme at Prague (Bill Rose Collection)

3. Simulation of 'foo fighters' shadowing USAAF B-17 bombers during a raid on Nazi Germany. (Artwork by Bill Rose)

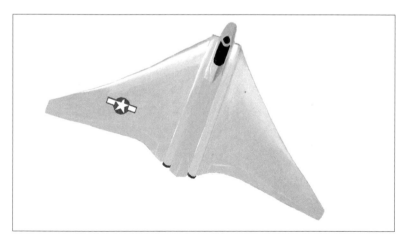

4. Mock-up of an aircraft directly based on the Gotha Go-229 flying wing designed in Germany during the Second World War by the Horten brothers. The aircraft has been stretched to allow for afterburning turbo-jets, and has a number of features common to advanced US/German experimental aircraft of that period. If this aircraft existed, it may have been responsible for the Kenneth Arnold sighting of 1947 which gave birth to Ufology. (Artwork by Bill Rose)

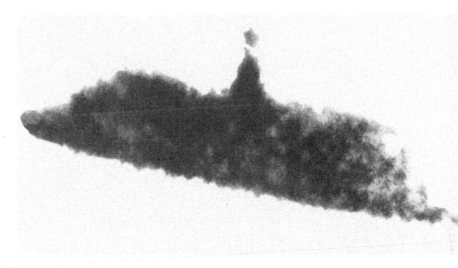

5. The famous McMinnville UFO sighting of 1950 which seems to have been completely authentic. This highly enlarged computer-enhanced image reveals what seems to be a tail fin; the disc, 30–40 foot (9–12 m) in diameter, may have been an experimental jet-powered 'Flying Pancake'. (Bill Rose Collection)

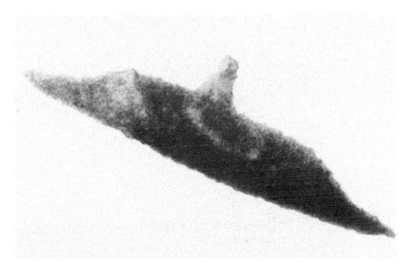

6. This UFO was photographed above Rouen, France in 1954. Computer enhancement shows it to be strikingly similar to the McMinnville craft. Was this another US jet-powered 'Flying Pancake' on a secret mission? (Bill Rose Collection)

7. Charles Horton Zimmerman, who designed the US Navy's 'Flying Pancakes'. (Bill Rose Collection)

8. This boomerang-shaped aircraft is a modern-day B-2 stealth bomber. There was an earlier version, supposedly cancelled in 1983, and that design looked very similar to the UFO reported in the Hudson Valley during the 1980s. (Air Combat Command, US Air Force)

9. 'UFO' seen on 6 March 1971, Atlantic City, NJ. This rare photograph shows the 'deltoid pumpkin seed' Aereon 26 during a successful test flight. (Aereon Corporation)

10. Massive triangular 'UFOs' are, in fact, hybrid lighter-than-air (LTA) vehicles constructed from very tough composite materials. The combination of materials and triangular shape makes for impressive stealthy performance. The *Air Force 2025* survey suggests that such craft could be used for forward area transportation by the military. The Aereon Corporation is thought to be designing similar craft for use as radar-sensor platforms. (Aereon Corporation)

11. The Aereon Corporation also worked on huge LTA vehicles for the US Navy during the 1970s, including the 'Dynairship' concept, shown here. (Aereon Corporation)

12. 'Tier 3 minus' DarkStar was a stealthy unmanned aerial vehicle (UAV) built by Lockheed Martin and test flown from 1996. Could this type of unmanned aircraft be mistaken for a 'UFO'? (NASA)

13. Virtual Reality Control for UAVs: a Predator UAV being operated by a ground controller. The USAF Scientific Advisory Board Study, *New World Vistas,* claims that the UAVs are the weapons of the future. (US Department of Defense)

14. The British Aerospace Special Projects Site at Warton, where security is extremely tight. The regime was developed with help from experts at the Lockheed-Martin Skunk Works. Construction began in 1992; several witnesses have since seen UFOs in the area. (B. Wilkinson)

15. A concept produced by British Aerospace relating to the Future Air Offensive System. Note: triangular craft are shown flying in the background. (British Aerospace)

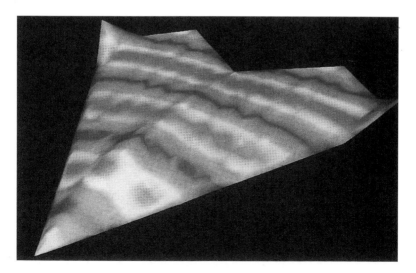

16. Supposedly a 'generic stealth concept' developed by a joint team of experts from British Aerospace, GEC-Marconi, the Defence Evaluation and Research Agency and Cray Research Limited. Many people claim that the conceptual aircraft is what they saw in the air. (British Aerospace)

17. Stealthchasers keep an eye on classified projects. This still was taken from a telemetry video showing an unidentified aircraft performing high-*g* turns off the Lancashire coast near the Special Projects Site at Warton. Local people have reported many sightings of small 30-foot (9-m) triangular aircraft. (Steve Austin)

18. Defence Test and Evaluation Organisation (DTEO) test facilities at West Freugh, south-west Scotland. Researchers tracked at least one secret project involving triangular UAVs to this facility. (Tim Matthews)

19. SR-71 'Blackbird': the first generation of Dark Eagles was built more than 15 years before the F-117A. 'Blackbird's' role was reconnaissance, whereas the F-117A 'Nighthawk' was a stealth bomber. Both emerged from black programmes; both were built at Lockheed's Skunk Works. (Anthony M. Thornborough)

20. A 1997 picture of the once highly secret Lockheed F-117A stealth interdictor aircraft. It was developed at Groom Lake, Nevada in great secrecy and remained classified for more than a decade. (Photography by Bill Rose)

21. A simulation by Bill Rose of an unusual aircraft seen refuelling over the North Sea in 1989. Observed from the drilling platform Galveston Key, it is generally thought to have been the top-secret hypersonic 'Aurora' spyplane. Earlier versions of this picture were widely distributed. (Photography by Bill Rose)

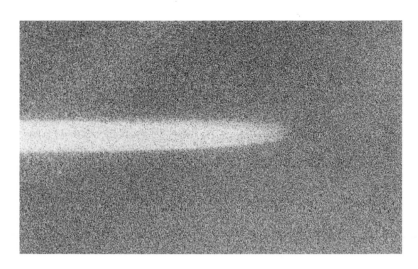

22 and 23. Invisible aircraft near a remote Scottish airbase. These remarkable photographs were taken by aviation and photographic expert Richard Sutton near RAF Macrahanish using infra-red film. Other photographs taken at the time came out perfectly. (Richard Sutton)

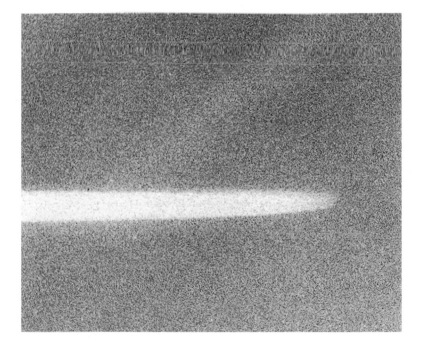

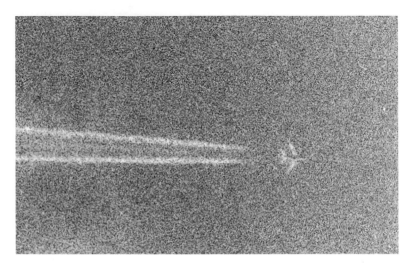

24. Visible aircraft: Sutton captured numerous other aircraft using the same camera and film at around the same time. (Richard Sutton)

25. X-24B: from the early 1960s to 1975, there was enormous research into triangular Lifting Body concepts. Here, a delta-wing research aircraft is seen over the Dryden Research Center in California. (NASA)

The first part of this account is taken from material that appeared in the British magazine *UFO Reality* (King). Initially a soldier named Mark reported the incident to Jon King, the magazine's editor. I spoke to Jon King in order to confirm the details as they had been set out.

What seems to have happened is that Mark and a group of other soldiers were 'volunteered' to take part in an unusual night operation, supposedly mounted in order for a reconnaissance unit to test new night-vision apparatus.

The group was required to walk in a straight line from Beach's Barn to Dunch Hill Plantation (*Ordnance Survey Landranger 184*; from map reference 186513 to 206486), which is located near several Danger Areas and military facilities. The exercise seemed unusually easy – the simplicity of the route they were required to take becomes evident through a cursory glance at an Ordnance Survey map.

The soldiers started walking at around 2 am and they were all of the opinion that this was a waste-of-time exercise, especially given that they had tested out the same equipment and that it would be easy to spot the group of them walking in a southerly direction.

The supposed 'reconnaissance unit' monitoring their progress was up at Sidbury Hill. As the group approached their final destination, a large black aircraft, said to be the size of a Hercules or even bigger, emerged. It appeared to be dark in colour and the soldiers noted that it appeared from within a sectioned-off Ministry of Defence area next to the footpaths on which they had walked. The map appears to indicate that this was situated to the south of the plantation. The craft beamed down a light on to the surrounding trees and operated in silence.

The only thing that the soldiers can remember is that the craft shot off in an easterly direction. The next thing they knew, the whole group was some 2,000 feet (600 m) away from their previous position, and none of them could understand how this could be. Mark himself had been on long hikes and standard military exercises where he was required to stay awake for two days; this should have been no problem.

Mark remembers being picked up by Land Rover and being driven back to his barracks with the other members of the group. Nobody said anything about the incident until much later on and Mark himself appears to have had great difficulty in recalling all the events. As a result, and because he had made contact with Jon King, he agreed to undergo hypnotic regression in order to shed some new light on what had transpired.

There are, it should be said, many problems with hypnosis, none more serious than the fact that there is no regulated training for regressionists, neither is its use officially sanctioned. False memories can be

implanted through a variety of means – leading questions or suggestion – and in several noted cases American courts have seen children
entirely invent scenarios under hypnosis where they claim Satanic
abuse and so forth. In other words, hypnosis can be very dangerous
and misleading (McClure, 'Yesterday Belongs to Me', *Abduction Watch*,
1998). It is highly controversial and there is a moratorium on its use by
most reputable UFO research groups. No doubt the use of a questionable technique in this case may lead some readers to dismiss the new
testimony revealed through Mark's interaction with hypnotist Robert
La Mont. That is a risk we have to take.

What encourages me to believe Mark is the similarity of an event
that took place several years later under almost identical circumstances
and involving highly trained military personnel. I have also had a long
conversation with La Mont about the witness and investigation and he
was both helpful and courteous.

Under hypnosis Mark recalled feeling cold as a bright light shone
down on him from the direction of the UFO. Becoming rather
distressed during the regression, Mark said that an American had
appeared from the direction of the wood and that he had started to
prod the soldiers with a stick-like device akin to an aerial. The
American was wearing a black zip-up outfit.

After this Mark said that a bright beam of pulsing light had encir-
cled the soldiers and that he had been able to pick out the shape of a
'wedge-shaped' black triangle. The aircraft was making a continuous
humming sound not unlike a generator. The encounter ended when
the triangle shot off to the east.

The Black Triangles of Boscombe Down

The second incident is very similar and was reported to my colleague
Gloria Dixon of BUFORA. Knowing my interest in possible military
UFOs, she contacted me in late 1997 with an amazing story taken from
a confidential report made to her by a commissioned officer.

Because all credible UFO organizations insist on witness confidentiality, it is neither possible nor ethical to release personal witness
details. Given the deeply personal and occasionally traumatic nature of
such experiences, we must protect witnesses. No one will come
forward if they believe that their stories will be used as sales fodder for
sensationalist magazines or newspapers.

The story relates to an incident that took place one night in 1996
during a military exercise. On this occasion approximately 20 soldiers
were making camp for the night when a triangular aircraft appeared

overhead. To their surprise the craft hovered very low over their position for several minutes before moving off. Upon returning to base, the captain felt it necessary to report the incident to his commanding officer.

The CO seemed to have prior knowledge of the incident. It was made very clear to the captain that under no circumstances was he to talk about this story any further and that serious consequences would result from a breach of the Official Secrets Act. Shocked and surprised by a man in whom he had implicit trust, he relayed the news to his men. They appear to have accepted the CO's orders, although the captain was most unhappy with the whole affair.

No other information about this story can be given here, but this is a convincing report. Again some readers may baulk at the necessary anonymity. One thing is clear: we have a situation where military personnel appear to have been treated as guinea pigs by shadowy covert forces operating within the UK. One of the places where these triangles have flown from is RAF Boscombe Down. It comes as little surprise that the base is only a few miles from the alleged incident at Dunch Hill. So, further weight is therefore added to the suggestion that Boscombe was a centre for secret military aircraft testing.

The Boscombe Down incident was reported in several newspapers including the *Daily Telegraph* on 19 December 1994 under the headline 'Secret US spyplane "crashed at Stonehenge"'. The report by Nick Cook of Jane's and Christy Campbell indicated that a secret aircraft, possibly the TR-3A 'Black Manta', had crashed and been brought back to Boscombe Down. To add weight to this claim aviation enthusiasts and 'Mil spotters' (those who monitor military radio frequencies for interesting and unusual activity) reported that distress calls had been picked up around midnight on 26 September. Several spotters were arrested by police and road blocks were put in place to restrict access to the area. The *Telegraph* report quoted Michael Crutch, RAF editor of the *British Aviation Review*:

> *People were reluctant to talk. They wrote down what they had seen — and we were amazed.*
>
> *One was a serving Air Force officer who saw an aircraft of unknown type disabled at the end of the runway, covered by tarpaulins. Twin inward-canted tail fins were poking out of the covering.*

Jamie Hunter, another Mil spotter, said that a flight plan had been filed for a USAF Galaxy transport to fly into and out of Boscombe just days after the crash (Long and Ruffle). It was destined to fly back to

Palmdale in California, home of the Lockheed Skunk Works. Air traffic controllers noted that two civilian jets had arrived at Boscombe two weeks after the incident. One of them, registration number N1178X, officially did 'not exist' and might indicate the involvement of an American intelligence agency – the CIA, for instance? The other covert civil aircraft was a Gulfstream GIV registered N604M; on 9 October it flew from Boscombe via Luton to Farmingdale, New York – home to a Grumman Aerospace facility. In addition to these aircraft, two USAF C-5 transports were also involved using a callsign LANCE 18.

(I am told by a reliable source that another 'Janet' registration number is N1177C; given the similarity of the number this may or may not add weight to the reports.)

The Defence Testing and Evaluation Organisation (DTEO), part of the Defence Evaluation and Research Agency, headquartered at Boscombe Down (Cooper) where it provides facilities for the Air Test and Evaluation Centre, hurriedly put out a cover story about a Tornado GR-1 that had been at the nearby Larkhill range towing a target. This had apparently got caught up and posed a safety threat, hence the closure of the main A345 road. In addition, it was claimed that a Defence Research Agency hover rig had been put under a tarpaulin after delivery and that its two V-shaped supports had been misinterpreted by over-zealous enthusiasts as the canted fins of an unidentified stealth aircraft. DTEO argued that no Galaxy C-5 aircraft had visited Boscombe after the alleged crash, despite the fact that Roger Long, an aviation photographer from Salisbury with sources at the base, photographed an unidentified C-5 approaching the runway on the day after the incident is said to have taken place – 27 September!

The conclusion that something untoward had taken place was supported by Robert Ruffle of the International Association of Aviation Historians, who suggested that those flying N1178X could have relied on Air Traffic Control (ATC) to fly unchallenged through UK airspace. Ruffle's wife saw an unusual aircraft flying from east to west not long before the events at Boscombe. It was grey in colour and operating at an altitude of 800 feet (250 m) below a cloud base of 900 feet (275 m).

It is tempting to believe that a secret aircraft was involved at Boscombe Down, partly because I was lucky enough to receive information about further US activity at the base. This took place in February 1997 at around 2 am. A large triangular aircraft was pulled out of a hangar. It took off vertically and was soon followed by an RAF Tornado escort. At the scene were the Boscombe fire crew. The vertical take-off was surprising enough, especially given that the aircraft appeared to create some sort of 'vortex' around it before shooting skywards at considerable speed.

This flight was observed by a female RAF witness who was at the base. Earlier that day she had occasion to speak with a few Americans and after striking up a conversation casually asked them what they were up to. One of them volunteered that they were on site working on a classified project for a limited period only. Surprised, the witness thought nothing of this throw-away comment until the early morning, where from a location inside the base she chanced on the strange flight.

Our witness hoped that the aircraft would return. Her detailed knowledge of aircraft suggested that what she had seen most closely resembled the 'cancelled' US Navy A-12 Avenger. The Avenger was a very interesting aircraft whose existence should indicate the true nature of the triangular UFO.

The A-12 is also thought to be a precursor to the AX-17/A-17 swing-wing stealth attack aircraft (Brown and Douglass; Rose 1997). Although supposedly cancelled by the US Department of Defense on 5 January 1991, the Avenger was a very sleek delta-wing aircraft built by General Dynamics/McDonnell Douglas and displayed in public for the first time at Carswell, Fort Worth, Texas in June 1996. It was a two-seat twin-engine aircraft carrier-based medium fighter for air-to-air or ground-to-ground all-weather day or night attack operations. It was to use two General Electric F412-400 non-afterburning turbo-fan engines creating 13,000 pounds (6,000 kg) of thrust and designed to carry AMRAAM and HARM missiles as well as 'smart' weapons. It was to be accommodated on board a carrier by folding its hinged 70-foot (21-m) wings to just 36 feet (11 m).

Back at Boscombe, the story took an unexpected turn the next morning. Knowing that she had probably seen something she was not supposed to have seen and that the American personnel had perhaps been a little loose-lipped, our intrepid RAF witness ventured over to the hangar where the aircraft was based and came across one of the firemen. She mentioned what she had seen the previous night and the fireman quickly took her to one side and told her not to say anything about the test-flight. He said that under no circumstances should the witness go any nearer the hangar nor should she make the mistake of making further enquiries. The man said that it was routine for the fire team to be available during such operations, but that it was made clear that they should keep very quiet about what they had seen.

To the casual observer this may seem like another tall story but the witness is highly credible. She was so moved by this sighting that she mentioned it to a contact of mine. It is further evidence that RAF Boscombe Down is a centre for the occasional test-flight of 'Most Secret' advanced aircraft. But there were unforgettable, perhaps alarming developments on the Continent, too, namely in Belgium.

NINE

BELGIUM REVISITED

RIANGULAR UFOS THAT can hover in near silence have haunted the UFO community since they were first reported. No one can quite agree when this was: some people claim that the 1950s was the decade in which these exotic aircraft appeared, although a more sensible conclusion might be that the 1970s was the first time that the deltas emerged in force.

The best-known evidence for the existence of triangular UFOs is arguably that which emerged in 1989–90 over the heads of several thousand Belgian citizens (Sheffield). This was a vitally important case because it seemed to start a process whereby UFOs were taken a little more seriously by the press and public alike.

The Facts

The facts of the Belgian case are well known although a brief recap may be necessary (*see* Derek Sheffield for further details). The sightings of unusual aerial phenomena took place on the night of 29 November 1989 around the town of Eupen, in the Hautes Fagnes of eastern Belgium. The next events occurred on 15 December near Liège and the final set of events related to 30–31 March 1990, around Wavre, Tubize and Brussels.

Approximately 75 of the witnesses were policemen and this fact seemed to add a certain weight to the reports. In addition to this, NATO Air Defense Ground Environment (NADGE) radar stations picked up a variety of spurious returns suggesting the presence of unexplained phenomena. The sightings were reported internationally and the Belgian military played a central role in the events and the subsequent enquiries into them.

On the nights of 29 November and 30 March events came to a head when F-16 aircraft from the Belgian Air Force were scrambled in an attempt to intercept and identify the unexplained aerial phenomena.

On the second occasion radar returns at Glons (local NADGE station) appeared to suggest that the unidentified objects were accelerating away from the F-16s at 'impossible' speeds. Both pilots had attempted to 'lock on' to the phenomenon, but failed to do so. Colonel De Brouwer of the Belgian Air Force claimed that this was certainly not a conventional aircraft and although the authorities were initially reticent about providing information regarding the events, they released a transcript of a conversation between the F-16 pilots and Glons Control Reporting Centre recorded on 30 March as well as copies of the radar tapes.

Glons control, like 80 other similar stations dispersed throughout Europe, is tasked to identify and track flights within designated airspace, to identify whether the aircraft are friendly or hostile, and to take appropriate measures if an aircraft is not identified. Most worryingly, from the point of view of the Belgian military, the radar returns appeared to show that the phenomenon had performed a series of violent manoeuvres amounting to 22g turns. On the face of it, something quite extraordinary had taken place.

Many UFO researchers thought that this was finally the evidence they had been waiting so long for – a Western government admitting that it had temporarily lost control of its airspace, making public a host of radar evidence and other evidence to back it up. It is hardly surprising that many concluded that the events had to be the result of some sort of extraterrestrial involvement in human affairs.

An Unclear Picture

Nevertheless, detailed analysis of the evidence suggests that the picture was not as clear as we might have been led to believe. Despite all the interest, the numerous sightings and the assumption that the military were on alert for any recurrence of these events, only one reasonable UFO photograph was taken.

The best and most impressive sightings by ground witnesses, including several gendarmes in Eupen, related to a large triangular object. The triangle was seen on 29 November by two sergeant-majors of the Belgian police off the road between Eupen and Kettenis. This was a structured aircraft and seemed to be hovering over a field next to the road. Three bright lights were seen on the underside at each apex with a red-orange light in the centre. The craft moved towards the men and they noticed the now typical humming sound as it flew overhead. It then proceeded to hover above a dam for 45 minutes. For two and a half hours a similar object was seen by witnesses in the area and an hour later the two original police witnesses came across the triangle again and they suggested that it was moving at approximately 40 mph (65 kmph). Two weeks later the Belgian Air Force tried for the first time (unsuccessfully) to make a visual identification of the phenomenon.

A few months elapsed before the panic of 30–31 March. It would appear that initially the Belgian government did not know what was going on. In a letter from Leo Delcroix (Belgian Defence Minister) to author Derek Sheffield, the police observations were confirmed, as were the spurious radar tracks, and it was stated that the Minister could not tell what these flying objects were. The US Air Force had confirmed that F-117A aircraft were not involved, but this should have been obvious from the police reports.

The Debate Re-opens

Sheffield's book argues that, despite encouraging signs early on in terms of official government and military attitudes, these soon changed. More particularly, the UK Ministry of Defence adopted an intransigent attitude and made claims at variance with the known facts of the case. Sheffield also found the Belgian authorities unwilling to 're-open the debate' on the subject of the UFO sightings. In addition, the attitude of the Ministry of Defence was unhelpful.

Nick Pope, now well known for his belief in aliens and his work at the MOD's Department Secretariat Air Staff 2a (better known as the 'UFO Desk') between 1991 and 1994 (Pope), was unable to provide any supporting data relating to Belgium. Pope even claimed in an official letter dated 26 November 1993 that:

> In answer to your specific question, Air Defence experts concluded that the Belgian UFO sightings posed no threat to the UK because there was no evidence of any such threat.

This kind of response will not come as any surprise to veteran UFO researchers and is indicative of the type of language used to deny the reality of UFO sightings. Clearly a triangular object had been seen by numerous witnesses. There is no doubt that as part of NADGE, the MOD would have been fully aware that their Belgian allies were seriously concerned about a series of unexplained radar returns and strange phenomena in the skies.

The Lord Hill-Norton, Chief of the Defence Staff from 1971 to 1973, and Chairman of the NATO Military Committee from 1974 to 1977, has categorically stated that there is no doubt that UK radar would have picked up such a target. He feels very strongly that UFOs are real. As well as supporting authors like Tim Good in their quest for the truth, he has formed his own pressure group, UFO Concern. Hill-Norton also suggested that Derek Sheffield should take little notice of Nick Pope's comments on the Belgian affair as the Sec AS2a officer was only a junior civil servant! Perhaps there is a clue in the Pope letter. I suggest that the phrase 'no evidence of any such threat' is important. It is around the question of 'threat' that we should look for answers.

Firstly, some of the evidence presented about the Belgian UFOs is in serious dispute. Research by Belgian Ufologist Wim Van Utrecht (Van Utrecht, 'The Belgium Wave' and *Fortean Times,* both 1997) has shown that a complete re-evaluation of the accepted evidence is required. The evidence presented above is taken from a number of sources which give the major details of the sightings in very similar terms.

It now seems as if the craft hovering over the dam (near Gileppe) was the planet Venus, very bright and in the same position on the night of 29 November. So while witnesses reported seeing a triangular object, it is unlikely to have been hovering for up to 45 minutes. In any case, the descriptions of the triangle seen from close quarters and reports of the object over the dam do not correlate. However, Van Utrecht is prepared to admit that a motorized blimp might have been responsible for the initial triangle sightings.

Most serious of all perhaps, from either side of the debate, was the radar evidence and the pilot reports. It should be pointed out (and was at the time) that, although the pilots admitted that the radar blips on their systems were rather unusual, they never made visual contact with the unidentified object. They did *not* see anything. If the object they were ordered to intercept was a structured craft, then how was it possible for them to have flown through it or for it to have changed shape, as claimed by ground observers? The answer may be simple: there was no relationship between the craft seen at low altitude and the supposed 'object' reported at just under 10,000 feet (3,000 m).

This explanation takes on significance when we learn that:

> the lights that baffled the gendarmes were identified as bright stars and planets, while a military study of the radar tapes revealed that at least one of the lock-ons (probably three) occurred when the F-16's radar mistakenly locked onto the second F-16. The others were almost certainly 'ground clutter' resulting from refraction of the radar beams by irregularities in the

atmosphere, causing surface objects such as cars to appear as airborne targets on a radar screen (Van Utrecht, Fortean Times, 1997).

Apparently, Colonel De Brouwer had jumped the gun. Was the later reluctance to talk about the events an attempt to hide 'weaknesses in the country's radar system'?

Further arguments from Van Utrecht focused on the question of the photograph taken during a skywatch organized by the SOBEPS UFO group at Petit-Rechain on 30–31 March 1990. Van Utrecht appeared to argue that there was some question as to the authenticity of the photograph; while this may be the case, there is still powerful evidence that the triangle captured on film was very similar to, if not the same as, the craft reported by witnesses. (On a separate note, the triangle is remarkably similar to delta-wing bomber concepts from the late 1940s produced by A. V. Roe Limited at Woodford near Manchester, from which the AVRO Vulcan once emerged!) Finally, Van Utrecht made the obvious point that many of the UFO reports made at the time and submitted to the police or SOBEPS did not relate to a triangular craft. We might expect this during a UFO flap.

Unfortunately there is a problem with the believer–sceptic dialectic. On the one hand, the 'believers', those who tend to argue for an extraterrestrial explanation for events, use the most doubtful radar evidence – supposedly showing a 'craft' dropping several thousand feet in a second – and official denials of knowledge to support their case.

On the other hand, the sceptics, those who tend to argue that all the sightings were explainable as misidentifications, hoaxes or evidence of strange natural phenomena, deny that anything relating to UFOs took place. This dialectic has hampered UFO research for years – the opposing camps refuse to believe anything put out by the opposition and engage in a desperate slanging match, while the UFOs make their excuses and leave.

Van Utrecht argues that the sightings at low level might have been caused by a cleverly orchestrated hoax undertaken by a Brussels businessman known to us only as 'K'. K approached Van Utrecht and claimed to have been responsible for some of the reports through the operation of a home-made remote-controlled blimp initially designed for advertising work. Initially, this seemed like a reasonable explanation and to some extent still does. Nevertheless, such people always seem to creep out of the woodwork during UFO flaps and never make themselves known to the public at large. This enables the sceptics to claim that UFO researchers are at the mercy of unseen hoaxers able to strike at almost any moment. Why have we not heard more from K?

In an article for *The New Ufologist* magazine Van Utrecht (1997) produced a photograph of one of K's airships: it is nothing like the craft reported by the witnesses at Gendarme. I find it difficult to believe that the small lights on the underside of the airship could have been responsible for the Belgian sightings.

Last but not least in the sad case of Mr K, we learn via Van Utrecht that the 'anonymous businessman' had asked the Belgian authorities for a huge sum of money in return for which he would give a full explanation of his airships and their involvement in the UFO flap.

Home Base: The UK

New evidence seems to suggest that there was rather more going on over Belgium in 1989–90. In 1998, it is possible to throw new light on this most important case: what little radar evidence there was seemed to indicate that the last known heading for the 'UFO' was south west – towards the English coast. This interested me a great deal given the almost certain knowledge that the UK and USA are engaged in a number of covert activities in the field of advanced stealth aircraft technologies. In addition, there was much evidence to suggest that just two years previously triangular aircraft had been tested in the UK. Given that the 'impossible manoeuvres' indicated by radar tapes could be explained as a technical failure, we are left with a triangular object able to move slowly in near silence.

Realistically, the only place that a secret triangular aircraft could have flown from was the UK. There are only a few facilities from which this aircraft could have operated: RAF Mildenhall, RAF Boscombe Down or perhaps RNAS Yeovilton. The last two bases are located in England's south-west. The first is a well-known site for the testing of prototype aircraft (the triangular Handley-Page HP-115 was flown from Boscombe in the late 1960s), and the second is a well-equipped Royal Naval Air Station facility and the headquarters for the Royal Fleet Air Arm. We now have a growing body of evidence that suggests that both these facilities have been used for covert activities.

The first piece of evidence comes in the form of an extended report (a copy of which was passed to me) made by a witness, Mr 'C', who lives in Street, Somerset. He was living there in March 1990 too; one Sunday afternoon between 4.45 pm and 5 pm he observed a large triangular aircraft ('the same size as a large aircraft') while walking home near a local park. A low humming sound was heard to emanate from the rear of the craft as it flew at an altitude of approximately 300–400 feet (90–120 m) and at a speed of around 30–40 knots as it passed by. The weather was clear and dry, and the sighting lasted for a minute – enough time to see the craft and to notice important details. This in itself was remarkable, but the series of events that followed only served to illustrate the nature of the UFO cover-up, who was doing it and why.

Concerned about the sighting and clearly deeply affected by what he had seen, Mr C did what so many others have done in the past: he rang the authorities to pass on the information in the hope that they might be able to shed some light on the encounter. He telephoned RNAS Yeovilton and they passed him on to RAF Uxbridge where he spoke to a wing-commander. According to the official, the sighting was of little or no interest to him. That should have been the end of it.

To his great surprise Mr C received a phone call from a woman claiming to be a 'Wren' from the MOD. At this stage the witness had not mentioned the sighting to anyone and the only people he had spoken to were military personnel. Therefore, the 'Wren' must have been calling on official business. She asked him many detailed questions about the sighting and specifically concentrated upon the possibility that Mr C might have noticed an 'unusual smell' coming from the craft. She wondered if he had noticed a burning smell. To the military UFO researcher this unusual smell might be evidence for the use of some sort of propulsion system using tremendous amounts of electricity, but the important point to make is that officialdom was very interested in the report.

It also seems as if the main concern for the authorities was the reports themselves, not the existence of a structured craft. Nick Pope himself in his book *Open Skies, Closed Minds* has coined the phrase 'structured craft of unknown origin'. My view is that these triangles are not of unknown origin – at least not to elements of the Defence Intelligence community and the upper echelons of the Royal and US Air Forces. Compartmented information and the Official Secrets Act serve to discourage any potential information leak.

Pope has confirmed both in his book and in interviews with UK researcher Nick Redfern that there was an unusually high level of interest in the triangle sightings of 31 March 1990. These sightings add weight to the belief that the triangles were stationed in the UK. There is no evidence to suggest that attempts were made by the RAF to intercept these triangles of 'unknown origin', and in any case, many of the sightings of triangular aircraft reported to my group involve the use of, for instance, RAF Tornados as an escort. This often enables spokespeople at the bases whence the triangles fly to claim that they did have aircraft up at the time of a sighting and that any reports are misidentifications of conventional craft.

On the other hand, quite often UFO researchers turn logic on its head by arguing that even at slow speeds, triangular aircraft are being chased and/or intercepted by RAF jets. The fact is that the unknowns are being escorted in the full knowledge of military commanders. A sighting that tends to confirm the military link was reported to me by a knowledgeable aviation enthusiast from Mablethorpe, Lincolnshire.

Military Link Confirmed

On 12 February 1997 this observer saw a smaller triangle under escort by RAF Tornados flying at subsonic speeds (wings forward) from his house a quarter of a mile (0.5 km) from the seafront. The triangle was around two-thirds the size of the escort jets. This observer has frequently attended airshows, including the international event at RAF Mildenhall, and has done a considerable amount of aircraft spotting at nearby RAF Coningsby and RAF Waddington, so there is little reason to doubt him.

He reported that the three aircraft were heading out to sea at very low altitude. This in itself would have been important, but at the time in question a military exercise reportedly named 'Northern Adventure' was in full swing with activity in the North Sea. It had also been suggested that the aircraft were on the way to use the Aircraft Manoeuvring and Instrumentation (ACMI) range owned by British Aerospace and situated out to sea. (I subsequently rang British Aerospace to confirm these details.) The range consists of electronic measuring equipment mounted on poles and hammered into the seabed. On the day in question, I have been told, the range was out of action. So were the craft off to join in the fun out to sea? Was this an opportunity for British Aerospace or whoever to show off their 'baby' under exercise conditions? It is likely that the triangle flew with the Tornados from the west coast on the designated Tacan route TB5 that runs across country. Maybe this kind of covert activity is followed by covert intelligence agencies, which would seem sensible. Nick Redfern has told me that from 1964 covert UFO research was undertaken by the Defence Intelligence Staff – just a short time after Nick Cook claims that a secret agreement relating to UK–US military UFOs came into force.

Various documents from the Public Record Office released under the provisions of the Thirty Year Rule Act indicate that DI55 and DI64, small specialist units within the Defence Intelligence Staff (DIS), have been involved in on-site UFO investigations (Redfern). Has this been done in order to find out what witnesses have seen and/or to put pressure on them to keep quiet? Given the secrecy relating to such an international agreement then the answer must be 'yes'.

A document from 1983 indicates that a UFO sighting was handled by DI55 (Randles, 1995). It would appear that these are the 'Air Defence experts' mentioned by Nick Pope in his letter to Derek Sheffield. Many researchers suggest that a covert agenda of UFO investigations has been effected to monitor unauthorized penetrations of the UK Air Defence Region. The truth may be rather different. Official and on-going UFO investigations have kept a close eye on public interest in UFOs and have sought to keep a lid on UFO reports for nearly 50 years (Redfern). Much of this would appear to relate to the activities of secret aircraft.

In the Belgian case we have some evidence that the UFO flew from Britain. We also have evidence that several intelligence agencies were concerned about the mass hysteria generated by the sightings. Documents released under the Freedom of Information Act (see Good, 1996, pp. 297–302) indicate that the US Defense Intelligence Agency (DIA) took a great deal of interest in the Belgian sightings. The distribution list for the unevaluated report is fascinating; it shows that the Defence Intelligence Staff at the Ministry of Defence received a copy, as did numerous other intelligence agencies and military establishments.

This clearly indicates that there are two levels of UFO investigation: one official – Sec AS2a – and one unofficial – shady elements within the DIS.

Shop Window/Empty Shop

Sec AS2a could be described as a beautiful shop window concealing an empty shop while DIS personnel can be seen as the real investigators who are routinely sent information relating to UFO sightings. This much is known. Matthew Williams and Chris Fowler have established, through correspondence with Kerry Philpott, Nick Pope's successor at Air Staff, that during Pope's work for Sec AS2a, UFO sighting reports were sent to RAF Rudloe Manor. The fact that Sec AS2a is neither the final nor the only destination for such reports indicates a cover-up of some sort (Williams).

That the DIS should be involved in UFO research is worrying to say the least, especially considering its role in intelligence-gathering, as well as its pivotal role in the 'defence of the realm' (Urban). In the past its operatives have been involved in counter-espionage and counter-subversion activities against Soviet agents. Officially speaking, DIS has been involved in making intelligence estimates of foreign weapons systems, reporting on the military strengths and weaknesses of these

PAGE:0014

```
INQUIRE=DOC100
ITEM NO=00503294
ENVELOPE
CDSN = LGX492   MCN = 90089/26566   TOR = 900891502
RTTCZYUW RUEXJCS5049 0891251-CCCC--RUEALGX.
ZNY CCCCC
HEADER
R 301251Z MAR 90
FM JOINT STAFF WASHINGTON DC
INFO RUEADWD/OCSA WASHINGTON DC
RUEKAAA/CNO WASHINGTON DC
RUEAHQA/CSAF WASHINGTON DC
RUEACMC/CMC WASHINGTON DC
RUEDADA/AFIS AMES BOLLING AFB DC
RUFTAKA/CDR USAINTELCTRE HEIDELBERG GE
RUFGAID/USEUCOM AIDES VAIHINGEN GE
RUETIAQ/NMCFTCBOHCGEGMEADEMD
RUEANCC/CNC CC WASHINGTON DC
RUEALGX/SAFE
R 301246Z MAR 90
FM ████████████████
TO RUEXJCS/DIA WASHDC
INFO RUEXJCS/DIA WASHDC//DAT-7//
RUSNNUA/USCINCEUR VAIHINGEN GE//ECJ2-OC/ECJ2-JIC//
RUFGAID/USEUCOM AIDES VAIHINGEN GE
RUFQAAA/HQUSAFE RAMSTEIN AB GE//INOW/INO//
RUEPAAA/UTAIS RAMSTEIN AB GE//INRME/INA//
RUHLCHE/CINCUSNAVEUR LONDON UK
RUFENA/USDELMC BRUSSELS BE
RUFENA/USMISSION USNATO
RUDOGBA/USNMR SHAPE BE
RUEAIIA/CIA WASHDC
RUFGAID/JICEUR VAIHINGEN GE
RUCKSAA/FICEURLANT NORFOLK VA
RUEXJCS/SECDEF WASHDC
RUEHC/SECSTATE WASHDC
RUEADWW/WHITEHOUSE WASHDC
RUFNBC/AMEMBASSY LUXEMBOURG
RUEATAC/CDRUSAITAC WASHDC
BT
CONTROLS
████████████████ SECTION 02 OF 02 ████████ 05049


SERIAL:  (U) IIR 6 807 0136 90.

BODY
COUNTRY:  (U) BELGIUM (BE).

SUBJ:  IIR 6 807 0136 90/BELGIUM AND THE UFO ISSUE (U)

MAR TV SHOW.
```

Witnesses' reports suggest that flying triangles operated from the UK during the Belgian 'flap' of 1989–90. Elements of the US and UK intelligence communities kept a close eye on events, as these distribution lists indicate.

and operating a network of intelligence-gatherers throughout the world. It is also tasked to provide detailed information relating to British interests abroad.

One of the most important elements within the DIS is the DSTI, also a recipient of UFO reports (Randles, 1995). DSTI – the Directorate of Scientific and Technical Intelligence – has been linked with advanced technology research within the Defence Evaluation and Research Agency (DERA), headquartered in Farnborough, Hampshire.

It has become apparent that DERA facilities are a focal point for sightings of UFOs. If DIS has expertise in the evaluation of foreign weapons systems, might we conclude that in 1990 it was carrying out a similar mission for its American allies?

The question remains: was the involvement of the DIS at the time of the Belgian triangle sightings evidence that the intelligence community knew all about the craft seen? Was this a secret military aircraft? The evidence suggests that this was indeed the case.

When the personnel at Sec AS2a claim that UFOs are of 'no defence significance', to some extent they are telling the truth. The intelligence community and those with access to 'Most Secret' information are aware that in many ways Britain is an American 'Airstrip One', and that they have been personally involved in a UFO cover-up of possibly Orwellian proportions for many, many years.

TEN

HUDSON VALLEY

THE HUDSON VALLEY is steeped in over 350 years of American heritage, taking its name from the English explorer Henry Hudson, who travelled up the Hudson River in 1609 looking for a short cut to China. The meandering river, green rolling hills and fields inspired the seventeenth-century traveller Daniel Denton to declare: 'If ever there be any terrestrial Caanan's, 'tis surely here where all the land floweth with milk and honey.'

Today, the Hudson Valley is home to the sprawling middle-class suburbs of Westchester County just beyond the boundaries of New York City. The world-famous West Point Military Academy is further north and if you travel up the valley you reach the beautiful Catskill Mountain ranges.

The Hudson Valley UFO

It was against this tranquil background, and above the heads of an unsuspecting public, that a series of most unusual UFO sightings took place in the 1980s. These were focused mainly, though by no means exclusively, on an area to the east of the Hudson River over Dutchess, Putnam and Westchester Counties, which border on the State of Connecticut (Imbrogno, Pratt and Hynek, 1987).

During a continuous wave of UFO sightings, or UFO 'flap', it is difficult for Ufologists to keep a sensible perspective on events. Anyone who has been involved in a similar flap knows what I am talking about: the press become interested in the sightings as more witnesses come forward. The press speak to some of the witnesses, and their sightings and experiences become widely known. The next thing that can happen is that the wider media become involved – radio and TV. Before

113

you know it, people are watching the skies and seeing all kinds of objects – most very simply explained. In many cases, for instance during the Lancashire Coast incident of October 1997, the same thing happened; it was only when local investigators had a chance to sit back and reflect on events that it became clear that only a handful of sightings could be taken seriously and warranted further investigation. Often in the later stages of an incident all kinds of ludicrous 'explanations' are put out by interested groups and individuals hoping to gain publicity for their particular theories on the origin and nature of UFOs. This confuses the issue, although it is easy to see how it happens.

Imagine then what the small group of investigators in the Hudson Valley area of New York State had to deal with from the early 1980s onwards. Author and researcher Philip Imbrogno notes that several thousand reports came in, and the media interest grew as time went by. The sightings were perhaps a good example of how the UFO community, and the UFO subject, can be used by shadowy intelligence agencies.

The First Reported Sighting

No one is quite sure when the sightings started, although Philip Imbrogno, one of the central figures in the unfolding events, argues that the date was New Year's Eve, 1982, when a retired New York City police officer went out to his garden to clear up some broken glass. He saw some lights moving very slowly and called for his wife to bring out his video camera. The object in question was a large triangular UFO emitting a deep humming sound.

As the object passed over his house at an altitude of some 500 feet (155 m), the multicoloured lights changed and three white lights were seen in a triangular shape. They illuminated the ground. After that, the lights changed back to the multicoloured arrangement. The video footage was remarkable although, perhaps unsurprisingly, any structure behind the powerful lights was impossible to discern. The local investigators soon found other witnesses to this UFO, which appeared to have flown in the direction of the main Interstate 84 highway. Edwin Hansen, a foreman, saw the lights as he drove along the highway; although his initial impression was that they came from a helicopter scanning the ground below, he soon realized that there was no sound at all. On closer inspection, the lights appeared to be coming from a large boomerang-shaped object with a triangular or V-tail. As it moved towards his car, it was possible to make out these vital details. In fact, this was most certainly a close encounter – the lights dazzled

Hansen and he became rather disconcerted. Nevertheless, something told him not to fear the craft hovering above.

The idea that UFOs are extraterrestrial craft interested in making contact with people, even 'taking' them, is deeply ingrained, perhaps not surprisingly given blockbuster movies like *Close Encounters of the Third Kind.*

The Unusual 'Boomerang'

On one occasion in February 1983 a mental health nurse named Monique O'Driscoll, who worked in Brewster, New York, chanced upon the unusual boomerang craft.

Travelling back with her daughter from a meal at her mother's house in nearby Kent, her daughter saw an illuminated object moving slowly near a small lake called White Pond. The object actually passed over the car before stopping above the lake. Initially, the lights had been very bright but as the object hovered over the water the lights went 'crazy'.

This was quite clearly a structured object, akin to a boomerang. Various blue and red lights were seen. Mrs O'Driscoll and her daughter noticed a larger amber light on the underside of the craft. Once again, the craft approached the witnesses and they became agitated. Even so, they felt drawn to the object and decided to follow it. Eventually, another car appeared and the three or four young men on board claimed to have been tracking the craft for some time. On investigation, it emerged that Mrs O'Driscoll had seen important details of the craft including 'the heavy metal part and then the crisscross effects, the diamond shape work, with tubular things here and there'. In fact, the O'Driscolls' story was backed up, as so often during the years of sightings, by another witness, Rita Rivera. Mrs O'Driscoll had understandably wanted others to see the craft, so she had stopped at a nearby house. This belonged to Mr and Mrs Donald Nandick, who confirmed the sequence of events, and also the fact that they had contacted the local police. Many others made similar calls.

On this remarkable night the object was also seen by some air traffic controllers travelling along Interstate 84. Again, the craft seen was a boomerang with lights on the underside and it operated silently as it passed above them at a height of approximately 1,000 feet (300 m). It was obvious by now that the witnesses had seen a large craft, perhaps 200 feet (61 m) long, with a most unusual ability to put on a light display and to operate in near silence – a slight hum having been detected on a few occasions.

The investigation undertaken by the small team affiliated to the Chicago-based Center for UFO Studies (CUFOS) began on 26 March 1983. A report appeared on the front page of the *Westchester-Rockland Daily Item*, resulting in a mass of reports and enquiries. This was most unusual for a start. As Philip Imbrogno points out, it was unlikely that a local investigations team would receive more than few cases each year – especially in a country the size of the United States.

A variety of people drawn from every part of the many Hudson Valley communities were witness to the UFO. In one case, local Yorktown police officers reported that their switchboard had been jammed between 8.20 and 9.30 pm on the night of 24 March. The craft seen was the boomerang-shaped one with numerous lights underneath. On this occasion, it had been moving slowly across Westchester County. It had been seen a week before at around the same time. Witnesses had described it as 'V-shaped' and as having 'rows of bright lights along its wings'.

Reappearance

The night of 24 March 1983 was one of the well-documented periods of activity. On this occasion the majority of sightings were reported from Westchester and Putnam Counties, where hundreds of people saw the UFO. By now a clear pattern had emerged. The same craft was being reported time and time again by all kinds of responsible people. The craft seemed to enjoy performing to the stunned audiences below. Around Millwood, on either side of the Taconic Parkway, cars had stopped to watch the UFO. Various bright beams of light were focused on to the vehicles below. Ed Burns, computer programmer, noted the way in which the craft travelled slowly, almost giving the impression of hovering. Coloured lights were replaced by white lights – the craft was not unlike a 'flying city' with panels of lights along the back. Taconic Parkway witnesses included police officers and a meteorologist with the National Weather Corporation. Bill Hele described this as a craft of approximately a quarter mile (0.5 km) in length – 'a large check mark or V with one of the V clipped off'.

Most interestingly, on the same night some 15 miles (25 km) north near Kent, Carmel, Lake Carmel and Brewster, the same type of craft was seen hovering above Route 301 in total silence before the now-familiar light display began. A family, the Holtsmans, were witness to this event, while a mechanical engineer with some experience of aircraft saw the V-shaped craft pivoting upon its axis at low level. So were there two or more of these huge boomerang-type aircraft?

Suitable Concern Is Shown

By this stage, the authorities were suitably concerned. Police spokespersons were unable to provide any serious comments, except a view that people were not making up the sightings and that the UFO had been seen by many hundreds of local people. As in all UFO flaps, the activities of sceptics and hoaxers surfaced. We cannot be sure of their real intentions, although the sceptics have a tendency to try to question the character of the witnesses, while the hoaxers try to confuse the issue as much as possible.

In the case of the Hudson Valley UFO, as time went on and the evidence increasingly suggested that something most unusual was going on in this sleepy part of the eastern United States, a small group of pilots appear to have attempted to muddy the waters by flying aircraft in formation over the area in which the sightings had taken place. Residents in both Putnam and Dutchess Counties reported flights of aircraft operating at a low level. However, these craft did not look at all like the UFO and made considerable noise as they passed overhead. Unfortunately for them, and luckily for the investigators, this did not fool anyone for more than a few seconds. Witnesses were angered by any suggestion that they were mistaken about the craft they had seen.

The flight of aircraft in formation did, however, encourage the Federal Aviation Authority (FAA), under pressure to make some official comment on the sightings, to suggest that aircraft in formation provided an explanation for all the sightings. However, they admitted to Imbrogno and his team that they had no idea where these aircraft were flying from. Assuming that they were telling the truth, this was a new twist in the tale of the Hudson Valley UFO.

John Tower, supervisor at the nearest air traffic control tower in Purchase, New York, made two interesting comments that appear to have passed the investigators by. Firstly, he said that the only thing that had appeared on radar at the time of the sightings was a small plane, and that the radar wouldn't have detected anything flying *below* 1,000 feet (300 m). Could this fact have had some bearing on events? In a final statement on events Mike Fedder at Dutchess County Airport commented that as long as the UFO stayed away from restricted areas and commercial air routes then there was little chance of action being taken. Quite what action could have been initiated is anyone's guess – attempts to make contact with the UFO had, perhaps unsurprisingly, failed.

The numerous and detailed reports of the UFO allow us to build up a picture of the craft. As we know, it was huge, boomerang-shaped and able to hover silently. It seemed to have a V-tail, almost as if a piece had been cut out of the back of the craft. Lights were arranged along the leading edge, the back and the underside and were able to present an impressive display.

A 'Close Encounter'

On 24 March John Wright and his family had a particularly close encounter with the UFO.

Wright, a correctional officer, was travelling with his two of his neighbour's children when they saw the object about 200 feet (61 m) above them near Mount Storm. Wright said that the craft was a 'single solid object' and that it looked as though it had been built from 'an erector set' (Meccano?). The flashing lights were coming through a series of windows. In addition, he could see a tubular inner structure. The craft was dark and nothing seemed to reflect off it. It moved away next to Interstate 84, where it was seen by other witnesses.

This was designated a 'Close Encounter of the First Kind' or 'CE-1'. One of the factors affecting the investigations was this use of the system set up by Allen Hynek, whereby sightings are put into categories – daylight disc, nocturnal light, radar-visual, close encounters of the first kind (a close-up sighting within perhaps 500 feet [150 m]) through to supposed 'Close Encounters of the Fourth Kind', where humans might make contact with the 'alien occupants' of an extraterrestrial spacecraft.

Of course the use of any classification system is problematic, but by the investigations team's own admission they were most interested in close encounters. In fact, Philip Imbrogno's view about UFO sightings seems to have become geared to an acceptance of 'Close Encounters' of the fourth and 'fifth kind'. This militates against the majority of evidence from Hudson Valley, where out of several thousand reports only a small number claimed to have any kind of contact experience. Much good work done, especially by researchers in the United Kingdom, indicates that these are, in the main, internal experiences perhaps stimulated by outside events rather than 'real abductions'. In other words, during the Hudson Valley flap, there was no reasonable evidence to suggest that anyone was taken on board the UFO and 'examined'.

Nevertheless, as the sightings tailed off in the late 1980s, a variety of 'New Age' researchers stepped into the frame and claimed that they had photographed aliens in the Pine Bush area of New York State and that this was an area where many 'Close Encounters' had taken place

(Crystal). Perhaps this had more to do with belief systems and wishful thinking than any hard evidence. After all, we are dealing with sightings of a structured object said to be perhaps 200 feet (61 m) in length.

More Sightings

Let us have a look at some other sightings from Hynek and Imbrogno's *Night Siege*.

- 25 March 1984 – Taconic Parkway, 8.20 pm. V-shape or boomerang-shaped aircraft. Described as a 'delta-shape' with six white lights and two green lights in the middle.

- 31 May 1984 – New Croton reservoir next to Taconic Parkway. Said by Joseph Marks to be a 'big V-shaped, wedge-shaped thing'. He speculated that this could well be a government-operated aircraft.

- Same night – David Boyd, local pilot, approximated size of object as 140–150 feet (43–46 m) in length.

All the witnesses to these events were sure that this was a single, huge object and certainly not a formation of aircraft or ultralights.

The UFO appeared to behave intelligently on several occasions, particularly in the way in which it started a light display *after* being spotted by witnesses. On other occasions when witnesses to sightings drove away from the scene of their encounters, the craft seemed to move off and follow them.

A sighting from late October 1983 was typical. Like many of the witnesses to the Hudson Valley UFO, John Cooke was hardly interested in 'the unexplained' and initially thought that he had seen some aircraft lights as he travelled back to his home in Mahopac, New York. What surprised him about the object he saw was both its size and the fact that it was hovering. It also operated in silence – a most unnerving discovery, especially at 2.15 am! More than that, Cooke had background in aircraft maintenance so this was an intriguing sight: a large triangular-shaped object above the Croton Falls reservoir – no more than approximately 15 feet (4.5 m) above the water. As Cooke looked on in amazement various lights started to come on – initially a cherry red colour. The lights moved from place to place and Cooke believed that they were 'interacting' with the water in some way. As other cars passed by the lights went out, only to come on after their departure. Cooke stood and watched – completely dumbfounded. The craft in question was approximately 100 feet (30 m) in length by 30 feet (9 m) in width. It departed vertically and faded out against the night sky.

Perhaps the operators of the aircraft chose to set off this light display in order to give a false impression that there was something unusual going on. In fact, I suggest that this might have been part of a psychological warfare operation. None of the witnesses could understand the lights. Why should they behave in this way? Surely this could not be a secret military aircraft? Surely it could not be tested in an area of fairly high population?

Nuclear Encounter

Many of the misconceptions surrounding the Hudson Valley sightings emerged after two sightings over the Indian Point nuclear reactor at Buchanan, New York, in July 1984 (Ecker; Imbrogno).

Although accidents at such plants are, luckily, very few and far between, the security which surrounds them is tight. The Indian Point facility is of strategic importance because it serves New York City (regulated by the New York Power Authority [NYPA]) and Westchester County as well as local schools, the New York subway and other trains. There was also a suggestion that military facilities were served by the reactor. Clearly, this was a vital installation, and with memories of the Three Mile Island nuclear accident (1979) not too distant, this was the last place that anyone expected to see a UFO. But that's exactly what happened.

The UFO appeared just twice over the reactor. The first sighting took place on 14 July, witnessed by three security guards. Ten days later, the craft returned and personnel at the facility were alerted through the internal communications system. The UFO, described by witnesses as the well-known boomerang, drifted over the only active reactor (number 3) where it hovered for up to ten minutes! The events of this night have never been explained to the satisfaction of Phil Imbrogno and he insists that all kinds of pressure were put on him to discourage him from discussing the incident.

As in so many cases, little hard evidence emerged, although Imbrogno was apparently sought out by workers at the plant. His sources appear to have suggested that there were documents relating to the incident held by the Nuclear Regulatory Commission (NRC). Freedom of Information Act requests resulted in little forward progress. The investigators suspected that the NYPA were working in concert with other agencies to keep a lid on the incident.

Perhaps unsurprisingly, these authorities hoped to minimize publicity. Readers can understand why – given the most controversial nature of nuclear power and the necessary security surrounding it. Nevertheless, one thing is clear: there was no real threat posed by the UFO. It did hover over an active reactor and send the officials and security guards into a panic. Talk of 'cracks' appearing in the reactor and equipment shutting down during the sighting seems to have been rather premature. There were also suggestions from 'inside sources' that armed security guards were thinking of opening fire on the UFO! It is also said that helicopters equipped with rocket-launchers were sent to intercept the UFO after calls were made to Camp Smith, a New York National Guard base just 10 miles (16 km) away.

There were many possibilities and equally many rumours. The fact is that nobody appears to have fired on the UFO and neither does there appear to be any evidence to suggest a malfunction of equipment or 'changes' within the reactor core. We might expect the authorities to make denials and Cliff Spieler, Vice-President of NYPA, argued that 'light aircraft' were responsible. It is also easy to understand why those in charge of such a potentially hazardous facility would want to keep quiet.

Some things do not, however, appear to make sense. Imbrogno claims to have spoken to various security guards. One of them estimated the size of the UFO as larger than a C-5a – which has a wingspan of 212 feet (65 m). Another member of the security staff and former police officer, 'Carl', estimated the size at 300 feet (91 m) in length. Other witnesses said 900 feet (275 m). These discrepancies are worrying.

Logic also dictates that guards would not attempt to shoot down an unidentified object. This could have allowed a security breach to become a fully fledged nuclear disaster! Imbrogno's sources expect us to believe that as the UFO flew over the operational reactor, guards armed with shotguns were 'waiting for the order to bring it down'. The hysteria surrounding the incident led one guard to speculate that the UFO had openings on the underside that could have been hatches for rockets! Perhaps this kind of woolly and illogical thinking was one reason for the resulting security shake-up at Indian Point.

Perhaps an effort to discredit Imbrogno's investigation was launched, and it might have been hastened by the Indian Point episode. He was contacted by various people as a result, some clearly trying to make his work seem less than credible. The following is taken from an article on the events written by Vicki Cooper:

I am still being given information about certain things going on in there – in the nighttime, people seeing little creatures coming through the walls of the casing on the reactor, and military personnel indicating 'we're aware of these creatures and we don't care if they're from outer space'.

Whereas we have very good information from witnesses relating to the many UFO sightings in Hudson Valley, the information about Indian Point is tinged with unbelievable and illogical testimony and far too much anonymity. After all, if all these security agents were talking to Imbrogno 'off the record' they must still have been known to their employers. In one case we are told about 'Carl'. How many Carls worked at Indian Point and how difficult do you think it would be to track him down?

Most worrying of all is the typical Ufologist's prejudice. There were many suggestions put forward both at the time and subsequently as to the nature of the UFO – a secret military aircraft, 'anomalous lights' (!) or extraterrestrial spacecraft. Philip Imbrogno is quoted as stating: 'I don't think that our government could be so bold with a craft of the kind that appeared at Indian Point.'

He also stated his belief that the most tenable solution to this particular UFO mystery was that it was an 'extraterrestrial space-craft'. These two pieces of flawed logic are, I suggest, the perfect cover for covert activities. We already know that the CIA have lied about their handling of the UFO subject (Haines) and we know that they have operated a variety of 'Top Secret' aircraft – U-2 and SR-71 (Miller, *Lockheed's Skunk Works*, 1995). The Air Force had the F-117A which was operational for some eight years (1981 to 1989) before its existence was publicly admitted (Sweetman and Goodall, 1990). There was also the B-2 'stealth' bomber. It was always shrouded in mystery and cost a fortune (Birdsall, 1995; Gonsalves).

My feeling is that the Hudson Valley sightings would have remained largely unexplained, and the witness statements increasingly the subject of 'Ufological mystification', had it not been for the work of one researcher. The man in question was famous for rather less than 15 minutes within the UFO community and his work has remained largely unrecognized by the research community. Tony Gonsalves is a little-known UFO researcher from Providence, Rhode Island.

He developed an interest in the Hudson Valley sightings in the late 1980s and decided to put the many witness statements together in order to build an actual model of the UFO. As we shall see later, Gonsalves' work has indeed been a 'UFO revelation'.

Look at the Evidence

Some of the witnesses to the Hudson Valley UFO believed that they had seen something terrestrial. While one could argue that Imbrogno and his team were almost programmed to conclude that UFOs were 'most likely' to be extraterrestrial spacecraft, in the real world this was, to say the least, most *unlikely*. It was also possible that their conclusions were coloured by the intervention of Dr J. Allen Hynek, who visited the area in order to help out, and subsequently co-authored *Night Siege* with Imbrogno and Bob Pratt. Hynek was totally convinced that the majority of unexplained UFO sightings were strong evidence for extraterrestrial contact. While UFO researchers are happy to support the view that there is an all-encompassing 'cover-up', they have an annoying habit of accepting some of the worst examples of official military propaganda. Take this example from Imbrogno's book *Night Siege*:

> *There are several reasons why the aircraft theory should be ruled out.*
>
> *...The UFO was seen to hover overhead. Many witnesses said the object hovered directly over their heads, some said for as long as five minutes. Helicopters hover but make a tremendous noise. British-made Harrier jet fighters, some of which are used by the US Marine Corps, can rise vertically and hover as they move into horizontal flight, but their engines are extremely loud.*
>
> *Blimps also can hover but their engines do make some noise that can be heard up to a mile away. Again no blimps were flying in the area on any of these nights.*

Having seen many a blimp I think the suggestion that the engines could be heard up to a mile (1.6 km) away is a little exaggerated. In any case, many of the witnesses, including cases quoted in Imbrogno's own book, claim that the object was not totally silent – in some cases a distant humming noise was heard.

The book was published in 1987, and at that time neither the F-117A Nighthawk nor the B-2 were known about. Of course there had been speculation; as early as 1980 mention of a 'stealthy' aircraft had been made by spokesmen for Jimmy Carter. Once again it should be noted that the F-117A had already been operational for some time (it was seen in the UK in 1985 and possibly operated there from 1984, albeit in a limited way). By 1987 work on the official B-2 prototype was under way. In the case of the B-2 it was always made clear in official briefings that no prototypes, beyond small-scale Radar Cross Section testing models, had been constructed or tested (Miller, *Northrop B-2 Spirit*, 1995; Sweetman, 1997). The design work had supposedly been done on new all-powerful super-computers! Of course, such pronouncements were propaganda intended only for public consumption. Such statements were somewhat 'economical with the truth'.

Were the investigations team arguing that the only military aircraft that could have possibly been responsible for the sightings were a Harrier jump-jet or a regular blimp? It would seem as if they had little or no access to material about black projects. One could argue that they did not want to know about such projects.

Admittedly there were many problems facing the small investigations team during the flap. One was the lack of any kind of progress, even after thousands of witnesses had come forward. In addition, too many other confusing and unrelated subjects were linked in after the initial investigations. An article written by Don Ecker, editor of the California-based *UFO Magazine,* makes this clear:

> *According to Mr. Phil Imbrogno, during the research that led to the writing of* Night Siege – The Hudson Valley UFO Sightings, *by Dr. J. Allen Hynek, Philip Imbrogno has stated that on several occasions, Hynek specified that he wanted no mention of the dozens of human abductions that they had already uncovered at the time. Hynek was afraid of the adverse publicity if word of this aspect leaked out to the public.*

Quite often tales of mutilations and abductions are linked in with UFO activity (Imbrogno, 1997; Howe), maybe because a local person has seen a UFO in the same area in recent times. My position is that, especially in the case of the Hudson Valley sightings, the focus should be upon the actual craft seen. I have spoken to several East Coast UFO researchers, including Tony Gonsalves, and they have not supported the view that 'alien abductions' were a feature of the UFO flap. One cannot help thinking that such information is put out deliberately to mislead the public and to lessen the impact of the local sightings. If not, then it is the researchers themselves who are muddying the waters by allowing belief systems or unrelated material to affect their objectivity. Philip Imbrogno himself, writing in his books, links the activity of the V-shaped UFO with the 'Close Encounter' experience.

It is not made clear how many of the witnesses featured in *Night Siege* have had such experiences. In fact, the one main 'abduction' case emerged unsurprisingly after a hypnosis session conducted by the controversial Bud Hopkins. It was made clear that much of the information relating to so-called abductions actually emerged during a conference organized in conjunction with lawyer Peter Gersten of Citizens Against UFO Secrecy (CAUS), held in 1987 and featuring the usual suspects – Whitley Strieber, Bud Hopkins and Ellen Crystal. These three speakers are entirely convinced of the reality of extraterrestrial contact, although Gersten appears to have developed an opinion that the craft seen was a military UFO.

Of 900 participants in the conference some 200 are said to have claimed to have contacted 'the UFO intelligence'. Of these 200, 120 were said to be unreliable, leaving 90 cases of which just 19 related to 'abductions'. Other reports related to a host of New Age experiences including 'channeling', 'entity communication' and 'sighting with telepathy'.

Conclusion: A Structured Craft

I have seen no evidence to suggest that the craft seen was anything other than a secret military aircraft. Perhaps its operators knew that the investigation team would come to all the wrong conclusions and cover up the reality behind the UFO sightings. Initially, reports were taken referring to a structured aircraft of unknown origin. Later on, thanks in part to the non-emergence of a solution to the sightings, a host of speculation, New Age beliefs and 'Ufolore' made its way into the equation, resulting in the suggestion that the UFO was involved in more than just test flights. Perhaps there was an element of psychological warfare involved here.

For instance, some witnesses, for example 'John Wright' and the two teenagers in his car, who had seen the UFO near Mount Storm on 24 March 1983, claimed to have had UFO-related dreams after their sightings. Given that they were scared by this powerful experience then perhaps we should not be surprised. Another witness, Mrs O'Driscoll, submitted herself to hypnosis as the result of a subsequent 'missing time' episode and was regressed by Bud Hopkins, whereupon she claimed to have seen 'aliens' on board a ship: more evidence of the power of a UFO sighting – especially one so close.

What is interesting about both these examples is how witnesses claim to have had vivid dreams or perhaps an encounter experience several months *after* their actual sighting. It is very worrying to note that when a UFO is seen, a *small number* of witnesses will claim to have been in contact with it or that they had a 'missing time' experience. OK, one can lose track of time when looking at a spectacular object deliberately made to look like a 'flying city', but to suggest that a missing time relates to a period where 'aliens experimented' on the witness is quite ridiculous. Luckily, many British researchers have conducted objective research into the 'Close Encounter' experience. Their considered conclusion is that even if such events are 'real' to the witness, they lie within the paranormal field of study.

Unlike the researchers involved, let us not lose sight of what the witnesses had reported: thousands and thousands of people reported seeing structured craft. The vast majority suffered *no adverse effects* beyond vivid recollection of the light patterns on the craft they saw. If Imbrogno is right and some 19 people at a conference claimed to have been abducted then this is a tiny number of people compared with the thousands of witnesses to the UFO. Indeed, we might expect a tiny number of people to have such experiences *regardless* of UFO sightings.

As author John Spencer points out, nobody has ever seen anyone being abducted. Secondly, 'abductions' are almost entirely the result of questionable hypnosis techniques (Spencer; McClure, 'Yesterday Belongs to Me', *Abduction Watch*, 1998).

Bud Hopkins, one of the speakers at the 1987 conference, has hypnotically regressed and tested children (Bryan, p. 359) despite the dangers involved, and the evidence indicating that such procedures can lead to implantation of false memories. It should be pointed out that up until now, no definitive evidence has emerged that close encounters with 'aliens' are taking place. In the USA there has been an unquestioning approach to the question of abductions (Bryan), and much of the energy behind the use of hypnosis has come from US 'therapists'. The pseudo-religious overtones are clear:

1. UFOs represent a 'non-human intelligence'.

2. Witnesses are 'chosen' for reasons never made clear.

3. There is little or nothing that they can do about it.

In the case of a UFO conference, it is perhaps not surprising to find that many participants will believe that they have contacted such an intelligence! Nevertheless, as secret military aircraft researcher Steve Douglass has pointed out, it is much more likely that any aliens that exist come from the Pentagon and that they wear grey suits!

ELEVEN

HUDSON VALLEY EXPLAINED?

WAS THE HUDSON VALLEY UFO of alien origin, as many want to believe? Looking closely at the evidence, Tony Gonsalves came to rather different conclusions.

He spoke to many witnesses and undertook a lengthy study of the events. I spoke to him about supposed abductions and he rejected the suggestion that these had anything to do with the activities of the UFO. He had heard of only a small number of paranormal events that had taken place during the period in question, although he did comment that he had no problem in believing that such things *could* happen. Back in the real world, the anonymous controllers of the structured aircraft must have been laughing at the researchers on the ground.

The following report (Imbrogno, Pratt and Hynek, 1987) was made by Donald Wecon, a 44-year-old electrical engineer who lived at Mount Kisco, and included an unusual observation:

> *It was some type of large airship, and as it passed over you could feel the mass behind it and get a sense of the power that would be needed for an object that size to move so slowly.*

Other witnesses said that it was travelling at the speed of a blimp. Don Duhart (mentioned in Imbrogno's *Night Siege* in connection with sightings at Bethel and Danbury) suggested that the craft involved was a large blimp with lights on it. He argued that such a vehicle could have been made using lightweight plastics and operated by remote control. Perhaps Duhart was closer to the truth than he realized.

Of course, the suggestion that any kind of blimp could have been responsible was ruled out by the authors of *Night Siege*. They cited adverse weather conditions where the wind blew in gusts up to 35 mph (56 kmph). They also added that during the incident at Indian

Point, the wind had been particularly strong and that no blimp or light aircraft could hover in these conditions.

By concentrating on the reports, and not speculation, Gonsalves built up a working picture of the unknown aircraft in his head: boomerang with triangular tail, size approximately as large as a football field, dull grey metallic-type finish. It was undoubtedly the B-2 bomber, but not the official version unveiled at Palmdale, California, in 1988 (Miller, *Lockheed's Skunk Works*, 1995). His view was simple: if it looked like a B-2 then it probably was a B-2, or something very close at least.

Lights to Use, Confuse, Intimidate

The most important element of the investigation was an explanation of the varying light patterns reported by witnesses. By arranging numerous lights along the leading edge and the underside of the aircraft it could present itself in many ways to a ground observer.

The majority of lights were white, although there were various red and green lights interspersed. These were not, however, randomly organized. Gonsalves argued that they were functional. For instance, many people had remarked on the white light located in the central area of the underside of the craft. Gonsalves argued that this aircraft would hover before landing and that such a light would be essential during a smooth landing. At last some common sense was being injected into new investigations.

White lights on both the leading and trailing edges were essential for landing operations, especially in a situation where the ground crew, however small, was largely unable to hear the craft approaching. The actual lighting patterns reported by witnesses suggested that white lights indicated a flying-wing shape with a triangular tail. Gonsalves argued that lights on the trailing edge would be used in order to light up the ground behind an aircraft. He argued that this was a tactical aircraft designed for use in any number of difficult situations, hence the need for illumination at low level. As the craft came in to land at a military facility, the white lights would very likely be replaced by red ones. He had worked on three aircraft carriers as a technician and had seen the use of red landing lights on numerous occasions during night operations.

There was nothing particularly extraordinary in the actual positioning of the lights on the craft. Their use could also be considered from a psychological point of view. The aircraft could be very intimidating – this much was clear from the testimony, especially where the forward spotlight was focused on a target – a car, a witness or group of witnesses. This light was probably located behind the forward landing-gear door.

For the craft seen in Hudson Valley, it was possible to build up a detailed picture, not only of its shape but also of important details. For instance, when seen head-on, eight lights, four on either side, were noted on the leading edge. On the official B-2 the leading edge could easily accommodate such lights. Head on, it is easy to see why some witnesses thought they were seeing a disc-shaped object – the point of the nose would be difficult to see and would of course be hidden through the use of powerful lights. From the side, the aircraft would not appear to be a flying wing either – again it would look more saucer-shaped.

Various photographs were taken during the flap, the majority of showing little more than a few lights. The best video footage, shown on a Home Box Office television show entitled *American Undercover* (and later on a CBS show), was taken by Mr Bob Pozzuoli on 24 July 1984 at around 10 pm. It was fairly clear and showed an object with a string of six bright lights in its centre with two more conventional running lights at each end. This arrangement of six bright lights was common to many reports. The footage was an excellent example of how a wing shape could, through the placement of a small number of lights, be used to confuse any witnesses.

To demonstrate this and other reported light patterns Gonsalves built a 1/43rd scale model of a B-2 with a triangular tail. There was little guesswork involved here. Note: The shape of the B-2 bomber was altered, supposedly at the design stage, during 1983 at a cost of $1 billion! The original trailing-edge configuration, as shown in Miller's book entitled *Northrop B-2 Spirit* (1995) on pp. 20–1, involved the use of a triangular or 'V' tail. The new design looked more like a sawtooth (*see* Sweetman, *World Air Power Journal*, Volume 31, Winter 1997). The wing with V-tail was integral to early designs. On p. 50 of his book we see three slightly different though familiar flying-wing designs dating back to 1979 based on work by Northrop's Hal Markarian. By the time Gonsalves came to build his model, throughout 1989, many official pictures had been published in the aviation press.

The major contribution made by Gonsalves was to realize what had been staring Ufologists in the face for eight long years: this was an American-made aircraft. Fundamentally, a flying wing is designed for use *within* an atmosphere, not outside, and this rule might be applied to both flying saucers and other 'UFOs' of delta planform. According to Gonsalves, nuclear physicist and UFO researcher Stanton T.

Friedman agreed with much of his analysis, particularly regarding the use of flying wings (Birdsall, 1995).

The Most Important 'Flap'

I had the opportunity and good fortune to speak at length with Don Ecker, editor of the California-based *UFO Magazine,* at the British UFO Research Association Conference in August 1997. I asked Don about Hudson Valley, and he claimed that this was the quite possibly the most important UFO flap in US history – especially considering Indian Point. He had even run a couple of Gonsalves' articles in his magazine and seemed favourably disposed towards the idea that a man-made UFO might be responsible for the sightings. Nevertheless, he disagreed with some of Tony's findings; but at least some people were prepared to give this vital work the coverage it deserved. Ufologists have been very slow to understand the implications of the flap, for their subject and for the belief systems it continued to engender.

In writing a book on the subject of secret technologies one inevitably takes flak from both the aviation enthusiasts who believe what they are told through the official aviation press and through its writers, and from Ufologists who are either uninterested in or not knowledgeable about the various stealth programmes or have an almost religious belief in aliens. These opposing belief systems leave a lot of ground uncovered. Are we really being told anything approaching the truth about the B-2 programme?

Stealth Programmes

The B-2 appears to have grown out of a requirement for a long-range nuclear bomber with the ability to penetrate Russian air defences (Sweetman, 1989) and to remain undetected at every stage of an operation. By 1978 the 'Have Blue' programme was under way (Rich and Janos). The F-117A grew out of the programme. In addition, and not generally known by Ufologists, there were other stealth programmes including a nuclear bomber design by Lockheed. It emerged that Northrop was chosen to develop an aircraft based upon its classic B-35/YB-49 design of the late 1940s. Apparently, these flying wings had been studied throughout the 1970s (Sweetman, 'B-2 Spirit', 1997).

These have always been United States Air Force programmes. Other aircraft, developed under almost paranoid security, including the U-2 and SR-71, were used for reconnaissance by the CIA. The need for a new aircraft had been discussed as early as spring 1977 when General Al Slay, Chief of USAF R&D, worked together with a small group in order to develop an aircraft rather more effective than the failing Rockwell B-1 bomber.

The group included William Perry, Paul Kaminski, General Robert Bond (USAF) and Majors Ken Straton and Joe Ralston. Although one of the designs submitted was not unlike the diamond-shaped Have Blue, other competitors had come to similar conclusions about a stealth bomber. The flying wing was excellent for stealth.

Lockheed's design is still classified, while Rockwell and Boeing put out a series of concepts in 1979–80; two Rockwell designs are of note – one focused on a medium-sized all-wing design with buried engines and fins under the trailing edge and a perfectly triangular design with small ventral rudders. From the point of view of supposed 'triangular UFOs' it is clear that these designs are 20 years old. There had been a history of such designs stretching back into the 1930s (Sweetman, 1986; 1989).

A Dichotomy of Views

From the point of view of the Hudson Valley sightings, there are several areas to consider. The first is the question of the triangular tail. The official histories of the B-2 note a mandatory design alteration made in 1983 (Miller, *Northrop B-2 Spirit*, 1995; Sweetman, 'B-2 Spirit', 1997; Gonsalves) which required a new trailing-edge configu ration; this was done in order to reduce structural loading, to improve control surfaces for stability and in order to fulfil the requirements of the ATB (advanced technology bomber) mission. All the information about these changes comes from official sources and has been faithfully passed on by a variety of writers. Other noticeable details on the UFO were clear, see-through panels on the underside. Many photographs of the official B-2 show similar panels (Miller). There is the question of the zigzag tubing within the UFO: this is clearly the internal structure of the craft. Look at any of the few diagrams of the official B-2. See what you think.

There has been some suggestion within the UFO research community, by Dr Richard Boylan and Dr Paul LaViolette, that in fact the official version of the B-2 utilizes 'anti-gravity' technology. It is not made clear how this works, but the fundamental point appears to be that an aircraft not unlike the B-2 has been seen hovering.

This could not be the jet-powered version as well, unless we are prepared to invoke a dual-propulsion system whereby the jet engines are for public show and the 'anti-gravity' technology for military use. Once again, we see the dichotomy of views: the Ufologists consider advanced US technology to be possibly of alien origin – a theory ultimately reducible to the Roswell 'UFO crash retrieval' – while the aviation enthusiasts stick to the official story – that four modified General Electric turbo-fans power the official version and that this is the only version. Gonsalves treads a middle course between the two. He claims that there might have been a nuclear propulsion system in use. This is possible although I doubt that even the operators of such a craft would dare to fly it over a populated area. Of course, it is difficult to understand the mindset of these people.

Nuclear-powered aircraft could well operate quietly and might enable an aircraft to hover. Quite who would be brave enough to fly the aircraft is open to question unless a pilot was thoroughly shielded from the possibility of exposure to radiation. Note too that the Americans and the British were interested in operating nuclear-powered aircraft from the late 1960s under the project name AST 340.

Invisible Planes, Invisible Finance

In fact, it may be possible to explain the Hudson Valley sightings. One thing is for sure. The cost of the B-2 programme was hidden for a long time and the final cost may never be known. The programme was always rumoured to be the subject of much internal investigation relating to expenditure (Sweetman, 'B-2 Spirit', 1997). The question of cost is central to our understanding of the programme.

It appears to have been a honeytrap for funding which enabled numerous other black aviation projects to emerge (Birdsall, 1995; Gonsalves). The anonymous, though knowledgeable, 'J. Jones' indicated in his Stealth Technology – The Art of Black Magic (1989) the existence of some 20 other black projects during the 1980s, some of which undoubtedly involved Northrop. One of these is described as the 'tactical stealth aircraft' or TSA. According to Jones, the pen-name for a suspected 'insider' (Douglass), Northrop signed contracts with the US Air Force in 1982. In addition, the Tactical High Altitude Penetrator (THAP) was linked by Jones with the Northrop Corporation. This particular all-wing aircraft was said to have been tested at Groom Lake throughout 1983. Having ensured both a contract and massive financial maintenance for the B-2, Northrop were able to develop both an official version, several other prototypes and a range of other all-wing stealth aircraft. Bill Sweetman ('B-2 Spirit', 1997, p. 75) indicates the massive amounts of money involved:

In April 1997 the US Department of Defence finally revealed the total programme costs of the ATB/B-2. As part of a Selected Acquisitions Report...the B2 was quoted as costing $45 billion in toto. Crudely expressed, this equates to an individual cost of $2.14 billion per aircraft, which is twice what most previous public estimates had been. The USAF would never express individual aircraft costs in such terms, preferring instead more nebulous calculations such as 'flyaway cost' or 'then-year dollar price'.

And there was much evidence for financial irregularity to the extent that on 1 March 1990 *The Washington Post*, so long the scourge of corrupt political and business activities, reported that the Northrop Corporation had admitted to some 34 counts of fraud and misrepresentation.

The Corporation was fined $17 million and as a result of the guilty plea another 141 charges were dropped! Northrop agreed that it had overcharged the Air Force during the B-2 programme (Birdsall, 1995). Was the Corporation encouraged by the Pentagon to put its hands up to these charges, in order to bury any further revelations reaching the public domain?

Gonsalves' Thesis

Given that by any estimate each aircraft cost hundreds of millions of dollars then other worrying anomalies emerge. These were pointed out by Gonsalves to lawyers involved in the Northrop trial and they reportedly became increasingly depressed as he presented his thesis:

- The landing gear on the first B-2 (AV-1) was constructed in Federal Year 1982. Admittedly, the Lockheed Have Blue team had raided the parts bin in the early stages but it had been operating under much greater financial pressure. At several hundred millions per unit per B-2 one might expect decent landing gear to have been designed.

- Despite all the computer-aided calculations, the aircraft undercarriage sank into the tarmac during a roll-out run in 1988.

- Modification to the wing design in 1983 supposedly cost $1 billion – a ludicrous figure, especially given Northrop's insistence that the designs were all undertaken on high-powered CAD/CAM computers.

By 22 November 1988, and billions of dollars later, only one aircraft (and a few small-scale prototypes), AV-1, had been delivered (*Jane's All the World's Aircraft*, 1997–8).

Major Success

On the positive side, the B-2 programme had achieved major success, mainly in the fields of materials and avionics – advanced electronic control systems able to make minute alterations to pitch and yaw in order to ensure maximum stability (Miller, *Northrop B-2 Spirit*, 1995). The particular aircraft shape, the most important factor for stealth, was a variation on an established theme, whereas some 900 new materials were supposedly tested and validated in the early stages of the programme. The best materials for stealth were plastics and 80 per cent of the aircraft was built from composite materials over an aluminium/titanium substructure. The composites were carbon, graphite and glass fibres woven into a plastic-like polymer.

Radar Absorbent Materials (RAM) were used selectively to reduce the Radar Cross Section. To reduce the infra-red (IR) signature, various IR paints were used. The weakest element in the stealth make-up of the B-2 was perhaps its contrail. As a result, certain chemicals were designed to be injected into the contrail. The dark grey colour of the underside of the aircraft was carefully chosen in order to minimize the visual signature of the aircraft at an average altitude of 50,000 feet (15,000 m). Efforts were also made to limit the engine noise produced.

It has been said that Northrop would still make a profit if just 15 aircraft were constructed. In 1998 only 21 are scheduled to be built – originally 132 were scheduled. Although the threat from Russia diminished, there are, and always will be, zones of instability – the Middle East (Iran, Iraq), the Far East (China, North Korea), the Balkans and many of the newly emerging independent states on Russia's borders. Few of these are especially friendly to the United States of America or her NATO allies. Many questions remain to be answered about the B-2 and the Hudson Valley UFO flap.

An Advanced Stealth Prototype

Perhaps the most damning indictment of the Intelligence Agency responsible for the operations in New York State comes from those witnesses who argue that the B-2 stealth bomber *most closely resembles* the 'UFO' they saw in the 1980s. The Hudson Valley UFO flap had typical ingredients of a cover-up: reports from numerous credible witnesses, official denials, the activity of shady and suspect intelligence agents, and attempts to confuse the local community by flying aircraft in formation. Perhaps our faith in the ability of the witnesses to correctly evaluate and describe the UFO they have seen can be restored after this examination of the incident.

Finally, new information about the supposed 'abductions' has emerged via Philip Imbrogno (Imbrogno and Horrigan). His own evidence leads us to conclude that the 'Federal Hypothesis' is essentially correct: UFOs are controlled by a loose underground network of intelligence personnel and figures from the military/industrial complex. Imbrogno suggests that most 'abductions', encounters and events of 'high strangeness' take place between 2 am and 4 am. We know that most of the UFO activity during the Hudson Valley flap was reported between 8 pm and 10 pm. So where is the link? He also proves the theory that such interests will act to cloud the issue. In this case Imbrogno was approached by a man who claimed to have flown the light aircraft in formation over Hudson Valley, and that these were specially prepared for CIA use.

I think the witnesses were right: they saw one of several new advanced stealth aircraft prototypes. Once again the 'spaceships' came from earth.

TWELVE

LIGHTER THAN AIR

OW IS IT POSSIBLE for aircraft to hover? They would have to use advanced Vertical-Take-Off and Landing (VTOL) technology, and Philip Handleman, aviation writer and documentary maker, clearly feels that Lockheed Skunk Works has developed this.

One of the major criticisms of military UFO research is that none of the high-speed aircraft, for instance the almost mythical 'Aurora', have the apparent ability to hover and travel at slow speeds (Van Utrecht). As we have seen in our examination of the Hudson Valley UFO case, reports indicate that many witnesses state that structured UFOs – saucers or triangles – can hover or fly at walking pace.

Often there can be a confusion between hovering capability and very low speeds. Although the Chance-Vought flying flapjack could fly at particularly slow speeds of 40 mph (65 kmph) some 50 years ago (Angelucci and Bowers) and flying saucers would appear to have similar characteristics, UFO researchers still get excited about reports of slow-moving or reportedly stationary objects. It would appear that there are several solutions to this and it seems that a range of new, and not so new, technologies enable black-project aircraft to operate both slowly and almost silently.

Most UFO researchers will have looked into cases relating to triangular or all-wing UFOs and some reports stretch right back to the immediate post-war period (Redfern and Bott). Most of these early sightings probably relate to either the Northrop experimental flying wings or perhaps the Armstrong Whitworth 'bat' (AIR 100-203-79). Both could have been mistaken for UFOs; official histories of the AVRO Vulcan note that during initial test flights many local people in northern England reported seeing UFOs to local police stations! Leaving aside the possibility that military UFOs are invoking some kind of magnetic or 'electrogravitic' propulsion systems, many people find themselves stuck for further explanations.

I suggest that the answer is simple: many of the UFOs said to hover, especially the triangular ones, are hybrid airships – part aircraft, part airship. What is more, experiments and test flights of similar craft can be found in the late 1960s (White).

Aereon 26

The Aereon Corporation of Princeton, New Jersey was at the forefront of hybrid designs and concepts in the 1960s. The company was founded in 1959 and by 1977 had invested over a million dollars of private money into its work. Although one of the original designs, the triple-hulled Aereon 3, which looked back to the classic cigar shape of the 1930s, at first seemed promising, it was abandoned in 1967.

It was replaced by a 'deltoid pumpkin seed' design that used helium cells integrated into the aircraft hull. This was the Aereon 26 (see illustration no. 9) and its shape and performance were shown to have great potential after a series of manned tests with an orange-coloured prototype in 1971. The craft was 27 feet (8.25 m) long and weighed 1,200 pounds (545 kg). Although it is conceivable that a similar craft painted grey or even black could be mistaken for a UFO, it is quite possible that something not unlike the proposed Aereon 340 would have been much more likely to give rise to reports.

The 340 has raised some eyebrows in recent months as a result of my proposal that such a craft has been developed and has been flown in both the USA and the UK. Looking at artists' impressions of the 340 we see a large flying triangle 340 feet (104 m) in length with a wing-span of some 256 feet (78 m)! It was initially conceived as a cargo transport capable of carrying heavy loads. Four Rolls-Royce turbo-props were envisaged as the powerplant for the 340 and the helium gas was to be carried in large envelopes, making this a lighter-than-air (LTA) craft (White).

The military showed great interest in the 1970s in the possibility of using such hybrid designs for oceanic surveillance, and the resulting concept was known as the 'Dynairship' (see illustration no. 11). This was a huge craft of 600 feet (183 m) in length with the ability to remain in the air for days at a time. Although it was most likely to fly slowly, the ship would have been able to reach over 200 mph (322 kmph) if necessary. It was estimated in the 1970s that a few tens of millions could get the programme off the ground and be enough to build a prototype – much less than the money needed to develop and build the C5A and similar aircraft.

A small number of us have consistently argued that many of the UFOs seen are using a combination of helicopter and aircraft technologies.

137

We saw with Silver Bug the military need for both dispersed-base operations and an ability for a Vertical-Take-Off and Landing (VTOL) aircraft. One of the most fascinating concepts to emerge from Aereon, again in the mid-1970s, was the 'Aer/lighter' craft to be used for a variety of missions including long-range transportation of heavy loads. It combined VTOL with Short-Take-Off and Landing (STOL).

A New Kind of Airship

At the same time as these developments were taking place, a gifted man called Michael Walden was working on similar concepts. I entered into correspondence with him in the summer of 1997. In fact, Mike had believed since 1967 that airships were the future (Walden).

The first series of lighter-than-air vehicles he worked on was the XEM series. The XEM-1 was a fully functional solar-powered aircraft built in 1974, while the XEM-2, built in 1978, holds an unofficial flight duration record of just over three months (February to May).

Following on, the XEM-3 featured a fully geodesic frame equipped with a radical Density Controlled Buoyancy (DCB) system. XEM-4 was a radio-controlled test model for a series of full-scale, manned and rigid-hulled airships; this series of designs was built in conjunction with a Mexican team. The 1980s Mexican Lighter-Than-Air vehicles (the MLA series) were the first modern rigid-hulled airships to fly for 60 years. More importantly, they were saucer-shaped (Windle).

MLA-32B measured 105 feet (32 m) in length and was given extra manoeuvrability through the use of a vectored thrust system. Built of light materials,the hull was very strong and the airship actually flew in a crosswind of 35 knots. If we remember the Hudson Valley UFO flap we now have evidence that in the 1980s it was possible for poorly funded amateurs to build a saucer-shaped airship able to operate in difficult conditions. So much for the claim made by investigators that the flying-wing UFO could not be of terrestrial origin:

> Carl had no doubt that it was a solid object and not a formation of aircraft, partly because winds were gusting up to twenty-five knots an hour that night (Night Siege, p. 147).

In fact, the MLA-32B designed by Walden, and his Mexican associate Señor Roldan, would have been fully aerobatic and could have used more powerful engines. Perhaps the most important element of the Walden story is the fact that he worked at Nellis Air Force Base, where the XEM-1 was demonstrated in August 1977 in conjunction with the Department of Energy (DOE).

The US Department of Defense (DOD) was interested in his work to the extent that some of it is still classified despite requests for the information to become freely available. In fact the tests resulted in 'classification at the highest levels'.

Hybrid Designs

In the meantime Walden has continued his work on a wide range of hybrid designs through his Lighter Than Air Solar Corporation and has built up a reputation as being the foremost thinker in terms of advanced airship technologies (Windle). When considering airships the reader should dismiss any thoughts of the *Hindenburg*, the Graf Zeppelin or the Goodyear blimp! The systems technologies developed by Walden have raised some eyebrows, and more and more people are coming to the conclusion that the larger triangular aircraft seen in our skies, especially those that appear to have pipework patterning on their underside, are helium-filled LTA vehicles.

Looking around the current technologies associated with such aircraft, we find computerized control systems, mission analysis tools, specialized hull construction and manufacturing techniques, vectored thrust systems, self-levelling landing gear which eliminates the need for guy ropes and ground crew, the possibility of high-*g* manoeuvres and even advanced propulsion systems using laser detonation (Windle; Gunston, *Warplanes of the Future*, 1995). Some or all of these technologies are being used in more conventional-shaped airships. For instance, the Hornet Aerial Work – a non-rigid, hybrid buoyant aircraft – is controlled by an advanced fly-by-wire system and can operate from most airfields. The craft is controlled by a simple joystick. The company responsible for the Hornet, Advanced Hybrid Aircraft, has also built a remotely piloted airship with vectoring winglets that enable it to take off and land at steep angles.

Michael Walden also claims that his airships could be used in sub-orbital conditions or as a hypersonic Single-Stage-To-Orbit (SSTO) system.

His ionic airflow engine could allow for very high speeds and this seems possible given the tremendous advances made in the construction of lightweight composite materials in the last 20 years. These are many and varied but most of those used in advanced technology aviation manufacture are inherently stealthy.

Materials used to reduce the Radar Cross Section need to be able to absorb radar energy and to dissipate it (J. Jones, 1989). Carbon composites are popular, especially where high temperatures are concerned, whereas ceramics also help to lower an aircraft's infra-red signature.

Kevlar could be used if the craft was going to be flown at relatively low level, as it is damage-resistant to gunfire and because a minimal radar signature would enable the aircraft to penetrate enemy defences to the extent that small-arms fire might be the only option for hostile ground forces, assuming that they could even see their foe. Kevlar is a particularly effective material and much stronger than many metals.

On a more general note, we might expect to see triangular craft of the sort mentioned above being tested at low level over differing terrain; if they are destined to operate at low level for the covert insertion of troops or forward-area military supply work then they would need to hover or fly at low speed (*Air Force 2025*). They would need to be self-sufficient – able to land by themselves either through manual or remote control. Silent or (more realistically) near-silent operation effected by use of ducted turbo-fans or similar propulsion systems would make this an ever more desirable weapon.

Walden's Solution

In concluding, it might be best to allow Michael Walden to relate his own solution to the question of flying triangle sightings that I put to him in mid-1997 via e-mail:

I put together a picture of what the combination of the 'Deltoid Pumpkin Seed' form modified for high speed 'waverider' aerodynamics and a drive unit using my 'ionic airflow engine' and the Laser fired pulse engine would look like.

Seems it has all the characteristics reported in the 'Triangle' craft sightings.

1 – It is large. LTA craft by their nature are big...and bigger the higher they have to fly. Fortunately high speed friction will heat the lift gas so it isn't humongous...only 400–600 ft long and 200–300 ft wide.

2 – At low altitudes it would emit a slight humming sound or no sound at all if higher than a few hundred feet up. Occasionally there would be a bluish discharge from the ionic corona of the engines and if pointed down these would look like bright search lights to a person on the ground with some attendant electrical effects as this is a charge flow of air...might short out ground-based electronics if close.

3 – At high altitudes the 'go fast' engines are turned on (saves fuel to float up and less noise too). The 'go fast' engines use a laser pulse to detonate hydrogen fuel. The contrail thus looks like a set of puffs on a string. If set up as a 'ring' combustion chamber this would result in the donuts-on-a-string seen near triangle activity. A series of low rumbles would result from its operation. Speeds somewhere between Mach 6–10 in this configuration. You could be anywhere in the world within an hour or so.

Nothing flies as high.

Nothing goes as fast.

It only shows up on radar if it wants to – all composite.

What do you think they would use it for?

Hypersonic Flight

Not everyone agrees entirely on a definition of hypersonic flight, but it is perhaps best described as a speed of approximately 3,600 mph (5,794 kmph) or Mach 5.4; the air in front of the aircraft stagnates and is trapped, making for very high temperatures.

Although there are several problems with the use of hydrogen, there is increasing evidence to suggest that hypersonic flight has been a reality for some time (Sweetman, 1993) and that a number of exotic propulsion systems have been developed. The use of composite materials is commonplace and craft of the approximate size mentioned have been proposed.

Walden attempts to answer the whole triangular UFO mystery in one fell swoop. His work has concentrated on lenticular (round) aeroforms, and on a very limited budget he has met with some success. There is also some evidence that the military intend to use triangular hybrid airships similar to the 1970s Aereon designs. The *Air Force 2025* report shows a picture of the Aereon 340 proposal in relation to a possible 'future' ('future' often means 'present' in the black world) stealthy forward-area cargo-lifting role; Chapter 3 – 'System Description' – notes the need for increased air mobility and an increase in airship use, perhaps to replace the C5-B transport aircraft. What is required is 'a 500 ton useful lift capacity, maximum airspeed of 250 knots, maximum range at maximum gross weight of 12,500 miles, and a defensive/stealth capability'. These requirements are possible within the current technology, as we have seen.

Another potential use of advanced airship technologies is as 'atmospheric satellites', sensor platforms. In a recent and fascinating conversation with William Miller Jr of the Aereon Corporation he told me that the US Navy had shown an interest in the use of his airship concepts as massive radar platforms. The company has been the recipient of various small business grants relating to similar conceptual work. As if to prove the theory that hybrid lighter-than-air craft are responsible for some UFO sightings, a huge black flying wing was seen over built-up areas of California in the late 1980s.

The Federation of American Scientists said that the craft stopped, hovered vertically and pointed its trailing edge to the ground. The Federation concluded that 'this could be a lighter-than-air craft pushed by slow-turning propellers' (FAS, 1997).

Considering Michael Walden and his many achievements, one can only wonder exactly what his counterparts in the black world have been able to develop along similar lines with their immense resources.

THIRTEEN

UAVS AND UFOS

M ANY OF THE Unmanned Aerial Vehicles (UAVs) developed in the last 30 years have been triangular. The problem for Ufologists is simple and was spelled out in the March/April 1995 (Birdsall, 1995) edition of *UFO Magazine* (UK). It reports on 'unconventional flying objects, possessing amazing manoeuvrability' and notes that many of the sightings near Area 51 are of RPVs (Remotely Piloted Vehicles) and UAVs:

> *unmanned vehicles may account for the vast majority of sightings recorded in the Groom Lake region....When these are viewed from a distance, even twelve miles, it must make for a spectacular sight.*

A Talent to Confuse

There is a major attempt to confuse the issue here: our information about UFOs comes from a variety of sources including witness reports. If you or I were at Groom Lake and we saw a UAV performing 12g turns, then would we not have seen an Unidentified Flying Object? The chances are that we actually saw a black-project aircraft the real name or designation of which was known only to a handful of people with the relevant security clearance. So we saw a UFO – unidentified, unknown to all but a few, and 'non-existent' as far as the military-intelligence communities are concerned. We might report the sighting to a local UFO group. Are proponents of the extraterrestrial hypothesis trying to cloud the issue? Are they saying that 'unconventional' craft are terrestrial and 'unidentified' craft are of extraterrestrial origin? Who decides?

One of the most important UFO flaps took place in the most unlikely of places – Barnsley in South Yorkshire. There were numerous sightings in the winter of 1987–8 of what seemed to be the same object. Unsurprisingly, witness reports and drawings of the objects they saw varied (Clarke).

Uttoxeter Flying Triangle

As we shall see in the chapter on the Silent Vulcan (Chapter 15), on Tuesday 22 September 1987 there was a spectacular sighting of a flying triangle near Uttoxeter in Staffordshire. This was covered in the local newspapers and a wealth of details were forthcoming from the witnesses. As a result of this and other sightings, local Member of Parliament Bill Cash asked the MOD for answers. He got nowhere (Potter, 1989).

Just three days later at Houghton near Thurnscoe, South Yorkshire, Mrs Sandra Taylor and her daughter saw an object moving towards them making no sound. It was triangular, at an altitude of around 100 feet (30 m) and had three white lights and four orange lights on its underside. These were very bright indeed as the craft flew overhead. The craft disappeared from view after passing over some nearby fields. It was a clear night – a few stars in the sky, a gentle breeze.

There were a number of other sightings in October and November, but at the end of December a sighting was reported that was to be repeated by many local people in the area over the next couple of months. Security officer Derek Anders of Goldthorpe Road, Goldthorpe, South Yorkshire, saw a triangular object with eight orange lights and one white light 'jetting across the sky' early on the morning of New Year's Eve at 7 am. *The South Yorkshire Times* newspaper reported him as commenting that:

> *I had just taken my dog into the garden when the lights caught my eye. I'm not a believer in UFOs but this mystified me because there was no sound at all, and I watched it move across the sky to the west, disappear, then come into view again from the south-east. The object was definitely of a triangular shape and was so clear that somebody else must have seen it.*

In a later interview he said that the object had been in view for three minutes and, although he was surprised by it, he felt that there must be a rational explanation. Mr Anders printed his telephone number in the newspaper and received 30 calls from people claiming to have seen the same object. A similar sighting was reported as taking place at 7.30 pm on 10 February 1988 in nearby Wombwell, Barnsley. Mr Hoyle observed a diamond-shaped UFO approximately 200 feet (60 m) above the ground moving slowly over the rooftops. Other people saw the object, which was described as 'fantastic'. It moved off in the direction of Hoyland. Ten minutes later a woman and her daughter leaving an aerobics class in Hoyland saw a large black triangular UFO in front of them as they negotiated the local one-way system. It had an assortment of bright green and red lights arranged underneath and the witnesses described it as a black metallic craft set square behind the lights. This was no misidentification – the two witnesses got within around 150 feet (46 m) of the craft.

A seemingly unimportant detail to the witnesses was the fact that as the triangle moved off it followed the path of some electricity pylons towards Harley and Wentworth. The witnesses were lucky enough to view the same object moving in a westerly direction with the many lights pulsing in the night sky. The woman later commented that she thought the object could have been man-made.

Later that night at 10.15 pm a dull-metallic diamond-shaped object was seen by a lady driving three friends home from an event at Holmfirth Community Hall. They believed that this was neither an aircraft nor a helicopter and it seemed to be moving erratically in a northerly direction at an altitude of 600 feet (180 m). On the cold, dry night they were able to discern three very bright spotlights on this object. Its back end was said to be no larger than a double-decker bus.

The following Saturday, 13 February, shift worker Mr Jeff Goodwin of Maltby reported that he had seen a large triangle-shaped object while walking his dog at 2 am. The initial bright white light visible on the underside of this craft went out as it moved towards the man and changed to reveal three new white lights. The man watched the object for a considerable time as it flew towards Rotherham. The craft made a buzzing sound as it passed by at an altitude of around 500 feet (150 m).

Five days later at Wadsley Bridge near Sheffield Elise Oxley, a student working towards a degree in Biomedical Technology at Sheffield University, saw a large equilateral triangle which she subsequently drew for investigators. She had been driving to her home in Binstead Gardens from college at 6.20 to 6.30 pm when she first saw the object and stopped the car because of the strange noise it was making. When she got home both the witness and her husband heard a strange noise and went to the back door. They saw a large triangular craft making a turn and heading north.

Interestingly, the witnesses reported that the sound they heard was most unusual; when the craft was nearest to them they said that it was very loud but as soon as it moved away nothing could be heard at all.

A couple of weeks later four students were travelling on their usual route from Manchester to Sheffield via the A628. Both Jacqueline Hetherington and E. D. Rogers reported that a triangular craft was moving towards the TV mast on Emley Moor. They said that the craft was travelling point first – like a delta-wing. At an altitude of approximately 3,000 feet (900 m) the craft was visible for three minutes.

A Secret Test?

These sightings were but a dress rehearsal for the events of 20 April 1988. Described as 'weird and intriguing' by Independent UFO Network (IUN) investigators, a report from an 18-year-old caterer blew the mystery of the triangle sightings wide open. The Barnsley woman was interviewed in her home by Andy Roberts on 11 June and he felt that she was honest and truthful.

Miss Cook and her boyfriend Gerald had been walking down Warren Lane, a piece of open land between Staincross and Woolley, when they saw an unusual sight – a triangular object that appeared, making only the faintest sound. As the triangle emerged, three or four cars sped along shining bright lights into the field where there was a man and a car. The witnesses had seen the man for around 15 minutes from a bench situated nearby, and noted that he had been behaving rather strangely – getting into and out of the car. As he did so he twiddled the aerial. Sharon and Gerald noticed that the man had a device in his hand, and appeared to be looking into the sky. The triangle had around ten lights on the underside and made a hissing sound as it appeared. The witnesses felt that the man and the triangle were in some way connected and they noted that he drove off in the same direction as the other cars on departure.

Was this a secret test of some sort? It certainly seemed so. The location was quite convenient for this kind of covert activity and it was simply a case of good luck (or bad luck for the operators) that the couple had been there. The man in the car did not appear to have noticed them.

Most Special Model Planes

Events were to take an even more fascinating turn when UFO researcher Albert Budden drew IUN investigators' attention to an article printed in the 11 August edition of *Executive Post*. It featured an interview with Mr Ray Jones, founder and director of Wrexham-based Dragon Models. The report stated that:

> model aircraft have now gone beyond the provision of entertainment, becoming the basis of a retail, photographic and media-support business which is trading worldwide and discovering new roles for radio-controlled machines.

Mr Jones said that his company had designed 25-foot (6.5-m) scale models of the B-52 bomber for use in films and that specially designed multi-purpose reconnaissance craft for use by the police, local authorities or councils had been developed and used to great success. Perhaps the clincher as far as Ufologists are concerned comes in the following comment: 'The Ministry of Defence is currently doing business with Dragon Models on a confidential military project.' You bet!

The nature of such a confidential project might be apparent in subsequent sightings of a similar UFO in Barnsley featured in the Clarke report on the same and following nights.

The history of RPVs/UAVs shows us that the technology to fly an aircraft by remote control is 50 years old. The *Wasserfall* remote-controlled bomb was used from 1944 by the Germans (Klee and Merk; R. V. Jones). The Americans used drones based upon pre-existing bomber designs to attack V-1 sites in Europe (McDaid and Oliver). This was done under the banner of 'Project Anvil' – a joint Navy–Air Force project based in England: Special Air Unit One, based at Fersfield.

We have already seen how there may have been some limited German involvement in the post-war years in terms of flying-saucer technologies. In addition to this, a dozen former V-1 rocket specialists were sent to work at the US Navy's Pilotless Aircraft Unit at Point Mugu, California in 1947 as part of Operation Paperclip. Throughout the 1950s and 1960s technological developments allowed for much wider use of UAVs for reconnaissance. One of the companies best known for its UAV system was Teledyne-Ryan, whose Firebee drones excelled in Vietnam. The UAVs involved in secret intelligence-gathering missions were Ryan Aeronautical model 147 series aircraft funded through an Air Force programme administered by Air Force Flight Logistics Command at Wright-Patterson Air Force Base.

By the end of the Vietnam War UAVs could operate at 75,000 feet (23,000 m) and carry a 300-pound (136-kg) load. A new package called COMMINT was installed into UAVs from 1970, and allowed them to listen to enemy messages and had relay and control equipment as well as extra fuel capacity (McDaid and Oliver).

Serious Abilities

UAVs have come of age. Their abilities have serious implications for the UFO researcher. The variety of systems and capabilities of the modern-day UAV makes life rather complicated (Munson, 1988; 1997). Nowadays, a UAV might well be able to perform turns between 12g and 18g. Such manoeuvrability can easily confuse a witness – especially one looking at an object over a military facility – into thinking that he or she is seeing something quite 'alien'.

The advantages of UAVs are clear: added manoeuvrability, higher possible speeds and the removal of the political consequences relating to pilot casualties. In addition there is a major strategic gain associated with the UAV: the ability to field several units at once whereby the loss of even a few to hostile action enables the others to carry on with real-time data relay (*New World Vistas*).

It is quite remarkable how many UAVs are triangular. A look into UAVs past and present shows us a firm belief in the advantages of the delta shape, from the tiny HDH-10 Enmoth in Australia during 1975, the Dornier Tactical mini-drones involved in the Lockheed Aquila programme, the NASA Hyper III, South Africa's Kentron Lark to British Aerospace's HALO.

One of the fastest UAVs was the D-21 drone, initially developed for use with the A-12 spyplane (Miller, *Lockheed's Skunk Works*, 1995). It reached very high speeds and was designed for maximum stealthiness, mainly through the use of RAM treatments. The D-21 was cancelled in 1966 but the idea that a UAV could be launched from a much larger platform, dare one say mothership, was to be revived for much later concepts and studies.

Another inherently stealthy mini-RPV was the Teledyne-Ryan 262, developed under the US Navy Ship Tactical Airborne RPV programme of the mid-1970s (Munson, 1988). It was specifically designed to produce minimal infra-red, radar and acoustic signatures. This was done by using glass fibre and composite materials in construction. The noise reduction element is very important given reports of near-silent UFOs of triangular shape.

This was achieved with the 262 by using a ducted propulsion system housed on top of the wing. The craft used an advanced Honeywell electro-optical sensor suite and Raytheon radar system. It is suggested that this smaller craft might have been used as a tech-nology demonstrator for a much larger manned delta stealth aircraft.

The US Air Force firmly believes in the benefits of the UAV. In a study entitled *New World Vistas* this is made clear. The most impor-tant feature of this huge report is the distinction made between

Uninhabited Reconnaissance Air Vehicles (URAVs) and Uninhabited Combat Air Vehicles (UCAVs). It appears that a UCAV may be classified as a cruise missile and therefore be subject to verifications and limited (McDaid and Oliver, p. 155). Until the last few years it was policy not to use UAV systems for attack. Central to the study is the question of survivability or low observability. Therefore stealth is required in order to take out what are described as 'mobile and protected' targets:

Together, stealth and performance will reduce the reliance on electronic countermeasures with an accompanying reduction in cost and system volatility, and when directed by offboard information and passive sensors, they have the surprise value of a silent force.

The study also discusses the use of 'revolutionary' high-technology systems and the comparative advantage they give the warfighter who uses them. The idea of a 'silver bullet', the perfect weapon, is seen to be of interest. Nevertheless, and reading between the lines, the idea seems to be that stealth technology is a revolutionary concept the evolution of which has given the USA a distinct advantage over its perceived enemies (Sweetman, 'The Invisible Man', 1997). This comes as no surprise to those of us who have argued that the active disinformation surrounding not only stealth but other leading-edge technologies needs to be targeted on the UFO community – the most likely group to investigate sightings of these new aerial weapons systems.

In terms of the *New World Vistas* report, which introduces the idea of 'Global Reach, Global Power' to the reader, UCAVs are seen as a central tool. These will be controlled from a special control centre by virtual reality (Gourley). The only problem facing the future UCAV designer is the question of autonomous control whereby software bugs could be problematic. Nevertheless, the use of fuzzy logic systems is thought to be reducing this potential problem even now. Regarding the supposed 'impossible manoeuvres' performed by UFOs, we might do well to take the following paragraph from the report to heart:

UCAV survivability can be increased by increasing maneuverability beyond that which can be tolerated by a human pilot. Acceleration limits for inhabited aircraft are, typically +9G or 10G and −3G [and that is pushing it]. A UCAV can be designed symmetrically to accelerate in any direction immediately. Anti-aircraft missiles are usually designed with a factor of three margin in lateral acceleration over that of the target aircraft, although a few missiles have acceleration capability as high as

80G. A UCAV with a +/– 10G capability would outfly many missiles, and an acceleration of +/-20G will make the UCAV superior to nearly all missiles.

The UCAV may be required to travel at high speed. The triangular craft or wedge-shaped craft would seem to be a sensible option. For use against mobile targets it is felt that active stealth might be used. The identification is a particular problem given new camouflage techniques and underground facilities. If a UCAV could hover then it would perhaps be better able to deliver its precision-guided munitions. There is great discussion of loiter ability for the UCAV/URAV. Hovering is even better.

When people report triangular UFOs that hover perhaps we should offer them a copy of the USAF Scientific Advisory Board's *New World Vistas* study and then they may understand why they are seeing these craft performing supposedly impossible manoeuvres. I believe that many of the video clips we are shown on TV programmes about UFOs are of UAV systems being tested. A rule of thumb Ufologists might like to develop is this:

When the military talk about developing a system they probably already have developed it. By the time you hear about a system that has been developed then the designers and technicians have already moved on to something else.

In this chapter we have seen more than enough evidence to suggest that UAVs can perform unusual manoeuvres (usually hovering), and that at least from 1987, probably earlier, these systems were being developed and tested in the UK.

Late in 1996, when in conversation with a stealth expert associated with a black project, I was informed that the British were particularly advanced in terms of the UCAV and had been testing such systems for a decade in conjunction with the Americans. He had read a copy of my *Stealth, Lies and Videotapes* report, first published in 1996. He said that many of the things put forward in the document were entirely correct and that copies had been passed around the British Aerospace facilities at Warton!

No wonder the powers-that-be spread so many rumours about aliens and UFOs. It simply wouldn't do for more researchers to watch their local military bases, look into stealth, come down from the hilltops and abandon the hope that they may meet extraterrestrials through a contact experience.

FOURTEEN

ADVANCED UNMANNED AIRCRAFT

A S IF TO VALIDATE both the shape of the Hudson Valley UFO and the
reality of an aircraft able to hover at low level in almost total
stealthiness leading to many UFO sightings, we now learn of
the existence of a little-known, and supposedly cancelled Lockheed
Martin Skunk Works aircraft known as Tier 3.

Much of the research into the evidence for the existence of this
advanced unmanned aircraft comes from US researcher Dan Zinngrabe,
whose Black Dawn web site is a favourite place for secret military
aircraft researchers to start their enquiries (Zinngrabe). The Black
Dawn site features some information about Britain's HALO programme
courtesy of this author.

Tiers 1, 2 and 3

Why Tier 3? Very simply, until recently Unmanned Aerial Vehicles
(UAVs) were not organized into any classification system reflecting
their capabilities. Nowadays such a system exists, but the Tier designations are really procurement project names and not official military
designations. In fact many of the UAVs that have been developed come
under the aegis of the Defence Advanced Research Projects Agency
(DARPA) and two other agencies: the CIA and the Defense Airborne
Reconnaissance Agency (DARO) (Gehrs-Paul).

Tier 1 was procured by the CIA in the hope that a tactical recon-
naissance/surveillance UAV could be operational as soon as possible.
The General Atomics 'Gnat 750' was chosen and modified. The Gnat
has the ability to operate for up to 30 hours between 5,000 and 15,000
feet (1,500–4,500 m) with a small electro-optical payload. These have
been used over the former Yugoslavia and are also used for research by

Lockheed Martin. Tier 2 is also made by General Atomics.

The 'Predator' is a strange-looking craft and can carry a sensor payload of 450 pounds (200 kg) up to 25,000 feet (7,600 m). This is a relatively new development, having had its first test flight in March 1994.

One of the advantages of these craft is that they are very cheap to produce at around $3 million per unit. The Predator has been used over Bosnia and can carry electro-optical and infra-red cameras. Although initially limited to line-of-sight data links, Predators now have the ability to relay data via satellite for over-the-horizon flights. The Predator has also taken place in the Roving Sands integrated air defence exercises, having been initially tested at El Mirage Airport, California, the joint CIA/General Atomics test site.

The Tier 2 Plus – built by Teledyne-Ryan Aeronautical – like all advanced systems, was developed by major players in the military/industrial complex including E-Systems, Rockwell International (wings), Loral Communications, Allison Engines, Hughes Aircraft Radar Systems, GDE systems and Heroux Inc. (landing gear). The HAE (High Altitude Endurance) system gives a relatively cheap aircraft with a flyaway cost of only $10 million, although it is part of a much larger programme to develop a non-stealthy long-endurance surveillance UAV. It can reach 65,000 feet (20,000 m) with a payload of 1,800 pounds (816 kg). It is expected to be the workhorse in the developing mix of UAV systems.

Of greater interest is the Lockheed 'DarkStar' – a Tier 3 minus flying-saucer-like stealthy reconnaissance vehicle (*see* illustration no. 12). It was developed at the Skunk Works (Lockheed Martin Advanced Development Company). There has been input from Boeing Defense and Space Group's Military Airplane Division.

DarkStar is one of several UAVs under development since the early 1990s. It will no doubt be responsible for a share of UFO sightings. Like many modern-day stealth aircraft, it is constructed from graphite composites. These are built over an aluminium fuselage, and a single engine is incorporated into the body for maximum RCS reduction. Importantly, UAVs like this will need to loiter over an area for up to eight hours. DarkStar's top speed is 300 knots and it can reach an altitude of 45,000 feet (14,000 m).

The ability to fly UAVs successfully has existed for 40 years, although it is only since about 1995–6 that an overall plan for their use in future military operations has been developed. The most obvious advantage of UAV systems is their cost-benefits. UAVs and their future uses form an important part of strategic planning documents; this is reflected in a number of studies including *New World Vistas* produced by the US Scientific Advisory Board and the Air University of America's 'Global Reach, Global Power'. The advantages are clear. Admiral William Owens, Vice-Chairman of the Joint Chiefs of Staff, said in June 1995:

> *I was looking at Predator [imagery displays] yesterday.... It was flying over an area...at 25,000 ft. It had been up there for a long time, many hours, and you could see the city below, and you could focus in on the city, you could see a building, focus on a building, you could see a window, focus on a window. You could put a cursor around it and [get] the GPS [Global Positioning Satellite] latitude and longitude very accurately, remotely via satellite.*
>
> *And if you passed that information to an F-16 or an F-15 at 30,000 ft, and that pilot can simply put in that latitude and longitude into his bomb fire control system, then that bomb can be dropped quite accurately onto that target, maybe very close to that window, or, if it's a precision weapon perhaps it could be put through the window.... I'd buy a lot of UAVs in the future.*

These are all aircraft that we know a great deal about. Numerous articles have been written on them and now books are starting to appear on the subject of the UAV 'revolution'. As usual in these matters we are expected to believe that these are the only drones under development. There is obviously much more going on than we are allowed to know. Note that none of the official versions, except the much-vaunted NASA 'LoFlyte' (Low Observable Flight Test Experiment), are triangular in shape (Butcher; Chittenden).

LoFlyte is interesting because, although only tiny scale models of up to 12 feet (3.7 m) have been tested, there was a suggestion in the quality press in late 1996 that this was the craft responsible for the Belgian Triangle sightings of 1989–90! The craft was probably not even on the drawing board at the time. It is worth bearing in mind that LoFlyte is projected to reach hypersonic speeds in the relatively near future, is triangular and might utilize a waverider approach (*see* p. 223) to the problem of defeating the shockwaves that build up at the front of an aircraft at Mach 5. Don't expect LoFlyte to be flying over a neighbourhood near you for some time yet!

'Strategic Reconnaissance and Intelligence is vital for the defense of both the US and her NATO allies' (*Air Force 2025*). As a result, flexibility is needed and craft for a wide variety of missions are required. The Tier 1, Tier 2 and Tier 3 minus, though useful, are limited. One thing that is important to realize about these craft, and most UAVs, is the fact that they can be operated via a small ground station. The ground stations could be mobile and as small as a Land Rover motor vehicle.

Other methods involve the use of high-powered satellites (KH-11 and KH-12), TR-1 and SR-71 spyplanes, E-3 AWACS, RC-135 (Electronic Intelligence – ELINT), tactical reconnaissance and targeting aircraft like the F-14, F-15 and F-16 and possibly also the much-vaunted near-hypersonic US spyplane tested from Groom Lake.

The hypersonic spyplane, the TR-3A 'Black Manta' aircraft and the Tier 3 are most likely to be responsible for UFO sightings (FAS). Officially, no Tier 3 aircraft has been built. The evidence suggests otherwise.

During the Gulf War, gaps in US airborne overhead assets were noted, with complaints from commanders that they were finding it difficult to acquire accurate and timely intelligence on which to make important strategic decisions.

The Americans had not helped themselves: during the drawn-out Iran–Iraq conflict, the USA had supported the Iraqis in the hope that they could dampen down the flames of the Islamic Revolution. They largely failed to do this and, even worse, the USA provided the Iraqis not only with weaponry but also with detailed and classified satellite data. This showed Iranian troop concentrations and fixed targets, and, more importantly, gave the Iraqis a good idea of what kinds of equipment and facilities would need to be camouflaged from view and how to do this.

The truth is that despite Gulf War propaganda, Desert Storm was not overwhelmingly successful because the Iraqis had used their US satellite knowledge to conceal many of their high-technology facilities – especially those associated with their nuclear-bomb programme. Some of these facilities were discovered after the war was over by inspection teams (Burrows and Windrem). Note that it was stealth technology in the form of the F-117A (possibly in combination with the Black Manta, if the rumours are correct) that took out many of the high-value targets during the conflict with pinpoint precision.

Given the fluid international situation and the many possible war scenarios involving the USA and its allies in the Middle East, it seemed sensible to develop a range of UAVs to fulfil intelligence-gathering and covert attack missions. One of these was Tier 3 or more precisely the Advanced Airborne Reconnaissance System (Zinngrabe). It would seem that this unmanned aircraft has been tested in both the UK and the USA. This would have been demonstrated to the UK, first possibly under the terms of the secret formal agreement in terms of stealth technologies and advanced aircraft that several writers including Bill Sweetman and Nick Cook believe to have existed for perhaps 40 years (Cook, *Interavia*, 1995).

Aviation Week and Space Technology, so often a fairly reliable source of information on black projects, reported on 17 January 1994:

> The two month old Defence Airborne Reconnaissance Office (DARO) is expected to field this 'stealthy UAV that could stay up for days without refueling...to assist the overhead [satellite] assets', a senior defense official said.
>
> The relatively slow UAV is 'more advanced than Raptor', the Ballistic Defence Organizations (BMDO) UAV programs, and should be operational within 'three to five years', he said. The official would seem to have been talking about something rather more advanced than Tier 3 minus.
>
> Satellites are not perfect in an intelligence-gathering role, mainly due to their fixed orbit and consequent predictability and their huge cost. They can be tracked by radar and telescopic means and their windows of operation can be reasonably calculated by an enemy. They invoke a huge cost – several hundred million dollars each plus a launch of around $200 million. They provide imagery through the use of very powerful telephoto lenses [while an aircraft can use a much smaller camera and is far less predictable] (see Burrows).

Best Solution

Therefore the best solution would be a stealth aircraft with the manoeuvrability of a UAV, the ability to hover undetected at any altitude and the ability to use natural features for added cover. Is this a description of the Tier 3?

Solutions to the gaps in intelligence-gathering given added weight during the Gulf War resulted in various proposals for new reconnaissance aircraft including one based predictably on the B-2 bomber submitted by Northrop and E-Systems. During hearings before the Committee on Armed Services in May/June 1993 relating to authorization for Appropriations for Fiscal Year 1994 for Defense Intelligence, Senator Exon asked:

> If we have the satellite intelligence that you collectively would like us to have, would that kind of system eliminate the need for an SR-71, as Senator Glenn has referenced?

Admiral Macke responded by arguing that he required not only information relating to a specific moment in time, but also a system that gave him real-time or near real-time data relay. He said that in the specific case of Serbia his troops would need to know not only, for instance, that the Serbs had had arms, tanks or artillery at a specific location but what they had done with them subsequently. Hence the need for a UAV of some sort: the 'integration of strategic and tactical'.

In reply to a following question about the SR-71 a Mr Hall claimed that UAVs would remove the lag in time between mounting a reconnaissance mission and retrieving the data. Therefore he wanted a unique UAV system, and said that:

> There was a system conceived to do the job, called Advanced Airborne Reconnaissance System, which we have recently determined would meet the requirement but is not affordable because it carried a price tag in the neighborhood of [deleted in official version]. Those are the two major shortfalls, and we are looking at an alternative means of doing that that would cost [deleted] which is the system solution that was developed as a replacement to the SR-71.

It should be pointed out that the money could well have been made available for this or a similar scheme. Stealth technologies take a much bigger slice of the Special Access Required (SAR) or 'black' budgets. In this case we have only certain details from which to make a determination.

Too Advanced to Use

As I suggested before, there were several designs similar to the B-2 put forward from the late 1970s to the early 1980s. One was the Northrop wing with triangular tail, and the other was a remarkably similar version by Lockheed. This latter design was modified to fit into the requirements for the new proposed advanced UAV, although it was much smaller than the 172-foot (53-m) B-2. The Lockheed design was redesigned using the latest computer technologies, and a new ultra-low-speed propulsion system was incorporated based on STOVL concepts. Most interestingly, Dan Zinngrabe adds that this aircraft featured an active stealth system, whereby incoming radar signals would be absorbed through the composite skins and a 'phase conjugated pulse' directed toward enemy radar systems (US Patent Server). This effectively cancelled out the enemy system and made the Tier 3

UAV invisible to radar. In the past, aircraft shaping in conjunction with Radar Absorbent Materials had been seen as a winning formula in RCS and infra-red signature reduction: hence faceting for the F-117A and the sleek shape of the B-2. Other stealth aircraft testbeds utilized a triangular design to this end (Sweetman, 1989).

Now, active stealth could be combined with the latest in 'smart skin' technologies (Douglass and Sweetman). These are very advanced indeed and involve the use of electrochromic plates through which a charge can be passed. This can change the colour of the skin to match local surroundings. Another similar leading-edge system uses polyaniline Radar Absorbent Materials which can change colour and hue instantaneously. Sensors mounted on the aircraft provide an on-board computer with information about the colour of the sky and the ground below, thus enabling the skins to alter their appearance. Similar white-world applications would include windows that can change from opaque to frosted at the push of a button (*see also* Loewy).

According to Douglass and Sweetman, this system was thought to be most effective at low altitude where the UFO witness would be most likely to see it. It also enabled the aircraft to survive inside hostile enemy territory where it would be at greatest risk. Although it was conceived as an unmanned aircraft, the programme managers apparently insisted that a pilot was used and this pushed up the price considerably. There was a concern that such an advanced system might be prone to a 'software bug'. Even at the slow speeds that observers reported, the craft was difficult to pick out against the night sky (Zinngrabe).

It was also tested in the UK. Given that a small prototype was tested in 1992 and a manned prototype by 1993, the timeline would seem to fit in with reports of a new wave of triangle sightings that hit the UFO research community in that year. Although such a craft would be demonstrated to military personnel, and probably representatives of companies like British Aerospace, it would perhaps not exclusively be tested within established test areas out to sea and along the British coast. Delta test areas around RAF Boscombe Down or Farnborough might have been bases of limited operations while certain of the RAF facilities on the east coast – Coningsby or Mildenhall – might also be worthy of consideration. The 1993 sightings certainly related to a military UFO and this was not the first advanced aircraft to be tested in the UK, as we have already seen (Fowler). The Tier 3, with its remarkable abilities, is a good candidate in our search for the elusive slow-moving and near-silent UFO. Observers reported that not only were the camouflage patterns most unusual, but the craft was boomerang-shaped and could fly at 'near-walking speeds' – shades of the Hudson Valley.

Such was the advanced nature of Tier 3 that US officials were supposedly unwilling to use their asset in case it crashed. Dan Zinngrabe suggests that the crash landing of such an aircraft over hostile territory would have required that the country be 'bombed back into the stone age' in order to protect the technology.

Technology does not exist in a vacuum. It is developed over time. Given that we know that advanced radial-flow jet engines were predicted for use in the mid to late 1950s, might we conclude that the technology to enable an aircraft to hover with ease is rather older than that demonstrated by the Advanced Aerial Reconnaissance System?

FIFTEEN

SILENT VULCAN

T HE ENGLISH COUNTY of Leicestershire was a focal point for two major triangular UFO flaps – one in 1978 and the other in 1985. Sceptics will argue that the aircraft seen could not have been of terrestrial origin. The reasons for this may already be apparent but they relate mainly to three factors:

1. Very silent operation of the aircraft at low altitude.

2. Ability of aircraft to travel very slowly or hover.

3. Unusual lighting configurations.

It is clear that these factors in no way indicate an extraterrestrial spacecraft, but most likely do indicate the operation of a secret military aircraft. In fact, we might suggest a rule for UFO investigations:

All triangular or circular-planform aircraft are of terrestrial origin. They are secret military aircraft perhaps based upon unconventional or 'leading-edge' technologies.

October 1978 in Leicestershire

The UFO sightings of October 1978 can be explained in these terms. The case is quite remarkable in that it appeared to strike a chord with local people – especially those who saw the UFO. Between 6 pm and 11.46 pm on the night of Monday 23 October 1978 Leicestershire's small UFO research groups were inundated with calls from local people who had seen a triangular object with three or four very bright lights on the underside.

The investigators, including Mark Brown, Trevor Thornton and Graham Hall, did a remarkable job of collating all the reports and they left no stone unturned in their efforts to get to the truth of the matter (Brown and Hall).

The majority of witnesses seemed to live in Hinckley and Nuneaton. A peak of activity was noted between 6 and 6.30. During this 30-minute period, 55 of the total 67 completed reports occurred. This seemed to indicate that reports from later on that evening may not have been related, and may have been misidentifications of stars or regular aircraft lights. The newspapers certainly seized on the reports and helped to publicize the events and also on the phone number of the local investigations teams. Some 200 telephone calls were logged. Of the final and completed reports, 36 were obtained through personal interviews, the rest through postal questionnaires.

Most of the witnesses to the half-hour of most important activity agreed that the aircraft had been in sight for several minutes, moving in a north-westerly direction. A majority of respondents also noted mainly bright white lights, while several others saw a variety of red lights on the underside as well.

What was so important about these early evening sightings was their similarity:

> I was travelling home and I was between Littlethorpe and Cosby at 6.20pm when I noticed 3 white lights travelling towards me. I thought at first it was an aeroplane going to land at Castle Donington with its landing lights on.
>
> As it got nearer the lights got very bright and formed a triangle, this in itself seemed an unusual formation. I slowed down to view it more safely and realized there were no other lights as on normal aircraft, on wingtips, tails etc. I stopped my car and opened the windows as it got closer. I could see the shape as a black silhouette, it was like a Vulcan bomber, triangular shaped with a light on each point and large. The other strange thing was that I heard no noise at all, no sound of engines etc. – after it passed the lights were no longer visible and it disappeared from my view into the dark. I have never seen the like before and that includes three years in the RAF when I saw aircraft day and night. (Mr K. Porter, Church Drive, Lutterworth, Leics. Aged 41.)

> Being ex-RAF I would have said the object was a Vulcan bomber flying South to North on the flightpath used by East Midlands airport. However, the object was stationary for 3 minutes. Imagine a Vulcan with bright lights on each wing tip and two very bright landing lights in the centre. It then moved towards us

and overhead gathered speed. When overhead I could see what looked like a red navigation light in the centre and another white light where the tailplane would be. THERE WAS NO NOISE. I rushed to the front of our bungalow (taking a few seconds), and it had completely vanished. (Mr R. Mayne, 89 Forresters Rd, Burbage, Leics.)

We saw what we first thought to be an aircraft but later when we got out of the van we realized that it couldn't be because it was moving too slow. We saw three big very bright lights, the outer two were much bigger than the centre one.

The lights moved very slowly across the sky making no sound that we could hear. This, and the slowness of speed made us think that it was very high up, yet the lights were too big and seemed near. We watched it for about ten minutes and then it disappeared behind a cloud. (Mrs D. Morley, 19 Lochmore Drive, Hinckley, Leics. Aged 21.)

Sceptics might be tempted to argue that people were merely seeing Venus or another bright star. The following report would seem to argue against such a simplistic explanation:

I left school around 6.45 pm on Monday 23 October 1978. I walked towards our house which is in the grounds, my two Grandchildren came to meet me. As we walked up the side of the house, in front of us in the sky was a reddish-orange light. We watched it for a few minutes then I called my husband and sons out of the house to look at it. We watched it for about five minutes then I went across to the school to ask the Deputy Headmaster (he gives lessons in Astronomy). I thought that if it was a star he would be able to explain it. He was talking to the Headmaster and I asked him if he would be able to explain it. He was talking to the Headmaster and I asked him if he would come outside and have a look. When we got outside and looked towards where the light had been, it had gone. Then looking down on the field due South we could see three bright lights coming towards us. My youngest son came over to us and asked Mr. Goodman what it was. It then came nearer to us and looked to me, head on, very much the shape of a Vulcan bomber, or half-circle. As it went right over us it looked to have a dull red light underneath it. We thought it was a plane but as it went over there was no sound whatsoever, also there were no navigation lights on it.

Also as we turned round to look at it, it was completely black at the back and we could see nothing. It was travelling south to north but not on a flight path. After we got back in the house we rang up UAPROL [local UFO group] to report it. After talking about it and saying it looked from the front very much like a V bomber, I rang up Bitteswell (where the V bomber that comes over is stationed) I asked them if it had been up in the last hour and a half and they said no, if it had, we definitely would have heard it. (Evans family, School House, Hastings High School, Burbage, Leics.)

Many of the witnesses attempted to draw pictures in order to indicate the positions of the main lights on the aircraft; although their efforts varied widely, in terms of quality and accuracy, it was clear that a triangular shape had been evident to most witnesses while some others opted for a diamond shape. There was a suggestion from certain witnesses that the lighting patterns on the underside had changed during their sighting. Only a couple of witnesses claimed to have seen a flying saucer – interesting given the powerful imagery of films of such craft etched into Western consciousness by films like *Close Encounters of the Third Kind*.

There were several attempts to film the UFO, largely unsuccessful, mainly owing to the use of incorrect film. A ciné film was taken by Mr Evans (his sightings noted above). The final report on the Silent Vulcan incident described the film in the following terms:

The approximate footage shot was 3 feet, this represents 30 seconds of film – the film shows the object in three distinct phases, although these phases may have been partially caused through visibility deficiencies rather than them being actual differences.

Phase 1 – the object appears as an indistinct circular mass of yellow/white light, this lasts for approximately 8 seconds and gives the impression of the object's progression towards the cameraman.

Phase 2 – after this initial 8-second period the mass of light appears to separate (presumably due to diminishing distances), into 3 white/yellow lights, in which the centre light appears to be slightly advanced or raised from the other outer two.

Phase 3 – the second phase lasted 15 seconds before the centre

light appears to go out. This appearance of going out quite
suddenly with no apparent dimming beforehand, and leaves just
two white/yellow lights visible with a gap between them. The
film runs its remaining seven seconds with just these two lights
visible.

Although the film is not without its problems, I made strenuous efforts to get hold of it and any photographs relating to the incident; although nothing has emerged yet, there is reason to believe that some material may become available in future. In addition to this, various East Midlands newspaper archives were searched for new information on the sightings.

The report written by Brown and Hall was incredibly detailed and every effort was made to identify the object. Some sceptical researchers argued that this was merely a misidentification of a Vulcan bomber, although there was little evidence to support such a view. The witnesses insisted that this was *not* a Vulcan – and many of them were used to seeing the aircraft. The UFO they reported was able to travel at very slow speed, and we know that the Vulcan's stall speed was not slow enough to allow it to be mistaken for the UFO.

The size of the UFO was estimated to have been between 100 and 200 feet (30–60 m) wide. Although the Vulcan had a wingspan of 111 feet (34 m) and a length of 99 feet (30 m), many witnesses stated that the UFO was larger. The lighting arrangements on the Vulcan were completely different: two forward-facing white landing lights, a mid-airframe red rotating beacon (on top of the aircraft) and two red flashing lights on the underside as opposed to the overly bright white lights reported on the UFO (Cubitt and Ellis).

Although local RAF bases were contacted, the personnel who spoke to the investigators were either unable, or unwilling, to disclose any sensitive information beyond the routine and operational. One of the main questions to be answered related to the actual projected flightpath of the UFO, said to be flying from south-south-east to north-north-west near built-up areas and over open countryside. The craft was seen from Nuneaton, Hinckley, Leicester, Newbold Verdon, Coalville and Ashby between approximately 6.30 pm and 7 pm.

Let us assume – and the evidence to some extents supports our assumption – that this was indeed a structured craft of some sort. Is there any evidence that could lead us to conclude that this was an extraterrestrial spaceship? No. Such a conclusion would be a matter for speculation. It is much more likely that this was an experimental aircraft flown on only one occasion in the area. There could have been numerous reasons for this, and during the 1970s other sightings of seemingly 'unconventional' aircraft were reported. Set against the background of the UK–US special relationship and secret aircraft flights of US craft over British soil sighted in the early 1960s, then the events of 23 October make some sense.

Cornwall to Lincolnshire

In 1976, Brian James saw a sleek delta-shaped aircraft off the Cornish Coast moving at high speed. This was reported in the *Fortean Times* magazine in response to comments about triangular UFO sightings.

A much more detailed sighting came to light recently as a result of research undertaken by Scottish UFO researcher James Easton (web site). This relates to an incident that preceded the Leicestershire sightings by seven months. The sighting is said to have taken place on either a Tuesday or a Thursday night in March at around 11 pm near Ulceby Cross – a well-known Lincolnshire crossroads just 6 miles (10 km) from the east coast. The witness, Paul Hanmer, a chartered accountant, was travelling home when he was confronted by dazzling lights. These turned out to be coming from a very large triangular or delta-shaped object moving very slowly overhead at an altitude reported to be as little as 50 feet (15 m). Clearly, this was an unusual and shocking experience and although Hanmer knew of the Vulcan bomber this was a much larger craft with no sharp protuberances or similar features.

Interestingly, a bluish glow emanated from the underside of the craft and this could be seen as it slowly glided over the witness's car. During an interview with Easton, Mr Hanmer said that this seemed too real to be extraterrestrial, and it was obviously unlike anything he had either seen or heard of. The craft appeared to be of solid construction, rigid in appearance and fashioned from one sheet of material (he saw no joins or panels on the underside), so he speculated that it must be of metallic content. The craft was perfectly triangular and of equal depth throughout. In true terrestrial fashion, two bright lights positioned at the very front of the triangle beamed light down at an angle of 90 degrees on to the flat terrain below. The craft moved off in a southerly direction in the general direction of Boston at a speed of between 15 and 40 mph (25–65 kmph), and as this was a clear night Hanmer could see it as it departed.

One wonders why an extraterrestrial craft would be beaming what appeared to have been searchlights of some sort on to a deserted area of little strategic interest. No doubt somebody will come up with a theory – taking soil samples, abducting innocent members of the public, an extraterrestrial reconnaissance mission to judge humanity's husbandry of Planet Earth – but none of this should be taken particularly seriously. It may well be possible to explain this sighting too.

Sightings in the North-West

Of interest were a number of sightings reported in late 1978 in the north-west of England. Many took place in the immediate area of RAF Burtonwood (now closed down) off the M62, although investigators seemed to be curiously unaware of this at the time.

I have spoken to many of them, including Jenny Randles and Peter Hough (Hough saw a delta-shaped object himself at approximately the same time), and it seems that they did not necessarily believe that the UFOs seen could be secret military aircraft. I spoke to Peter Hough in July 1997 about the incident, and he argued that it could not have been of terrestrial military origin

Under these circumstances, they were the most likely group to investigate the sighting of a secret military aircraft; further investigation is limited to possibilities within a predetermined classification system. It is likely that sightings of a similar nature would be classified 'CE1' – 'Close Encounter of the First Kind'. Can one really have a 'Close Encounter' with a secret military aircraft, and doesn't the terminology adopted in such a system have an inbuilt bias towards strange, even 'alien', phenomena?

Possible Answer: The SR-71

One might conclude that these craft were of unknown origin. There are other more distinct possibilities. By the mid-1970s the CIA-sponsored SR-71 was operating regularly from RAF Mildenhall in rural East Anglia (Graham; Bowyer). Rumour has it that the aircraft actually landed in the UK in 1973 and that its appearance caused a rather nasty behind the scenes diplomatic/political storm regarding an American 'spy' plane being based in the country. The NSA station at Menwith Hill is still the subject of controversy because essentially it is an American outpost over which the UK has no real control.

The SR-71 was designed to operate at very high speeds in excess of Mach 3 in a purely reconnaissance role (Peebles). It was a prized CIA asset and all the staff associated with it had a 'Top Secret' clearance. When it officially touched down at the Farnborough Air Show in September 1974 via Mildenhall, the UK was one of the few NATO countries prepared to allow the aircraft to operate from its soil (Graham). This was a politically sensitive aircraft and could only heighten fears that the UK (and parts of Europe, especially Germany) were becoming merely 'aircraft carriers' for US forces overseas.

By the time the first operational deployment began in April 1976 the U-2 spyplane had been operating from Mildenhall for some time. The SR-71s were housed on the more secure part of the base, and had the use of a 9,000-foot (2,750-m) runway. The deployments were of a short-term nature between 1976 and 1980 and lasted between three and six weeks at a time.

The U-2 would tend to operate in advance of the SR-71 and, although a large, specially trained support crew was available for each aircraft, there were technical areas common to both aircraft. The kind of operations the spyplanes were involved in were sorties in support of NATO military exercises; during such operations over 100 personnel and several KC-135 refuelling aircraft from Beale Air Force Base in the USA were required to ensure success. British air traffic controllers received unclassified data relating to operations, but they were not given any information relating to activities above an altitude of 60,000 feet (18,000 m) (Graham).

Attempts were made, especially by U-2 crews, to keep their presence at Mildenhall as quiet as possible, although the operation of the two aircraft was known. Nevertheless, the National Security Agency, concerned by the existence of numerous Russian fishing vessels in the North Sea, emphasized the need for radio silence as often as possible during take-off and landing, and no doubt elaborate procedures to confuse the enemy were put in place.

There were, as noted above, numerous Lockheed technical experts on hand to assist with operations. In terms of secret flights of other 'unidentified' aircraft, it is reasonable to suppose that technical experts and teams associated with these could be spirited into Mildenhall without raising much suspicion.

If Mildenhall was not the centre of operations for the 1978 Leicestershire UFO, then perhaps nearby RAF Alconbury was. Later, in 1983, Alconbury was chosen to host a whole wing of U-2/TR-1 reconnaissance aircraft because more extensive intelligence data was required by both the CIA and NSA.

The much-vaunted 'special relationship' between the United States of America and the United Kingdom appears to exist on a number of levels, from well-known treaties and agreements through to much more secret links that researchers are forced to speculate about. As we have seen, the UK government was willing to allow the SR-71 to be flown from its bases. Undoubtedly the UK has always been the weaker partner, and in fact this goes right back to the end of the Second World War. After the end of the conflict a new alignment emerged whereby the Soviet Union came into its own and the Iron Curtain came down across Europe. With a rapidly failing Empire and the emergence of two superpowers Britain's role was reduced to that of a satellite off Western Europe. Through the North Atlantic Treaty Organization (NATO) Britain retained some influence, although it was only through close ties with the USA that this could be maintained. Winston Churchill defined the new relationship as 'spheres of influence' – quite clearly the UK had to look to the USA, rather than Europe, in economic and military terms.

Or – Silent Vulcan

The other possibility is that this UFO was a early test-flight of a hybrid lighter-than-air vehicle. The reported characteristics of the 'Silent Vulcan' UFO – slow operation, large size – sound not unlike the configuration said to be typical of the Hudson Valley UFO.

Remember, by 1978 Aercon Corporation had carried out successful test-flights of their deltoid craft and had produced several impressions for a large triangular airship. Only two years before, the publication of White's *Airships for the Future* had heightened interest in modern airships. This had been entirely ignored by the UFO community. But Britain continued to develop its own secret technology.

SIXTEEN

BRITAIN'S SECRET TECHNOLOGY

RAF BOSCOMBE DOWN is the headquarters of the Defence Testing and Evaluation Organisation (DTEO). The DTEO is part of the Defence Evaluation and Research Agency (DERA), a focal point for the development of several advanced technologies. Many of these technologies relate to stealth aircraft concepts. All of this is admitted on the DERA website at www.dra.hmg.gb

The aviation enthusiast might claim that, although the UK is working on concepts, there are no actual prototype aircraft in existence. In other words everything is at the design stage or on the drawing board.

But the evidence suggests otherwise, and, as I pointed out in my 1996 report, numerous sightings of a small triangular aircraft of around 30 feet (9 m) in length have been reported to UFO researchers throughout the North-West and along the west coast.

In addition, the release of material by the Ministry of Defence after the December 1994 incident at Boscombe Down (p. 99) bore the hallmarks of an officially sanctioned disinformation campaign.

There is little doubt that the Americans are involved in this project, given their desire to maintain supremacy in terms of stealth and to work with the British in order to make further technological breakthroughs. It is an old joke that British scientists develop new technologies only to have the Americans come along and see the project through to the end – either through lack of UK funding or because the USA has flexed its muscle and invoked the terms of the formal agreement between the two countries. It is unclear exactly what the UK has gained from the relationship, but we know that in the mid-1980s the F-117 Nighthawk landed at RAF facilities in East Anglia. It also seems to be the case that RAF pilots have been allowed to fly other undisclosed stealth aircraft in the USA (Bissell).

The DERA Umbrella of Technologies

According to information made available to the public via their own web site, the Defence Evaluation and Research Agency (DERA) is an agency of the Ministry of Defence and was launched on 1 April 1995 as a trading fund.

Over the four years from 1991 to 1994, the Defence Research Agency had successfully brought together the bulk of the MOD's non-nuclear research establishments. They are now sectors within DERA: the Defence Research Agency (DRA); the Defence Test and Evaluation Organisation (DTEO); the Centre for Defence Analysis (CDA); and the Protection and Life Sciences Divisions (PLSD). The DERA also includes the facilities at Porton Down – the Protection and Life Sciences Division (Barnaby). Within these four main sectors are many other specialized groups working on a host of technologies relating to land, sea and air systems, weapons, materials and electronics. The organization employs over 12,000 people and has an operating budget of over £6 billion a year. DERA admits to having a 'close working relationship with the defence staff in Washington [DC]'. In addition to boasting that it employs many leading scientists and internationally acclaimed experts, DERA has a number of ranges and test facilities under its control. These are dispersed throughout the country and are available for use by any of its customers, the main one being the MOD.

In our search for the answers to the many UFO sightings along the west coast of Britain, and the appearance of US stealth aircraft on British soil, the DERA is a sensible place to look. Although it has been in operation only since 1995, the facilities and technologies now used and developed under DERA have been around for years. For instance, Boscombe Down has been a centre for flight-testing since 1914. In 1924 the testing centre became known as the Aeroplane and Armament Experimental Establishment (A&AEE), becoming part of the Directorate General of Test and Evaluation (DGTE) in 1991, before joining DERA in 1995. In 1997 Boscombe became the headquarters for the Aircraft Test and Evaluation Centre (Cooper).

Radar Absorbent Materials

As J. Jones points out in his *Stealth Technology – The Art of Black Magic*, Britain has been at the forefront of stealth technology development. Plessey Limited have produced various Radar Absorbent Materials (RAM), including narrow-band flexible plates and wide-band camouflage netting.

They have also developed stealth camouflage for hiding large structures that might reflect radar energy, such as aircraft hangars, command posts and ground equipment. One RAM treatment developed by the company is made from Kevlar and is strong enough to be used on airframes. In fact, it was British scientists at Farnborough who invented carbon fibres back in the 1960s. Similar lightweight composites would be used to construct stealth aircraft, and the Structural Materials Centre (SMC) within DERA has developed several new technologies along these lines. The SMC was the first DERA Dual Use Technology Centre from 1994 and drew together materials, science, engineering and processing skills that support current and future air requirements. The SMC has facilities at Farnborough, Fort Halstead in Kent and Rosyth in Scotland. It is continuing to develop new systems including acoustic dampening, stealth and polymer matrix composite technologies. Official SMC propaganda states that:

> The SMC has extensive skills and facilities related to the development of all aspects of stealth technology, including acoustic, magnetic, radar and infra-red signature control, either as palliative treatments or intrinsically stealthy structures.

Negative Luminescence

Other work done by the SMC at Malvern was reported by Andrew Gilligan of the *Daily Telegraph* in July 1996. It raised eyebrows in the UFO and aviation research communities:

> In a quantum leap in military strategy, staff at the Ministry of Defence Research Agency...have bent one of the fundamental laws of physics to produce a material which can give off 'negative luminescence' at room temperature (Gilligan).

The material is based on indium antimonide semi-conductors and could be used to make tanks, guns, personnel carriers and indeed soldiers invisible to thermal imagers, giving troops a decisive advantage. Most conflicts will be fought at night in future, and the new infra-red chameleon could be used to reduce even further the IR emissions of stealth aircraft.

Although Dr Tim Ashley of DRA claimed in an interview with Gilligan that only tiny amounts of the material had been developed, it seems highly unlikely that such a development as this would not receive the maximum possible advantage. This is a good example of the typical propaganda to which we have become accustomed; admit to the technology, then deny its current use. The material in question is quite remarkable – it absorbs light but doesn't emit it (Sutton).

Evaluating Stealth Technologies

Because the DERA has some of the world's most effective air defence and battlefield systems, it is able to put stealth technologies through their paces. In terms of weapon systems, the organization has a great deal of experience in terms of evaluating the interaction between weapons, stealth, electronic support measures (ESM) and electronic countermeasures.

There are other indications that Britain is at the heart of secret technology developments. An article by the *Times* Defence Correspondent Hugh McManners, written on 29 September 1996, stated that Vickers was developing a plastic tank for stealth warfare and that 'alternative plastic skins' would allow for automatic changes in the colour of vehicles in order to camouflage them and also drastically reduce their RCS.

The first real indication – beyond reports of a small, possibly unmanned, triangular UFO operating off the west coast – that the public was not being told anything approaching the truth about Britain's stealth programme came in an article. It was written by defence expert Paul Beaver for the September 1996 edition of *Air International* magazine. Entitled 'RAF 2006', the article dealt with various issues surrounding future developments including missiles, helicopters and conventional jet aircraft like the Eurofighter 2000. In addition, the article included, on p. 167, an impression of a 'future' stealth aircraft. The caption beneath the picture stated:

> Shape of things to come for the RAF? A theoretical 'generic' stealth concept aircraft conceived at the new Farnborough Supercomputing Centre by a collaborative team of British Aerospace (BAe), DERA and GEC Marconi and Cray Research Ltd.

The 'generic stealth concept' was remarkably similar to the UFO reported as operating in our skies. Coincidence? Hardly.

'HALO' Programme

In fact, in April 1996 a report in the respected *Flight International* magazine indicated that British Aerospace (BAe) had flown small-scale prototypes of a 'mini B-2' UAV.

This was associated with the company's second HALO programme. The first programme had started in 1989 and related to Hawk Low Observable Studies, while the second HALO programme was 'High Agility Low Observable' – an unmanned stealth vehicle. Perhaps this admission was designed in order to appease an increasingly interested press. Various local newspapers in towns and cities (for instance, Lancaster, Morecambe and Southport) along the west coast had featured reports on triangular UFO activity, while UFO publications, selling more and more copies at the height of a massive increase in popularity, were beginning to focus on secret military aircraft programmes. Artists' impressions put out by British Aerospace showed a small grey triangular UAV with a section of coastline below. This led several people to jump to the obvious conclusion that prototype UAVs were responsible for UFO sightings.

Nevertheless BAe, under pressure from all sides, soon changed its position and claimed that the sightings were not the result of test flights. This seemed to be an impossible change of stance. Perhaps US pressure caused the change of mind.

We know for certain that experts from Lockheed were involved at the British Aerospace facilities at Warton during the construction of dedicated facilities on the southern tip of their land. The Special Projects Site was constructed at a cost of around £100 million from 1992, and the work was documented in an enlightening article written by Nick Cook for the July/August 1995 edition *of Interavia Business and Technology* magazine.

BAe officials reveal that engineers recruited for the south-side facility are being screened as rigorously as any employee of the Lockheed Martin Skunk Works – an entity that has become synonymous with stealth.

I spoke to an expert associated with British Aerospace and he told me that HALO referred to a 'classified defence programme' under way within the company in conjunction with DERA, and that it would in a few years' time result in a manned stealth aircraft. In addition he claimed that BAe had invested the money in their Projects Site only in the certain knowledge that secret funding would be made available by the UK government in the near future. *Jane's All the World's Aircraft, 1995–6* (p. 452) stated:

BAe Advanced Aircraft Studies.

TYPE; Low Observables (LO) combat aircraft to replace Tornado GR Mk4.

PROGRAMME; £100 million spent in 1992–4 on stealth aircraft development; purpose-built research and development facility, including secure hangar, nearing completion at Warton plant in 1995. BAe urging government go-ahead for stealth demonstrator in 1997: production aircraft then to be available in 2013; international collaboration likely.

NOTE: US press reports, quoting Washington sources, allege UK already proceeding with LO aircraft for frontal area stealthiness.

UK media allege LO aircraft assumed to be American destroyed in accident at Boscombe Down on night of 26th September 1994. No evidence to substantiate either.

Warton and Stealth

Jane's All the World's Aircraft, 1997–8 gives details of the continuing work at Warton more generally within British Aerospace. This relates to extensive studies into 'low observable' or stealth technology.

UK defence expert Paul Beaver, in an article written in *X-Planes* magazine (*Air Forces Monthly Special*, February 1998), is more specific:

Even industry is unusually reticent to talk about what goes on at British Aerospace's Warton, GEC Marconi's Stanmore or Short's Castlereagh plants.

He goes on to claim that:

Most of the United Kingdom's electronics companies regard the Farnborough-based Defence Evaluation and Research Agency as the custodian of 'black' technology, theoretical and practical.

He appears to believe that much of this will end up in the development of future UCAV systems. Of course, my position is that prototypes of these have already been flown and they have been responsible for their fair share of UFO sightings.

Beaver also notes in the article that in the South-West the development of an anti-terrorist airship involved local residents being 'unwitting witnesses to the development of a unique spy in the sky'; it would have remained a secret had it not been for a US contractor inadvertently giving away some classified information. One wonders about the many other occasions where people reporting UFO activity have been the 'unwitting' witnesses to the development of secret aerial technology programmes.

The Projects Site at Warton was built in order to facilitate research into a host of new technologies including stealth, low-speed, Short-Take-Off and Vertical Landing technologies (STOVL), and unmanned control systems. Every aspect of stealth would be studied by small teams and it was said that these might come together in order to build a manned full-size stealth aircraft in the near future.

The 'replacement for the Tornado GR Mk4' we now know to be the Future Offensive Air System (FOAS) (*see* illustration no. 15). FOAS replaced the Future Offensive Aircraft programme (FOA) and involved some radical designs described by the *Independent* newspaper's Chris Bellamy on 17 December 1996. In an article bearing the fascinating title 'Don't worry. If you see a flying saucer, it's probably one of ours', Bellamy reported that the MOD had opted to spend just £35 million on future concepts which could include Uninhabited Combat Air Vehicle (the new politically correct name for the UAV!) flown by virtual reality. Again, DERA was said to be involved although BAe was destined to receive only £3 million. An important point to make is that the MOD announcements highlighted a change in direction: unmanned craft were now to be used in a combat role – previously they had been used for reconnaissance. Bellamy closed by noting the possible highly controversial use of 'non-lethal' weapons on the new aircraft.

Knowing that something big was indeed coming together at Warton, triangular UFO sightings did not surprise us. Many reports came in from Barrow-in-Furness where from April to July 1996 witnesses in the Abbey Road and Bigger Bank areas of the town reported seeing a small triangular craft making its way towards the Lancashire coast. On several occasion two Tornados appeared to be escorting the smaller craft.

In one case in early June four witnesses standing on Walney Island saw the triangle at 4.30 pm travelling in a similar direction. On 10 June the craft was reported by several witnesses approaching Warton via the coast.

At around that time my wife and I visited the Lancashire Coastal Path in one of our first attempts to find out the truth behind the rumours. Looking across in the direction of the Special Projects Site I saw a dark aircraft descend vertically behind the buildings. The sighting lasted only seconds, but was enough to convince me that there was an element of truth to the sightings. As if to provide corroboration of sorts, I received a phone call a couple of nights later from a Heysham man claiming to have been previously employed as a security guard at Warton. He claimed to be interested in UFOs and asked for detailed information about our activities. After a general conversation about the possibilities of extraterrestrial life the man, who called himself Derek Hanson, said that the one thing we shouldn't 'waste our time on' was the British Aerospace facilities at Warton.

This was a strange comment, to say the least, especially given my visit to the base just days before. My informant insisted that 'all the rumours' were untrue or exaggerations and that our UFO group should steer clear. I thanked him for the information, took his name and phone number and promised to tell him when our next meeting was. Intrigued, I dialled recall number 1471 to see if he had left his number in the system. He hadn't, and furthermore the number (and many variations of it) was bogus. I have never made much of my Warton sighting because it will be seen as far too convenient. In any case, we can listen to other witnesses in order to establish a pattern.

It appeared that a major breakthrough had taken place on Friday 29 August 1996 when a Fine Arts student (now at Lancaster University) contacted us about a remarkable incident that took place at 9.15 pm over the Sandylands Road area of Kendal in Cumbria. The young woman, 'Wendy P.', had been on the phone to her boyfriend at 9.10 pm, when she heard a strange rumbling noise coming from outside the house. It was quite frightening and her mother and father also noticed the sound. The lights in the house flickered on and off, so the three of them went outside to see what was going on. Some of their neighbours were standing in the street and outside their houses looking concerned. During the passage of what seemed like several minutes the sound changed from a rumble to a buzzing sound.

A small triangular object was hovering at the end of the road not far from the local convenience shop! Three red lights could be seen at each tip of the craft and a single bright light in the middle on the underside. As the craft moved around on its axis a panel of red pulsating lights could be seen along the 'back' of the craft.

Despite the appearance of this UFO, some of the witnesses went back inside while some teenagers stood entranced as the object proceeded to move off towards the town centre, only to return to its previous position at the end of the road. Luckily we spoke to three witnesses on the following Sunday and we were able to interview other locals before too much time had elapsed. The local newspaper, *The Westmorland Gazette*, received a few garbled reports. Wendy's father, a former RAF man, made the comment to us that 'this was no regular aircraft – I've never seen anything like it'. He suspected that this was a secret military craft, but could not imagine what it was doing over Kendal unless it had strayed from the testing area near Brough (Delta areas D407/407A). I dutifully contacted Sec AS2a and

From: Miss K Philpott, Secretariat (Air Staff) 2a1
MINISTRY OF DEFENCE
Main Building, Whitehall, London SW1A 2HB

Telephone (Direct dial)   0171 218 2140
(Switchboard)   0171 218 9000
(Fax)   0171 218 2680

Your reference

Our reference
D/Sec(AS)/64/3
Date
11 September 1996

Dear Mr Matthews,

1.   I said I would write to you following our conversation earlier this week when you asked if the MOD might be able to shed any light on a "UFO" sighting you are investigating which took place on 29 Aug 96 between 2115 and 2200 hrs over Kendal, witnessed by 20 or so people.

2.   As briefly explained during our telephone conversation the Ministry of Defence examines any reports of "UFO" sightings it receives solely to establish whether what was seen might have some defence significance; namely is there any evidence that the UK Air Defence Region might have been compromised by a foreign hostile military aircraft? The reports are examined, with the assistance of the Department's air defence experts as required. Unless there is evidence of a potential military threat, and to date no "UFO" sighting has revealed such evidence, we do not attempt to identify the precise nature of each sighting reported to us. We believe that down-to-earth explanations are available for most of these reported sightings.

3.   First I can confirm that the MOD received only two "UFO" reports for 29 Aug 96, one in Clwyd and one in Dundee, neither were deemed to be of defence significance. With regard to the possibility of the sighting being attributed to a military aircraft/helicopter I have ascertained that as Kendal has a relatively large population it is a military low flying avoidance area. As such no military low level flying would have been permitted over Kendal and this rules this option out, unless the sighting occurred on the very outskirts of Kendal. This would not of course rule out the possibility of it being a civil helicopter.

4.   The other potential option is that the shape seen was some form of advertising dirigible. Advertising balloons would of course be deliberately flown over centres of population to attract as much attention as possible. A dirigible which is manned is subject to the same air traffic regulations as other aircraft and would be required to display green and red navigation lights. This might also account for the humming sound you mentioned some

1

This is a typical response to requests to Secretariat Air Staff 2a at the UK Ministry of Defence, written after a series of remarkable triangular UFO sightings were reported to the author on 29 August 1996. The craft seen was thought by witnesses to be 'the next generation of stealth'.

spoke to Kerry Philpott. I was not surprised to receive a letter from her claiming that the witnesses might have seen 'an advertising dirigible'. Wendy and family were disgusted at this suggestion.

It was clear that some sort of 'official line' was being put out. Perhaps the company took advice from colleagues at Lockheed Martin. Further evidence came our way when contact was made with a group of Cumbrian aircraft enthusiasts. One of them had been lucky enough to record several minutes of telemetry footage on his satellite system. (Telemetry relays images by radio, which can be picked up; it looks like flickering images in its usual format, as several different types of information about the performance of an aircraft are given.)

The footage that had been captured was recorded on 2.36 GHz – an amateur all-modes frequency. This detail has led some people to conclude either that a mistake was made by BAe or that the footage was unremarkable. In fact the footage is quite remarkable. The Cumbrian group has since been in contact with various ex-RAF personnel and other telemetry experts including a former British Aerospace employee who had worked on the Experimental Aircraft Programme (EAP) – which led to the Eurofighter. (EAP was conceived in 1983; it led to the development of a technology demonstrator known as EFA – European Fighter Aircraft, flown at Farnborough Air Show, 1986.) The footage, and information about the sightings, was also shown to a select audience including ex-RAF personnel and air traffic controllers.

In their considered opinion the footage showed an aircraft performing at least 9g turns at 450 knots – the maximum for a manned aircraft. The first segment of footage, recorded in early 1995, shows an aircraft approaching Warton airfield. What is more fascinating here is that the aircraft appears to be able to effect the turns without losing much speed. In addition, the group concluded that this was neither a Hawk nor a Tornado jet aircraft. The suggestion that this was a Eurofighter was also discounted. Official information released by British Aerospace and publicized in an article about the aircraft in *Air International* suggested that the Eurofighter had not yet performed 9g turns. Given that the footage was 18 months old, it seemed likely that something else might be responsible.

Some very good sightings came our way. One of these was from 'Mrs GH', a 31-year-old mechatronics engineer from Bare in Morecambe. Her sighting took place in March 1996 (probably 28 March). Looking out from her back yard on this clear night between 9.30 pm and 10.30 pm she saw a triangular aircraft flying at very low altitude – approximately 500 feet (150 m) – passing overhead in a south-south-easterly direction. It was dark in colour, and had a most unusual large red glowing aura in the centre. There were no other lights visible as the isosceles craft of 40 feet (12 m) in length passed by at moderate speed. The witness drew a picture of the triangular craft.

Just a couple of days later, a witness, caretaker Kevin Flannery (he said he thought the date was late March or early April), was walking along the Promenade in Bare at 8.30 pm when he saw a similar sight – this time just off the coast hovering approximately 100 feet (30 m) above the water. This was undoubtedly a triangular craft, and it emitted a humming sound and beamed a powerful light from its underside on to the water below. It moved off after a few minutes.

These were by no means isolated incidents. Any UFO researcher reading this book will know that often cases come in several months or years after a sighting, possibly as a result of local press and media interest.

The next case was one of these and appeared to support GH and Flannery in their view that small triangles had been flying along the Lancashire coast. In August 1995 Douglas Marsden and his daughter (Mrs Pattison) of West End, Morecambe, were driving along Thornton Road towards to the Promenade in Morecambe near the Junction. At the junction of Thornton Road and Marine Road they both saw an object beaming a light down on to the water below. They initially thought that this was the police helicopter, but it soon became clear that this craft was something entirely different. They stopped the car as the object came towards them. It performed a number of silent darting manoeuvres and appeared to be under intelligent control. They could see the outline of the triangle as it moved overhead and they watched for what seemed like hours, but was in fact between 10 and 15 minutes, as the object drifted out to sea. There were lights at each corner of the craft, said to be two-thirds the size of a fighter jet, and although the witnesses could remember seeing white and green lights, they were unsure as to the specific arrangement.

The question is simple: how long had this activity been taking place? It would seem that in this particular case since early 1995, possibly late 1994. The first sighting of a triangular craft was reported by 'Mr Graham T.' of Longton near Preston.

There is little doubt that the British Aerospace factory at Warton was a focal point for this activity. I spoke to 'GT' and his wife in March 1997, and their recollection of events had not diminished. After visiting friends in Blackpool they had driven along the main A584 towards Preston. The night was clear and calm, visibility was good. The road passing the Warton plant is very straight and GT's wife had commented on the lack of traffic as they passed by. Just then, some way in the distance, a bright spotlight beamed down on to the road in front of them. Slightly concerned, and wondering exactly what kind of idiot would beam a light on to a main road, GT slowed down just in case this was in fact a police helicopter. After a few seconds the beam went out, but they could still see an object slightly ahead and to the right. GT stopped and wound down the window to get a better view.

This was not a helicopter, but a wedge-shaped object well camouflaged against the night sky. GT remarked that its shape was triangular, and he confirmed this in a detailed letter to me written on 8 April 1997. He said that it looked like an airborne 'Dairylea cheese slice'! As the craft passed by only a faint humming could be heard; the craft seemed to be a little larger than the Vulcan bomber that sits outside Blackpool Airport and which the couple had seen on several occasions. A 'Christmas tree' lighting scheme was noted, for the craft was 'ablaze with rows of multicoloured lights'. A row of red lights moving constantly from left to right and back again were seen on the back of the UFO as it flew towards the southern side of the Warton airfield.

In April 1996 four builders sitting outside the Little Chef at Walmer Bridge on the A59 saw a similar aircraft come from the direction of Warton (situated just a few miles away) and fly right over them in an easterly direction. I have spoken to two of the men and they said that it was 'most likely a stealth craft from Warton'.

It is obvious that something has been going on at Warton for a few years now (Beaver, 1998; Cook, *Interavia*, 1995). That is not to say that this larger aircraft was constructed at Warton, only that it operated from the airfield on several occasions. It is possible that the Vulcan-sized craft was on loan from British Aerospace's allies in the USA. It might have been a TR-3A, known to operate in secret from the UK. But why all the talk of aliens? Beyond the media fad, we might well ask why, given such impressive evidence, we are still told by Ufologists that 'nothing' is going on at Warton (Fowler).

The only conclusion that we could reach was that the UFO community was reliable enough to effectively bury the sightings behind an 'alien' smokescreen. One group from Blackpool even visited Warton and were shown round selected facilities. Of course, they never got to the Special Projects Site and accepted the word of BAe officials who scoffed at any suggestion that secret work was taking place – despite the fact that this has been admitted by company officials and in *Jane's All the World's Aircraft 1997–8*! A review of the majority of literature relating to triangles written in the UFO press and in local newspapers concentrated on the usual speculation about alien craft and extraterrestrial life. All kinds of ill-informed material appeared, including a booklet entitled *The Flying Triangle Mystery* by veteran UFO researcher Omar Fowler. Supported through a series of articles and lectures by *UFO Magazine,* Fowler argues that:

> *It will soon become obvious to the reader that what is being seen is not a new top secret Stealth aircraft. It is far more likely to be a new type of alien craft and does not originate on planet Earth!*

This kind of thing is music to the ears of the military/industrial complex. We can certainly disprove this claim, as we have many others along the same lines. Thankfully, it was not only aviation enthusiasts and UFO researchers who had become interested in triangle sightings. Military monitors (Mils) had also started to listen for unusual or unexpected traffic. Before I detail some of the results on military frequency monitoring (*see* Douglass's *Monitoring the Airwaves for Secret Aircraft*), it should be pointed out that by early 1997 we had a very good idea about the precise location of many of the sightings. By this time a great deal of progress had been made.

'Manchester Near Miss'

At a meeting organized by the Lancashire UFO Society in November 1996, I was approached by a young man who took me to one side and told me that he could shed new light on the 'Manchester Near Miss' incident so widely reported and the subject of an official Civil Aviation Report. The near miss took place on 6 January 1995 as a Boeing 737 to the south-east of Manchester Airport approached at an altitude of 4,000 feet (1,200 m). The two British Airways pilots, Captain Roger Wills and First Officer Mark Stuart, reported that a dark solid and lighted unidentified craft had passed by at high speed. The men had ducked as it flew by (Good, 1996).

The release of the report on the incident caused a storm of controversy, and several UFO researchers including Eric Morris and Steve Balon were asked to comment. The authors, the Civil Aviation Authorities' Joint Airmiss Working Group (JAWG), made it clear that the pilots' report had been taken very seriously and that they were to be commended for coming forward.

Beyond the rather patronizing comment about the pilots the report made the mistake of pontificating about the possibility of extraterrestrial life while at the same time claiming that it was not the job of the committee to speculate on such matters. How about this for double-talk:

> *To speculate about extraterrestrial activity, fascinating though it may be, is not within the Group's remit and must be left to those whose interest lies in that field.... There are of course [sightings] which defy explanation and thus fuel the imagination of those who are convinced that there is 'something going on' out there...'.*

This kind of rhetoric had no place in an official report. At the same time that the committee was claiming no interest in the extraterrestrial explanation, it was fuelling the fire of alien speculation. It seems difficult to believe that these comments were written in the report without the authors of it knowing the inevitable response from the UFO community. Luckily both Morris and Balon made it clear that they were of the opinion that the most likely explanation was that a secret military aircraft had been in the area and that a series of potentially disastrous mistakes had taken place, allowing it to fly into a busy approach route.

I find it difficult to believe that a British Aerospace employee with the requisite clearance to work at the Special Projects Site would approach me at a well-advertised public meeting held in a nearby town. Anyone could have seen him there – including the undoubted 'spooks' who attend such events in order to keep a finger on the Ufological pulse (Redfern).

Still, despite the two-second sighting, this incident received massive coverage, leading several researchers to suspect that even if a secret military aircraft had been involved, pressure had been applied behind the scenes. The mere suggestion of things extraterrestrial served to hide the real truth. Could a secret military aircraft have wandered into civil airspace? It seems very possible.

Was the possibility of a secret military aircraft taken seriously by the Joint Airmiss Working Group? No. One conclusion that will inevitably be drawn from this part of the triangular UFO 'mystery' is that when in doubt or danger shadowy elements in the background move to protect the true nature and extent of black aircraft projects.

Sub-scale West Coast Triangles

In early 1997 much progress had been made in terms of our research into the west-coast flying-triangle sightings. New reports were made by a variety of witnesses living in the Hesketh Bank area just across the River Ribble from Warton. These related to incidents on 17 and 26 September that took place at 2.30 pm and 4.30 pm respectively.

On a visit to photograph the Special Projects Site I had the good fortune to meet a man who insisted that both he and a friend had seen a small triangle taking off from Warton and that he had subsequently spoken to other local people. They had seen the triangle taking off accompanied by RAF Tornados. It appeared that the initial statements from British Aerospace were correct: subscale prototypes had indeed been flown. Nevertheless, we were not exactly sure how advanced these were. Given that the captured telemetry footage showed a craft operating over Marshside Sands at the mouth of the Ribble Estuary, it was possible that the prototypes were very limited in ability. If that were true, then why the need for an escort?

One of the best sightings we received came from Mrs Mary Brunt and her mother. They had both seen a small grey triangular aircraft under escort by RAF Tornados. She told me about the sighting quite by accident after discovering my interest in local sightings. The sighting took place on a clear and sunny afternoon in April 1996 from a location in Meols Cop, Southport. Mrs Brunt heard the sound of jets and looked up to see two aircraft heading south in the general direction of Liverpool.

Both jets left contrails in the sky but they had a smaller grey triangular craft in between them. The smaller triangle, approximately one-half to two-thirds the size of the jets (probably Tornados), dropped several hundred feet and then carried on. The escort aircraft then dropped down to match the new altitude.

The icing on the cake arrived on my doorstep in July 1997 from a former RAF flight-sergeant and aviation enthusiast who had been near Warton in August 1996. I quote from his letter:

> I myself was near Warton last year early one morning when I saw from a distance at the end of the runway a large triangle hovering and making a whining noise. Then it disappeared behind a large hangar on the far side of the airfield. I have always wondered what BAe has been doing in secret.

Although many people agree that something 'big' has been going on at Warton it is likely that many other facilities have been used to test the UAV.

West Freugh – Secret 'UFO' base?

One of these facilities is DTEO West Freugh, a suitably remote test facility situated on the south-west Scottish coast. The nearest town is

Stranraer. Triangle sightings at West Freugh can, rather remarkably, be traced back as far as the early 1970s where, according to a colleague of mine, a slender delta-planform aircraft came in to land. It was seen by an informed source who had been involved in servicing the computers there.

The DERA has several instrumented air ranges that provide a safe environment in which to demonstrate new weapons systems against aerial, sea and land ranges. These operations are fully backed up by experienced staff who can provide data analysis, high-speed photography, film, video recording and radar measurement. The airfield is fully operational.

The facilities at West Freugh should be of great interest to us. It would appear to be some sort of secret UFO base, in that several flying triangles have been seen there. One report came via a former member of the Manchester UFO Research Association (MUFORA) who moved to the area in recent years. He has been told that a triangular craft was seen coming in to land at the base. Other witnesses have seen a 'small triangular craft', described as 'definitely not an F-117A', landing and being taken down below the runway on a lifting device. These reports are credible given that the danger area around West Freugh extends 147 square miles (380 sq km), horizontally and to 35,000 feet (10,700 m), with a low-level approach corridor extending 3,000 feet (900 m) in height.

A quick look at Royal Air Force Flight Information publication *UK (L)2 – En Route Low Altitude Chart* – shows the location of coastal delta testing areas around West Freugh. These are designated D402A, D402B, D402C and D411. Delta 509 has a higher ceiling of 55,000 feet (17,000 m) and is situated to the north-west.

A working theory developed by our research group was that the small triangles flew out of Warton irregularly for testing on the West Freugh ranges. This was backed up by hard evidence in the form of radio intercepts reported to us by several military monitors operating in Scotland, north-west England and Northern Ireland.

It had been suggested to us that stealth testing was taking place over the Irish Sea. Monitors had heard references to a single aircraft given the unusual designation 'the package'. Let us be clear: this was a single aircraft. There was no evidence to show that this was a collective group of aircraft described as 'the package'. Beyond the ritual journeys on to hillsides armed with Thermos flasks, sandwiches, video and camera equipment for UFO skywatches, military monitoring provides an effective warm indoor alternative. On 5 June 1997 the monitors struck gold. This is the full transcript of a conversation reported to me:

1720 hours – June 5th 1997

Radio frequency – 264.4 MHz

Two aircraft are heard. The first, an E3 AWACS (Airborne Warning and Control System) Callsign – Magic 88 (Special Ops) operating out of RAF Waddington. The second, a Tornado using the callsign 'SAVAGE 1', is a little more difficult to pin down. The Tornado callsign indicates a clear link with RAF Coningsby but Mil spotters suggest that it could be a British Aerospace Tornado.

AWACS: Target 230 spiked range 9,000 hot. Package break right.

TORNADO: The package single threat only – 9K break 233 hard right.

[Pause]

Single man heading West. I have made contact with a triangle.

AWACS: Do you wish to make heading for ARA [Airborne Refuelling Area]?

TORNADO: Affirm.

AWACS: Break ABO.

Despite the brevity of the conversation, many things emerge from this transcript. Firstly, the Tornado pilot had to be vectored (directed towards a target from a secondary source) on to the triangle, suggesting that his instrumentation could not pick it up. An indication of stealth ability? Secondly, 'the package' was most likely a UAV; there was no third man in the dialogue. Thirdly, copies of this transcript have been sent to several stealth 'experts'. The only one with the courtesy to reply was Bill Sweetman. British Aerospace refused to comment. Finally, it seems most likely that the UAV could have been flown in two ways: from a virtual cockpit on board the AWACS or from a virtual cockpit at a nearby military facility. West Freugh is the obvious candidate. (There is also now an Airborne Refuelling Area off the Isle of Man.) The major criticism of my interpretation of these events is that the RAF would not allow an AWACS to be used for such a mission. A counter-suggestion is that the RAF could well have been involved, possibly with the help of British Aerospace personnel on secondment.

UAVs have been flown from an aerial platform – this much is clear. How else could Magic 88 have vectored the Tornado on to the triangle unless there was real-time data relay in operation?

Supporting evidence came in the form of other information from military monitors that they had heard 'the package' out in the Irish Sea being tested for its stealth abilities. Both infra-red (IR) and radar signatures were tested. On one occasion operators at Warton were definitely involved.

Still not convinced? Then listen to the story of the American stealthchasers. The story begins and ends with Steve Douglass.

SEVENTEEN

STEALTHCHASERS

MILITARY MONITORING IS not just a hobby, but a way of life for a small but dedicated group of Americans. One of their spokesmen is Steve Douglass, who until 1997 produced the *Intercepts Newsletter* from his house in Austin, Texas. *Intercepts* has been the magazine for enthusiasts, black-project researchers and military monitors. From humble beginnings it grew to a subscribers' list of several thousand before Douglass recently opted to use the Internet to get his message out. Douglass has gained both the respect and the attention of the FBI in his quest for the truth about secret aircraft – he found that his house had been bugged by persons unknown and the FBI tried to set him up on a 'bum rap' a few years ago (Patton, 1994).

Douglass, born in Idaho, initially developed an interest in the possibilities of radio monitoring when he used scanning equipment to tune in to local police activity while working for the *Amarillo Globe Times* newspaper in Texas. Douglass shot to fame in 1986 when he heard a Russian nuclear submarine in trouble and in need of help. The vessel had a major problem with its reactor core and he recorded panic-stricken sailors screaming that the radiation counters on board were going up.

Another major success for the intrepid frequency hacker took place three years later in 1989 when he heard a now famous communication between an aircraft using the call sign 'Gaspipe' in conversation with 'Joshua Control'. He managed to snap photographs of a most unusual contrail known to black-projects researchers as the 'donuts on a rope' pattern. Through this piece of luck Douglass was able to determine that the plane in question probably used an advanced pulse-jet engine (Douglass; Sweetman, 1993; Peebles).

Despite the fact that scrambling communications is very expensive, one would have thought that the operators of black-world aircraft could hide their activities a little more effectively. However, as

Douglass himself says, opportunities to pick up vital communications are few and far between. In addition, the monitor seeking access to the secrets of the black world needs to have a detailed understanding of aircraft designations, call signs and aircraft numbers, otherwise a few seconds of new information could be lost. Then there's the problem of where to look. There are thousands and thousands of frequencies across the spectrum and it sometimes seems like the hunt for the proverbial needle in the haystack (Douglass).

Behind the Lies

We have seen how UK military monitors associated with my research were so helpful in terms of the 5 June 1997 incident. Another example of the value of the monitors in stripping away the lies surrounding secret aircraft becomes apparent in the following example.

The transmission took place on a frequency of 6.812 MHz (Upper Side Band) at 11.10 pm on 12 October 1992. Douglass takes up the story:

> A general placed a phone patch from SAM (Special Air Mission) 294 through Andrews AFB to 'AF [Air Force] Public Relations'. A secret aircraft was discussed. The general quoted an article in the 'Post' as well as the previous article in 'Jane's'. The general said 'It's almost laughable the number of hokey inputs they had – it's kind of similar to the UFO flap. We need to develop a release in response to inquiries.
>
> 'The guts of this should be that we've looked at the technical aspects of the sightings and what the logical answers for them are. You can quote Dr Mori and site the Lincoln Lab physics and the FAA's efforts to debunk other incidents.
>
> 'Most of the sightings were accounted for in the Q&A yesterday in a media available press release. Go through three or four sightings, **take each one and conclude with a paragraph that says that fantasy of Aurora doesn't exist'** [TM's emphasis] (see Patton, 1997).

They went on to discuss the sighting in the North Sea from an oil-drilling platform. 'Someone saw something accompanied by three F-111s. The Secretary wants us to talk with McCann and say it was an F-117A. I'll get together with Alex – write up a memo to the Chief or the Secretary.'

This conversation explains a great deal about the modern-day UFO phenomenon. While much of it clearly relates to military aircraft, sightings are actively debunked by the military at the highest levels. Aircraft like the F-117, now over 20 years old, are being replaced by a new generation of stealth aircraft with technologies developed in highly secret laboratories and test facilities found behind a smoke-screen of secrecy and active disinformation (Rich and Janos; Douglass; Zinngrabe). The latter must relate in part to stories about aliens.

Secrecy: A Military Necessity

Why the secrecy? Quite simply because black aircraft and their coun-terparts give the USA a distinct advantage over its enemies. The magic of stealth technology has now been understood and passed on to coun-tries in Europe, the Middle and Far East.

The Russians are rumoured to have various stealth aircraft under development although finance may be the undoing of any future programme (Douglass). Even the Iranians have been able to develop basic stealth technologies through their dealings with the French. Military monitoring has helped us to understand the need for the UFO cover-up: it is based on military necessity.

Despite the secrecy, only those tasked to prevent leaks from Area 51 have chosen to encrypt radio transmissions. The only other way for the controllers of Air Force Flight Test Centre Detachment 3 to maintain secrecy is to prevent spotters from gaining visual access to Groom Lake. That is exactly what they have done through the closure of Freedom Ridge overlooking the base (Campbell, UFOMIND web site).

There are other ways to detect UFOs beyond seeing or hearing their operation. Steve Douglass and others have claimed that the real aliens are those responsible for the overbearing secrecy surrounding black programmes. These are the faceless men who inhabit lonely, anonymous and seemingly unimportant offices inside the Pentagon. There is always a great deal of paper generated by military programmes, and one man hot on the trail is Paul McGinnis, nick-named 'Trader'. He operates an anti-secrecy site on the Internet (*see* references) and when one fights one's way past obscure designations and the exhaustive details of Special Access Required ('black') programmes, further evidence of the UFO cover-up – and its tremen-dous cost – emerges.

One of the areas which seems to cause tremendous confusion is that of security and classification (Pike). The system that operates in the USA at least is much more complicated than that used in Britain, where the draconian Official Secrets Act covers just about everything relating to government activity whether it be civilian or military.

Secrecy Layered Like a Russian Doll

The system operating in the USA is used to protect the confidentiality of certain military, foreign policy and intelligence information. The money and effort required to cover this small part of government activity is enormous. According to John Pike of the Federation of American Scientists (FAS), the system has not changed much in 40 years and has 'grown out of control' with more and more information becoming classified regardless of its actual intelligence value. In fact, we might have a situation where some information will have been classified years ago and those responsible for its classification may be retired or dead!

The system operates on three main levels: Confidential, Secret and Top Secret. Besides these are nine other special categories including Department of Defense Special Access Programs (SAPS), Department of Energy Special Programs, and Director of Sensitive Compartmented Information Programs (DCI SCI). Special Access Programs, for instance Have Blue, limit access to classified information to those it is felt 'need to know' about a part or parts of a programme. This is not by any means dependent on rank. The number of people granted such access is strictly limited in order to protect the information. Every SAP is given a classified code word and often an unclassified nick name. Beyond this is Sensitive Compartmented Information (SCI), which relates to information that the US Government wishes to keep hidden and unacknowledged publicly. Pike says:

> *A code word is a single word (such as UMBRA, the code word for communication intelligence; RUFF applies to imagery intelligence, etc.) assigned a classified meaning to proper security concerning intentions, and to safeguard information pertaining to actual military plans or operations classified as Confidential or higher.*

UMBRA is a code word that frequently appears in UFO literature, despite the fact that there is almost no chance of anyone involved in a Special Access Program speaking to UFO researchers. Given the three main designations, Confidential, Secret and Top Secret, then why do we hear so many rumours within Ufology about the '38 levels above Top Secret' and 'Q' clearances (Ellsberg on McGinnis web site; Good, 1992). Perhaps the answer lies in the myths propagated by Bob Lazar and information received from Daniel Ellsberg. Much of what Ellsberg had to say has been taken to heart by modern-day researchers.

But Who Has an Overview?

Ellsberg testified before the Joint Senate Hearings held on 17 May 1973 by the Committees on Judiciary and Government Operations. He talked about a nested structure of security classifications – of secrecy like a Russian doll where you strip away one layer or grant access to certain information only to find that there is more and more beyond your reach. He was particularly concerned about the question of over-sight and argued that the system of classification was fully understood by so few people that it militated against the existence of a free society through American democracy.

He argued that the press was routinely lied to (as we have seen through our interception of the October 1992 patch through Andrews Air Force Base, p. 187) and that there were multiple levels of secrecy – some whose very existence was known to only a handful of people. The only way to keep secrets was to lie in order to keep people in the dark. Becoming involved in Special Access Program or with Sensitive Compartmented Information was tantamount to a 'conspiratorial honour among thieves'.

This is all very subjective of course. Depending on one's point of view, should black programmes be hidden and buried by a tissue of lies? How expensive or dangerous are the new technologies and for whose benefit have they been brought into being?

Hidden Black-budget Finance

These are the important questions, and a look at black programmes funding through Freedom of Information Act requests gives us cause for concern. The annual black budget figures indicate that tens of billions are available with some $15 billion to be spent on black-project research and development and $21 billion on black projects procure-ment (Sweetman, X-Planes, 1998). This means that more is spent on black programmes in the USA than on healthcare or education. The budget is documented in requests for funding decided by select Congressional committees. These are then published in limited form in order to hide projects from supposed enemies and from the public – and from elected officials. The black budget comprises two elements: procurement and RDTE (Research, Development, Testing and Evaluation).

Of specific interest to us in terms of UFOs is the Air Force RDTE budget. Looking at the limited amount of information available for classified military spending, we discover some intriguing figures and technologies. 'Program element 0207248F' is a special evaluation programme amounting to $53 million for a variety of aircraft at Groom Lake (see Chapter 19), including the Russian Sukhoi Su-23. It should be remembered that a number of MIG jets were captured by the USA from the Russians in the past to be tested there. US systems were tested against them as well. Program element 020742F is an evaluation and analysis programme allocated $85 million. It is said to be related to hypersonic aircraft studies. McGinnis points out that up to 1994 the studies might be related to the COPPER COAST programme. COPPER COAST and COPPER CANYON are two examples of the code names used. McGinnis believes that the USA is still fighting the Cold War. Certainly the bunker mentality continues to affect decision-making (see Zinngrabe).

In any case, a quick perusal of the classified Department of Defense programmes gives a clear indication of the vast sums of money being spent: the Army Operations and Maintenance (O&M) budget shows $1 billion for a reconnaissance satellite, a Navy RDTE budget of $8 billion, an Air Force Procurement budget for 'selected activities' totalling $4 billion.

The immense sums of money being spent on secret projects show that they are continuing to flourish, even under the Clinton administration, which has claimed to be committed to greater accountability. However, attempts to move away from the Reagan–Bush mindset and the reality of black-world funding seem either to have completely failed or to be a typical example of rhetoric and good intentions signifying nothing.

The growth in classified spending is most apparent in the US Air Force RDTE budget. It rose from $12.9 billion to $14.4 billion between 1993 and 1997. McDaid and Oliver (1998) note that the CIA has been responsible for covert sponsorship of advanced UAV systems like the Gnat 750 and the Predator, which now flourish in the white world. Undoubtedly their development is mirrored by black-world systems too. Quite clearly companies like Lockheed, Boeing and McDonnell Douglas continue to be funded by the various agencies to develop more and more advanced aircraft (Sweetman, X-Planes, 1998; Rose, 1997).

Billion-dollar Shadowcraft

These are the UFOs of today – and tomorrow – and that is why we should forget about the 'search for extraterrestrial intelligence' and instead focus on the billion-dollar shadowcraft that operate above our heads. As stealthchasers point out, the Lockheed Martin Skunk

Works' car park is still full and yet official pronouncements would have us believe that only a couple of reconnaissance UAVs have been built in the last few years (*see* Rich and Janos). Over the water at Warton in Lancashire the car park is also full, yet we are told that the only thing going on is a bit of study or concept work and limited research into STOVL technologies.

The truth about structured UFOs is that they have their origins in these hidden programmes. Who knows what quality of black aircraft is hidden behind the secrecy and disinformation? Never forget that in the USA alone a substantial amount of the money spent on each black project relates to the maintenance of secrecy and the extra measures that go with it (Rich and Janos). Therefore, leading Ufologists up the garden path by putting out stories through a variety of channels about 'alien crash landings' and secret government research groups like 'Majestic 12' would seem to be money very well spent.

Numerous researchers have claimed that a programme called 'Senior Citizen' has been responsible for UFO sightings. Some have claimed that it is an example of 'recovered alien' technology. Luckily, we have several means of attacking the glacier of government secrecy. Paul McGinnis would probably tell you that the devil is in the detail and his exposure of Senior Citizen not as a hypersonic aircraft, as was initially suspected by most black-project analysts (FAS), but a stealthy transport is central to our understanding not only of military UFOs but of military secrecy.

This case study indicates that by comparing the 1993 Department of Defense document DoD7045.7-H, the FYDP Program Structure indicates that Senior Citizen (Program Element 0401316F) is tactical lift aircraft. Several Short-Take-Off and Landing (STOL) aircraft have been funded under the 04013XXX Program Element. McGinnis believes that there are strong links between the tactical Vertical- or Short-Take-Off and Landing (V/STOL) and the conceptual aircraft described in documents produced at the Technology Exploitation Directorate at Wright-Patterson Air Force Base. These show an impression of a delta-wing aircraft. This is almost exactly the same as a picture put out by Boeing which shows an 'Advanced Theater Transport' aircraft. This concept was described as a 'next generation theater airlifter'.

A report in *Commerce Business Daily*, 1988 (*see* McGinnis web site), indicated that V/STOL technologies would be essential and that the company awarded the contract would have to be able to 'conduct programmes at classification levels up through Top Secret. Special Access Required'. For Ufologists the alarm bells should be ringing: an advanced-technology stealth aircraft able to take off vertically and almost certainly fly at low speed and/or hover.

Always ask yourself: what are they going to use these aircraft for? Given the 'Top Secret' compartmented nature of such a programme and the probable use of such technology for troop insertion and covert activities, perhaps we should conclude that the operators of such an aircraft would need to test it over dry land. There is no point in testing something like this out to sea because that is not where it will be used!

McGinnis and the other stealthchasers – the military monitors, the people waiting with their video cameras – are fighting the modern-day equivalent of the 'war of the flea' in their attempts to get nearer to the truth.

Perhaps they are doing more to help us identify 'UFOs' than mainstream Ufology has done in 50 years.

EIGHTEEN

STEALTH 101

HOW DO THOSE tasked with the development of a stealth aircraft programme carry out their job? There are many rumours within Ufological circles – most based on flawed information or wishful thinking.

To give just one example: the 'Have Blue' programme that led to the development of the F-117A can answer many of the objections that Ufologists have to the suggestion that secret aircraft are responsible for UFO sightings. Ask a UFO researcher where stealth technology came from, and more than likely he or she will say something about Groom Lake and/or the 'UFO crash' at Roswell (Hamilton; Randle and Schmitt; Hesemann and Mantle). If only things were that simple.

In actual fact the development of stealth technology emerged as a practical response to a specific military need: the need to remain unde-tected by enemy systems especially in the radar and infra-red spectra. Although the SR-71 spyplane had a relatively low Radar Cross Section (RCS), Russian systems could still detect it at a range of around 100 miles (160 km).

Although the 'Blackbird's' high speed would probably save it from missile attack, the use of the Soviet SA-6 missile had devastated Israeli air forces during the war with Egypt in October 1973. There were fears that advances in ground-to-air missiles might make US air forces obso-lete.

RCS Reduction

As a result of what was learned in the Israeli war with Egypt, a new system was required whereby the RCS of an aircraft could be reduced, and not just by a half, or even by 90 per cent. What was required was a new type of aircraft entirely given to 'stealth', which could not be detected by enemy systems until it was too late to respond. (Even the most advanced active stealth systems do not make an aircraft entirely invisible – a tiny return may be measured but there is no way that this will be detected *and* identified as hostile.) The term 'stealth' appears to have been coined by Charles 'Chuck' Myers, a combat pilot who was also an executive with Lockheed (Sweetman and Goodall; Sweetman, April/May 1997).

Stealth was not new, at least not the idea that a drastic RCS reduction would give an important comparative military advantage to the country able to develop it. As I noted in Chapter 1, the Horten brothers' flying-wing designs were inherently stealthy. The shaping, in combination with a primitive wood/glue/sawdust composite, made them simply years ahead of their time. Unfortunately, no one had quite been able to decipher the complexities related to low-observable technology, whereby one could calculate the RCS of a given shape. The answer was hidden inside obscure nineteenth-century equations devised by Scottish physicist James Clerk Maxwell.

In the meantime, a Russian expert in theoretical optics named Pyotr Ufimtsev had shown how to calculate the RCS of an aircraft (Rich and Janos). Denys Overholser, a young designer at the Skunk Works, called in to help develop a new low-RCS technology, cottoned on to this. By refining Ufimtsev's theories, he was able to determine that an aircraft whose shape allowed for incoming radar beams to be deflected or scattered *away* from source would have a very low RCS. This meant that an aircraft would have to comprise flat panels expertly angled. This technique was called faceting, and as long as the panels never faced directly towards a radar system, then stealth could be achieved (Sweetman, April/May 1997). The reader may be asking what any of this has to do with aliens. The answer is simple – absolutely nothing.

The work undertaken by Lockheed was a response to a Defense Advanced Research Projects Agency study code-named 'Harvey' which sought to develop the lowest-RCS aircraft possible. Other companies were awarded small grants to develop similar systems and these included both Northrop and McDonnell Douglas (Sweetman and Goodall).

It soon emerged that Northrop and Lockheed were the main competitors; it was decided that the different concepts should be tested against each other at the Radar Cross Section range at Holloman Air Force Base. Two experimental survivable testbed (XST) aircraft were tested. The Lockheed design had the lowest RCS.

The cut-diamond (nicknamed 'hopeless diamond') shape of the Lockheed design was most unusual – almost alien-looking in that it had no curved surfaces, and an unconventional tail. There were many problems to overcome; up until 1976 the project was entirely theoretical, and little thought had been given to the vital questions of the powerplant, flight control systems and so forth. How could stealth be maintained with the heat signature of the engines or a cockpit protruding at the front? After Skunk Works guru Ben Rich persuaded DARPA to fund a demonstrator programme starting in January 1977, the stealth project was given the code name 'Have Blue'. Now the biggest questions of all had to be resolved: where could the aircraft be developed and what new measures would have to be taken in order to protect this most vital technological asset (Rich and Janos)? The answers should tell UFO researcher a number of things.

Programmes like the Lockheed U-2 and A-12 'Oxcart' – although CIA-sponsored – paled into insignificance compared to Have Blue. The first photograph of the U-2 had appeared in 1956, so any secrecy had been maintained for only a short time. Both aircraft had been designed for high-altitude overflights of enemy territory (Miller, *Lockheed's Skunk Works*, 1995).

'Have Blue'

'Have Blue' was different – it was a tactical strike aircraft designed to get in behind enemy lines and get out without detection. As a result, the XST proof-of-concept aircraft was taken to the most secret place in the world: Groom Lake in Nevada. Ben Rich and Leo Janos recalled a conversation with Kelly Johnson relating to the new stealth programme:

> *Ben, the security they're sticking onto this thing will kill you. It will increase your costs twenty-five percent and lower your efficiency to the point where you won't get any work done. The restrictions will eat you alive. Get them to reclassify this thing or drop it.*

No reclassification took place, but at Groom Lake secrecy was pretty much guaranteed. Nevertheless, only months after the XST arrived at Groom Lake, UFO researcher and former CIA pilot John Lear found himself able to get within a reasonable distance of Groom Lake and take a famous photograph of the layout there (Sweetman and Goodall; Brookesmith, 1996). This kind of photographic intelligence might have given away just a few of its secrets, including the fact that Soviet aircraft were tested there (Lear captured a MIG-21 on film sitting outside one of the hangars), had it not been for the fact that the photograph was not published until 1990. Lear apparently did have a run-in with security personnel. In the book *Skunk Works* by Ben Rich and Leo Janos and the brochure *Lockheed Horizons* (Lockheed Corporation, 1992), Groom Lake is not mentioned in relation to the Have Blue programme.

At Groom Lake measures to restrict access to the programme included locking other personnel in a windowless mess hall during test flights. 'Special Access' requirements in themselves facilitated a great deal of necessary secrecy but early on sight-sensitivity could have been a problem. Just seeing the aircraft may not have been enough for a 'loose cannon' to have been able to determine its possible use, but the smallest leak to the press could have made life very difficult. Still, the powers-that-be determined that it was all right to test the aircraft during daylight hours. After all, one only arrived inside Area 51 with the highest clearance. Everyone else, including Lear, soon found security personnel on their heels.

Another reason to screen those in any way connected with Have Blue was not only the low-RCS technology, but its possible *use*. In 1978 it was thought that this kind of aircraft could be a 'silver bullet' – to be used to take out a perceived high-value enemy with 'full deniability'. Under a rather insane plan known as 'Downshift 02' the Soviet president was deemed a potential target.

Given the amazing possibilities offered by stealth, it was decided that an autonomous and fully equipped home for the project within the USA was required for further development. This was Tonapah, a disused Sandia National Laboratories airstrip within the Nellis AFB test ranges. Tonopah was approximately 140 miles (230 km) from Las Vegas and suitably remote. Tonopah afforded the operators the chance to fly their 'Top Secret' bird unseen. Of course, the arrival of technicians, engineers and strange aircraft would not have gone unnoticed, so a programme of active disinformation – of the sort that black projects and some UFO researchers have become accustomed to – was set in place.

Under this programme, and knowing that Soviet spy satellites could photograph the base from above, it was decided to create the 4450th Test Group with the cover story that this was simply a flight test unit operating A-7 aircraft associated with Nellis Air Force Base (Lake).

In order to encourage the view that nothing of great interest was going on, A-7s were routinely left outside the hangars at Tonopah and were painted with over-large '4450 TG' markings on their tails. Personnel involved in the work commuted between Nellis and Tonopah in Boeing 727 airliners operated by Key Airlines – a company associated with similar activities at the Skunk Works and Groom Lake.

There was no way that test pilots could be chosen through the usual means whereby they would respond to an advertisement, so they were selected, asked to attend an interview and told to maintain secrecy. They were also told that they would be flying A-7s. The pilots chosen to test the F-117A had to be the best. They had to pass through the test programme; there was no way that they could be allowed to make the grade only to drop out later. That situation could lead to an embittered pilot becoming a security risk. As a result screening was very tough – the pilots were not even allowed to tell their close families what they were up to. Potential pilots were flown to Tonopah in blacked-out helicopters for interview.

Aircraft testing took place at Tonopah exclusively at night and the pilots were housed 7 miles (11 km) away from the aircraft in dedicated accommodation. They had to pass through security before gaining access to the central operating compound and this included a palm-print scan. The compound itself was protected by the highest security measures.

F-117A: First Image

It was not until November 1988 that the first image of the aircraft was made public. The existence of stealth *technology* had been hinted at in a press conference in 1980, by all accounts a rather desperate attempt to save the Carter administration and one that failed miserably. Nevertheless for eight years – owing to a range of particularly effective measures – the F-117A was kept secret. In fact, it was a triumph of deception and active disinformation. Only the vaguest ideas about the potential shape of the aircraft emerged. Artists' impressions themselves were very vague, and some researchers – including those at *Quest* magazine in England – argued that the new aircraft would not look triangular (Birdsall, 1988). Although well-informed, even the pseudonymous J. Jones claimed in his 1989 book that the F-117A employed 'several thousand flat surfaces' in order to reflect radar. He also suggested that active camouflage using smart skins might be used.

The F-117A had been operational for several years by the time its existence was fully acknowledged. This should serve as a reminder to the UFO research community that, just because the military deny the existence of a programme and actively seek to debunk sightings related to it, this does not mean that the craft reported are of extraterrestrial origin. There is a further and salutary reminder to Ufologists: too many of them deny that US stealth aircraft could be responsible for

UFO sightings. In the specific case of the F-117A it should be remembered that as early as 1985 the F-117A was landing at UK bases. In 1987 RAF pilots were flying the F-117A (Cook, *Interavia*, 1995) and had been involved in exchange visits to Groom Lake from 1957 (Bissell).

We can see how other stealth technologies developed in the 1970s, and how at least one aircraft related to the competition for the original 1974 DARPA stealth technology demonstrator contract has been responsible for UFO sightings. These include the TR-3A – the 'Black Manta' – and other triangular aircraft: the next generation.

Although the F-117A was landing at bases in the UK from 1985 onwards on irregular occasions, it was not responsible for the majority of 'structured' UFO reports.

In fact, it appears that a grand deception was taking place over the heads of the least suspecting members of the public. They lived in the countryside of sleepy Staffordshire and near the gritty South Yorkshire mining town of Barnsley. What they saw were UAVs, and the UAVs were UFOs.

NINETEEN

GROOM LAKE – AREA 51

GROOM LAKE WAS almost unheard of when Lockheed pilot Tony LeVier set out to find a new remote location for the 'Top Secret' CIA-sponsored U-2 spyplane to be test-flown. It was April 1955 and he was under strict orders from Lockheed guru Kelly Johnson to 'find us a place out in the desert somewhere where we can test this thing in secret. And don't tell anyone what you're up to.' Le Vier thought that he had found the perfect place for secret operations – it was essentially in the middle of nowhere. He said much later: 'I gave it a ten plus. Just dandy. A dry lake bed about three and a half miles around' (Rich and Janos).

What was more, the surface of the lake bed was rock-hard. A few days after this initial discovery, Le Vier flew back out to the location with a man he knew as 'Mr B' – Richard Bissell of the CIA (Bissell). Even more conveniently, the nearby nuclear test site was off limits to unauthorized air traffic, which meant that prying eyes would be unlikely to see anything without considerable effort. Bissell might not have realized the irony when he named the new site 'Paradise Ranch' – a title that immediately captured something of the mystery and magic of the stunning setting and magical technologies that would come together just a few months later. The first U-2 arrived at Groom Lake on 23 July 1955.

A Most Secret Place

It is not known whether Groom Lake was seen as a permanent location at this early stage, but it soon became clear that this was the best place to carry out further classified activities. The U-2 project was well hidden through the use of both strict security measures and active disinformation. Lockheed Skunk Works employees who knew about the aircraft referred to it only as the 'article' or by its project names 'Aquatone' and 'Idealist'. A new and anonymous special office to handle the bureaucratic side of things was set up in Washington, DC in temporary wartime buildings while other facilities were located above a car repair shop (Patton, 1997)!

Everything was flown in to Groom Lake and even the pilots were not entirely sure where they were heading. Upon approaching 'The Ranch' they were given a new set of instructions from 'Sage Control', and only became aware of the remote runway at the last minute. Beyond these measures on-site personnel were able to contact their families only in case of emergency.

This kind of security ensured that secrets remained secret. Similar measures were used for all black programmes after that. By 1956 six pilots from Strategic Air Command were training with the U-2 and by June 1958 Roger Ernst, Assistant Secretary of the Interior, was creating an area of 60 square miles (155 sq km) for further use. Although the operations were hidden behind activities 'by the Atomic Energy Commission in connection with the Nevada Test Site', there was now a secure area around Groom Lake. Throughout the late 1950s and 1960s a great deal of building work took place. New facilities for the military and other contractors were built, a fuel farm with a capacity of over 1 million gallons (about 4 million litres) was completed and over 1,000 personnel were located on site (Patton, 1997).

The nature of the 'special relationship' between the UK and the USA is further demonstrated by the arrival of 'three or four' RAF pilots at Groom Lake who underwent training on the U-2 in 1957 in order to be able to allow overflights of the USSR to be undertaken from RAF Lakenheath (Bissell).

Depending on whom you believe, flying saucers and flying triangles – UFOs – arrived at Groom Lake early on. Some researchers I have spoken to say that the saucers arrived in 1959–60.

Area 51

Just about everybody has a view on Groom Lake and Area 51, and I have drawn on several excellent sources. The first is Glenn Campbell's Area 51 Research Center, located in the small town of Rachel, Nevada (where Pat and Joe Travis have their 'Little Ale'Inn), and on the Internet (www.ufomind.com). The web site includes everything one needs to know about Area 51: its purpose, the people who guard it and the people who want to penetrate the web of secrecy that surrounds it.

Campbell is the best-known and most effective advocate for release of information on what he believes is 'Air Force Flight Test Centre 3'. Air Force Flight Test Centre, according to Gunston (*Jane's Aerospace Dictionary*, 1986), is headquartered at Edwards Air Force Base. In addition to maintaining the UFOMIND web site, Campbell has written several articles on various aspects of the Area 51 mystery (Campbell, 1994; 1995) and has largely taken on the role of information-provider for Area 51 enthusiasts. His work has been the rock on which most subsequent research has been based. In addition to Campbell, Phil Patton wrote *Travels in Dreamland* (1997) – a comprehensive look at the 'secret history' of Area 51.

Lazar: Genuine, Fraud or Obscurant?

The central character around whom swirl many of the fantastic tales surrounding this most secret place is Bob Lazar. Lazar came to prominence after a 1989 TV documentary made by George Knapp for KLAS-TV. The Lazar story is not provable, because it is almost impossible to demonstrate that the secret facility 'S4' – located south-west of Groom Lake – exists. We can only make inferences and come to the most tentative conclusions.

Campbell's favourite book on the subject was written by David Darlington. Entitled *Area 51 – The Dreamland Chronicles,* the book allows the main players to have their say: Bob Lazar, Lazar apologist Gene Huff, Bob Uhouse (the man who claims, with little or no evidence, to have worked on 'alien' flight simulators), Pat and Joe Travis (proprietors of the Little Ale'Inn), John Andrews of Testors Models, and Tom Mahood, whose Blue Fire web site provides an in-depth critique of Lazar's background and claims. Timothy Good has, in my opinion, presented the most succinct and understandable report on the Lazar story in his *Alien Liaison* (Good, 1992).

Surprisingly perhaps, Stanton Friedman has taken issue with certain of Lazar's claims about the supposed propulsion system used to power the extraterrestrial flying discs that Lazar is reported to have worked on between 1988 and 1989 (Friedman). Michael Hesemann, co-author of *Beyond Roswell* (1997) and editor of the popular German-language *Magazin 2000*, interviewed Lazar and several other researchers for his video documentary *Secrets of the Black World* (1993); similar material appeared on *Dreamland,* a British-made documentary put together by Bruce Burgess and shown on British TV on several occasions in 1997.

Of course, it is said by supporters of the extraterrestrial hypothesis,

Wendelle Stevens (Hesemann, video documentary, 1993), for example, that S4 ties in with the Roswell UFO crash retrieval, because the craft (perhaps even the bodies!) were transported there via other military facilities sometime in the late 1950s or early 1960s. This is a problematic and reductive conclusion, especially given the increasing doubts about the Roswell episode that have surfaced in recent years (Jeffrey, 1997; Pflock).

The area around Groom Lake has been the subject of several governmental land-grabs, especially since 1995. Until 1995 one could hike up a mountain known as Freedom Ridge and by using high-powered binoculars get a view of the secret facilities some 28 miles (45 km) away that the US government denies exist (Powers; Campbell, 1995). Now the ridge has been confiscated in a further attempt to seal Groom Lake off from all prying eyes. Secrecy breeds a culture of mistrust and paranoia. No wonder observers and Area 51 researchers don't trust their government.

There are several strands of UFO research relating to Groom Lake and the surrounding Area 51 (technically speaking, this is a restricted box of airspace: the area above Groom Lake). The first is the question of Bob Lazar and the many allegations made by him in relation to a secret flying-saucer engineering facility located 15 miles (24 km) south at Papoose Dry Lake (Good, 1992; Patton, 1997).

There is no doubt that all kinds of aircraft have been flown from Area 51 since the mid-1950s, undoubtedly many more than the U-2, A-12, SR-71 and F-117. This was reflected in a widely circulated US Air Force statement released to journalists in 1994:

> There are a variety of facilities throughout the Nellis Range Complex. We do have facilities within the complex near the dry lake bed of Groom lake. The facilities of the Nellis Range Complex are used for testing and training technologies, operations, and systems critical to the effectiveness of US military forces. Specific activities conducted at Nellis cannot be discussed any further than that.

UFO researcher John Lear was able to get near enough to Groom Lake in 1978 to take a well-known photograph of the facilities there (Sweetman and Goodall; Brookesmith, 1996). Nevertheless, there seems to be a gap in testing between 1968 and 1977 when the Have Blue stealth prototype that led the development of the F-117 'Nighthawk' arrived: nine years and apparently little activity of note? Did other, more exotic aircraft arrive at certain of the facilities housed within the Nellis Range Complex appear during this period? It is likely.

Williams' Revelations

At some point flying saucers are said to have arrived. The evidence for this comes not only from 'physicist' Bob Lazar, who emerged in 1989, but also from an earlier source called Leo Marion Williams, a name known only to a few UFO researchers. Williams' story has been covered on only one occasion (Basiago) to my knowledge, and despite the fact that much of the debate about flying saucers and facilities located near Groom Lake focuses on Lazar, Williams' claims are unusually similar. It is said that although advanced and secret aircraft are flown from Groom Lake these are nothing, in technological terms, compared with the machines located at nearby Papoose Dry Lake (Hesemann and Mantle).

Williams died from cancer in 1989 (apparently as a result of coming into contact with certain toxic materials), the year that Lazar appeared on the scene, but it was some 12 years earlier that he is claimed to have first mentioned a secret saucer base to a close relative. Williams reportedly said, in 1976, that the facility was to be found inside Area 51 at a base known only as 'S4'.

According to Basiago, Williams had been with the CIA for 30 years and had been involved in counter-intelligence. After developing cataracts in the 1970s, he had to resign from the CIA whereupon he gained employment with Lockheed. At this time he was informed (it is not clear by whom) that he would be required to travel to a 'super-secret' base in Nevada where recovered alien technologies and alien entities were being studied. Williams was flown to Area 51, then driven to S4 in a bus with blacked-out windows. The base location was therefore unknown and its structure was integrated into the surrounding terrain in order to hide it from Russian satellites.

The base itself was of a most unusual level of security, higher than even Williams had ever experienced. There is a suggestion that even back in the 1970s these measures included retinal and hand-print scanning as standard (for an interesting and possibly related example of this see *Lockheed Horizons*, Lockheed Corporation, May 1992). He was told several things including stories that the stealth bomber was using principles based on alien technologies.

Basiago claims to have spoken to one of the man's relatives, himself a highly credible professional. It is said that Williams had told the story because he knew that he was dying of cancer and that he had little to fear from his former employers. If it is true that these allegations were first made to the unnamed relative in 1976 then other stories relating to S4 are more likely to be true.

A typical example of the anecdotal material relating to S4 is as follows and is said to come from a repair mechanic stationed at nearby Groom Lake in the late 1960s. He soon learned that there was little to do after work had finished beyond drinking, so he took to exploring the nearby area. Both he and other colleagues decided to see how far they could walk without being challenged and during these excursions they saw little of note. One of the few areas declared off-limits was Papoose Dry Lake (Campbell, Area 51 Research Center, and UFOMIND web site, *Groom Lake Desert Rat*, 1995).

Remember that even our mechanic would have had very high clearance to work at Groom; this fact might indicate that Papoose Dry Lake had higher or separate security arrangements. Certainly other workers have heard mention of a place called 'S4'.

Mark Farmer, aviation enthusiast and friend of respected Area 51 researcher Tom Mahood, has seen unusual things near Papoose Dry Lake. In January 1994 at 10 pm he saw a glowing light shaped like a squashed ball rise from behind the Groom Mountains from a location off Highway 375 (recently named the 'Extra-Terrestrial Highway') and perform a series of most unconventional manoeuvres including sharp changes of direction.

Other sightings made by a variety of witnesses are featured in the various Area 51 videos on the market. Researcher Gary Schulz was able to photograph a saucer-like object in 1990 (Hesemann, video documentary, 1993). It is not clear whether these are structured craft or lights resulting from some sort of energy weapons testing.

Bob Lazar's Story

Leo Williams' story is remarkably similar to that of Bob Lazar, who shot to fame in 1989 after exposing potentially the biggest story of the twentieth century. Lazar said that extraterrestrials had crashed on earth and the remains of the craft had been taken to S4 within Area 51 – the location of an alien saucer testing site! Lazar went into more detail than Williams, and he too claimed to have been transported to the secure location in a blacked-out bus. Specifically, Lazar claimed that he had been asked to work on the propulsion system of the 'recovered' saucer and that this involved some sort of 'anti-gravity' system using 'element 115' for fuel (Good, 1992).

This part of the story was especially problematic for a number of reasons, including our certain knowledge that terrestrial saucer development programmes had existed for some 40 years previously. In other words, the story would need to be credible in terms of the supposed 'anti-gravity' propulsion system.

Unfortunately, the idea that the highly unstable, nuclear and (very) short-life 'element 115' of the periodic table could be used to power such a saucer was met with derision by many within the UFO community. Heaven knows what mainstream science made of it all. Critical Ufologists included former nuclear engineer Stanton Friedman and his many colleagues who, although quite happy with the idea of secret facilities and saucers, were particularly scathing about the rest. Such materials have certain characteristics:

> They have very short half lives, existing on average for perhaps a millionth of second. Only very small numbers of these atoms are produced despite enormous effort to produce them in huge accelerators.
>
> They are all radioactive hence dangerous in one way or another, which means they decay rapidly. All elements above 90, including uranium, are radioactive. Uranium has a half-life measured in millions of years. Depending on the isotope, plutonium's half-life can be 27,000 years. Cobalt 60, which is used for medical purposes, has a half-life of 5.3 years. This is a relatively long life, and large amounts can be accumulated by exposing certain cobalt isotopes in reactors (Friedman).

Lazar claimed that a small amount of the material was used to power the flying saucer, to which he had only partial access. He had handled it and through nefarious means both he and John Lear had managed to spirit some of the material out of S4 only to have it stolen back by shadowy agents both unknown and unseen!

At this stage the Lazar testimony starts to look shaky. Beyond the obvious problems with the radioactive element 115 and Lazar's impossible claim that large amounts were stored at the facility, there is the whole question of certain other claims that he made from 1989.

He said that he had various scientific qualifications and that he had been looking for gainful employment in the Las Vegas area. Although supposedly the inventor of a high-powered jet car, he had been employed as a lowly photo shop technician. He was supposed to have passed his *curriculum vitae* to various people involved in the military/industrial complex (including Edward Teller, or 'Ed' as Lazar called him), apparently coming up trumps when he was invited for interview at EG&G (the security company Edgerton, Germeshausen and Grier). He was subsequently accepted for employment at S4.

There are tremendous problems with Lazar's story, especially in terms of his academic qualifications — which do not stand up to close scrutiny (Mahood).

Although we might be prepared to believe that a maverick scientist could gain access to a secret facility, we would expect him or her to have a degree of some kind in a relevant discipline. After all, there are many suitably qualified people within striking distance of Area 51, most notably in southern California's Antelope Valley, the home of the bulk of the US aerospace industry. Investigations into Lazar's supposed academic qualifications leave us in little doubt that something is terribly wrong with his testimony.

Born in 1959, he claims to have attended Los Angeles Pierce College even though school records from the W. Tresper Clarke High School in Westbury, Long Island, New York, indicate that he finished 261st out of a class of 369 (Mahood; Patton, 1997). This placed him in the bottom third, whereas entry to respectable institutions of higher education, including Cal Tech or Massachusetts Institute of Technology (MIT), which he also claimed to have attended and graduated from, required placement within the top 10 per cent of students.

Lazar further claims to have gained a Bachelor of Science degree in Physics and Technology from Pacifica University. Unfortunately, Pacifica was shut down by the State of California for selling degrees the same year that Lazar said he gained his qualification. Rather disconcertingly, he also argued that sometime in 1977–8 he attended California State University before moving on to Cal Tech. The student year books from 1977 to 1982 were checked by Tom Mahood and no entry for our man could be found. If he did not have a Bachelor's degree, then it is highly improbable that he attended MIT in 1982.

Mahood notes that both Stanton Friedman and Glenn Campbell checked with MIT and once again found no listings or supporting evidence. It appears that in the same year he might have been employed as a technician for one of the subcontractors at Los Alamos National Laboratory. A possible link with Edward Teller came through a supposed meeting that took place between the men before a lecture Teller gave at Los Alamos in June 1982 to a packed audience. Again, you either believe it or you don't – there is no corroborating evidence. Soon afterwards Lazar moved into the photo-processing business. This was only marginally successful and serious financial and marital problems hampered him. You might conclude that this made him the perfect S4 employee – easy to debunk with a colourful background. It was apparently in 1988 that Lazar met ex-CIA pilot and UFO researcher John Lear. The first claimed period of employment at S4 began in December 1988.

Lazar's journey to S4 was typical in so far as he flew from McCarran Airport to Groom Lake, as have thousands of other workers over the years, before being transferred on to the blacked-out bus for the 15-mile (24-km) journey to Papoose Dry Lake.

At this point it might be sensible to introduce a major player in the Area 51 story. 'Janet Airlines' is responsible for ferrying an estimated 2,500 personnel into and out of Groom Lake every day. The aircraft and personnel have been tracked arriving at McCarran airport in Las Vegas. The workers wait for a short time before boarding their flight for the half-hour journey to Groom Lake. The first flight leaves Las Vegas at 4.30 am and the last journey appears to be made at 7 pm, Monday to Friday. There is occasionally a stop at China Lake.

Factual information about the 'Janet' flights is the clearest indication that something major is going on at Area 51. Nobody knows for sure where the name 'Janet' came from, but we do know that false destinations and flight plans are submitted on every occasion that an aircraft leaves the terminal at McCarran, built specifically for Groom workers.

The important point to make is that parts of the story about Groom Lake are believable; we already know that flying saucers existed 40 years before anyone had heard of the bespectacled and ultimately believable Robert Scott Lazar.

During his brief 'period of employment' at S4 he claimed to have been shown a bewildering variety of documents relating to the real origins of flying-saucer technology. In a nutshell, these suggested that for thousands of years alien races had been monitoring mankind and that the saucers were extant examples of recovered alien technology. There were nine hangar bays built into the mountainside where differing flying discs were housed. The craft Lazar worked on, dubbed the 'Sport Model' (and sold in replica model form to many thousands of enthusiasts), was approximately 52 feet (16 m) in length. The other craft were of similar size and this means that altogether the hangar bays required the excavation of over 600 feet (183 m) of rock (by no means impossible according to Sauder).

There were two reasons why Lazar supposedly independently concluded that these saucers were of extraterrestrial origin: firstly, the documents he saw, and secondly, the internal dimensions of the craft, which excluded flight by even a small human pilot. Lazar also said that he had seen, towards the end of his stay at S4, a small grey figure in one of the rooms housed within the secret facility. He refused to be drawn into speculation as to whether this was the evidence of extraterrestrial life that we have all been seeking, and made no mention of seeing any 'live aliens'. Nevertheless, the whole story is suggestive of aliens, even though we could reasonably argue that extraterrestrials might have trouble breathing in our atmosphere!

Bill Uhouse, who provided variations on a theme of Lazar's by claiming that he had been involved in the construction of flight simulators for alien-based aircraft, had no problem with this. He was apparently given telepathic technical instructions and information by an alien called 'Jarod' (Hesemann, video documentary, 1993; Darlington)!

By this stage the S4 story seems dead and buried, if only because talk of aliens seems most unlikely and illogical. If these were crashed craft, then how had the aliens survived – or are we really expected to believe the John Lear or Cooper 'darkside' material which claims that a secret human–alien treaty had been signed years before? Alien technology in return for mutilated cattle and so on (Brookesmith, 1996, Chapter 6). To the sensible author this is either a cleverly erected disinformation ploy – or just plain fiction.

Perhaps the people at the Air Force Flight Test Center (AFFTC) at Edwards Air Force Base feel that advanced technology needs to be hidden behind an alien smokescreen? After all, they control Groom Lake. Do they control the release of disinformation too?

In the end, Lazar became tired of the overbearing and, in his view, unnecessary security at S4 and decided to tell John Lear everything he knew. Most unusually, having been caught showing John Lear, Gene Huff and his wife a flying-saucer test flight in March 1989, Lazar was not immediately 'taken care of' by the authorities. He wasn't the victim of the unfortunate 'accident' we might expect or immediate imprisonment. Those operating Area 51 (AFFTC Det.3) have a number of weapons at their disposal that ensures that hardly any information of note leaks out.

Workers compromising security protocols can have their 'Top Secret' clearances revoked and can be imprisoned for considerable periods of time. Although Lazar claimed to have been debriefed at Indian Springs Airfield on 7 April 1989, he expected us to believe that his clearance was not officially removed and that he was not brought up on official charges. If proponents of the ETH believe that we are living through a 'Cosmic Watergate' then how come Lazar was not buried at the bottom of a pit? If 'they' can cover up details of extraterrestrial–human contact then 'they' can silence whistleblowers. It's as simple as that!

Why go to the bother of flying and bussing the S4 personnel in with other Groom Lake workers? Given the supposed super-secrecy surrounding Papoose Dry Lake, might we be justified in expecting special transportation measures to have been taken? Why not fly the workers in by helicopters with blacked-out windows? More importantly, how did Lazar and/or Leo Williams know they were travelling towards Papoose Dry Lake? Theoretically they could have been travelling elsewhere. Why not fly them in direct, avoiding Groom Lake? Researchers like Mahood and Friedman argue that Lazar was never at S4.

Nevertheless, even if we remove Lazar from the equation we still have flying saucers, and given the fairly impressive segments of video footage shot from positions located along the boundary of Area 51 it appears that some sort of advanced technology is being tested (Hesemann, video documentary, 1993). Is it possible that the Williams story was invented in order to corroborate Lazar or had Lazar heard similar stories via John Lear? The subject is pregnant with possibilities and theories and we end up only with the certain knowledge that as the years have gone by more and more land has been given over to classified use and that every day hundreds of workers are flown into Area 51 in order to work on a variety of undisclosed projects (Powers; Campbell, Area 51 Research Center, UFOMIND web site).

There is, however, enough circumstantial evidence to support several points of view. Just when researchers thought that the contradictory and quite fantastic testimony of Lazar had died a death, an archaeologist, of all people, came along in 1997 and re-opened the Papoose Dry Lake debate.

An Intrepid Archaeologist

The well-known *Las Vegas Sun* newspaper carried a series of articles about a man in search of another elusive quarry. Jerry Freeman sought to track down an inscription made by a member of a lost wagon train that traversed the Nevada area back in 1849 (McCall). The 'lost '49ers', whose demise led to the adoption of the name Death Valley, most unfortunately died in exactly the wrong place: the area surrounding the supposed secret saucer facility! Having not the slightest interest in the dark, mechanical shadowcraft of Ufolore, survival expert Freeman submitted requests for permission to embark on his journey of discovery. He was refused, of course, and took a decision to go ahead in any case! This was an unauthorized trek of over 100 miles (160 miles) through anonymous brush into a 'Top Secret' military heart of darkness.

In this modern-day testament to the pioneering spirit Freeman encountered security, rattlesnakes and near-dehydration. He never found the inscription, but he did find evidence of the wagon train. He also discovered more than he bargained for at Papoose Dry Lake when he saw a security vehicle that moved from place to place. That was not all: from a distance of around 3 miles (5 km) he saw an even more interesting sight: what appeared to be a hangar door, a stationary light getting bigger and smaller in the place where Williams and Lazar testified to the existence of hidden facilities. Freeman could not say for sure that this is what he had seen. Desert rat Glenn Campbell said that the archaeologist had not been near the Groom Lake base but instead some 10–15 miles (16–25 km) south. Why the security vehicles and why the anomalous light? Coincidence? No doubt the unbelievers hope so (McCall).

Glenn Campbell was asked to comment on the story, given his detailed knowledge of the terrain. He agreed that Freeman had actually been within approximately 3 miles (5 km) of Papoose Dry Lake and that the moving lights were consistent with the actual location of the road on the north-east shore of the dry lake bed. The stationary light could have been almost anything although it did seem to indicate an unexpected human presence in the area.

Lazar under the Microscope

In many ways Bob Lazar was an unknown entity as far as his potential S4 employers were concerned: an under-achiever by all accounts, but technically minded, showing occasional flashes of brilliance. His dubious financial dealings throughout the mid-1980s and his maverick status arguably made him the perfect man for a job at S4.

Let us assume for a moment that he did get a job at S4 and that he was involved in working on flying saucers. Surely his past must have been checked out, his contacts and circle of friends put under the microscope? Can we still build a credible case that supports some of his claims? Perhaps the answer is 'yes'. The 'alien' claims are clearly nonsensical and illogical; we have seen how flying saucers were envisaged as 'Top Secret' aircraft from the start.

We have to remove the alien folklore element from our research and concentrate on the UFOs. Then the situation becomes remarkably clear. The stories of crash retrievals and recovered aliens are encouraged either through the dissemination of often cleverly produced fake documents (MJ-12) or through the machinations of anonymous characters who appear on sensationalist TV documentaries hosted by gormless celebrities.

Ultimately, we realize that the saucers do not have to be operated along magnetic or gravitic propulsion principles and that aliens and conspiracies are the result of a need to believe and a need to disinform. These elements come together in tales of saucer sightings stretching back to the 1940s.

The Canadian 'Project Magnet', headed up by Wilbert Smith, concentrated on the idea that UFOs were extraterrestrial vehicles using magnetic principles (Good, 1996) at the same time as the Canadian

Government was involved in an arrangement to develop highly advanced radial-flow jet-powered flying saucers.

In other words, the UFO believer element, whose ideas are always presented as standard fare to a befuddled public, make pseudo-scientific claims while the real work continues apace. This seems to be exactly what has happened in more recent years within Area 51 (Cook, June 1995; C. Pocock; Sweetman, 1998).

It is almost as if the Federal Hypothesists are right to claim that, at the same time that the US Air Force or the CIA deny knowledge of UFO sightings, they are (1) actually involved in the operation of secret aircraft, and (2) active in attempts to cloud the issue through the dissemination of alien-based propaganda – frankly unbelievable material that will be faithfully trotted out by UFO researchers who think that they are making a valuable contribution to the understanding of 'unknowns' (Brookesmith, 1981; 1996).

Alien propaganda is an all-too-convenient cover for the operation of any secret military aircraft. It reduces the majority of the group most likely to be interested in UFO sightings to a laughing stock and allows the intelligence agencies to carry out a variety of psychological warfare operations of immense value.

This is what has been happening with Area 51 for far too long. Area 51 is there for a reason: the testing and development of advanced aircraft and weaponry (C. Pocock; Sweetman, 1998). We know less about them than we like to pretend, although we can put the pieces of the puzzle together in order to get some idea of the dreams and realities behind the exclusion zone. Even now, researchers are suggesting that hidden facilities more secure even than Area 51 are home to super-advanced terrestrial technologies.

Beyond 'Aurora'

There is a great deal of information available about the A-12, SR-71 and F-117. What of the other aircraft flown from the remote location? The most important technologies could be said to be those relating to stealth and to hypersonics (Benningfield). Put them together and we have a lethal weapon.

The threat of hypersonic aircraft has bugged both the black projects and the UFO community for years: the mythical 'Aurora' – goddess of dawn, the military's 3,000-mph (4,800-kmph) aircraft (*see* Chapter 20). Certain facts indicate the existence of such an aircraft, or range of aircraft, although its name is less important than its mission (Sweetman, 1993).

Electrogravitics

Beyond 'Aurora' there may be another type of even more exotic aircraft – worth the secrecy and potentially giving the US a military advantage over its enemies for decades. These aircraft use 'electrogravitic systems' (Stirniman).

Probably more nonsense has been talked and written about 'anti-gravity' technologies within the UFO field than any other subject within the subculture. Such technologies and their 'Tesla' counter-parts (many relate to 'death rays') tend to be seen only as part of a huge conspiracy of hidden technologies controlled by elite groups of bankers (Deyo). An obvious point to make is that unless you can understand gravity, you cannot control it. I prefer Robert Stirniman's attempts to understand such unusual and challenging technologies simply from a scientific, rather than conspiratorial point of view.

Unfortunately for those Ufologists who insist that all relevant history is post Roswell or post-1947, Thomas Townsend Brown was attempting to control gravity back in the early 1920s (Gravity Research Group). Brown worked closely with Dr Paul Biefeld, Professor of Physics and Astronomy at Dennison University and who was a former classmate of Albert Einstein; the men experimented with the possibility that an electrical condenser suspended by a thread might have a tendency to move if an electrical charge was applied to it. Experiments involving heavy lead balls indicated that there was such a tendency.

Similar work using condensers indicated that if placed in free suspension with the poles horizontal, the condenser, when charged, exhibited a thrust towards the positive poles. By reversing the polarity the direction of thrust was also reversed. This was known as the Biefeld–Brown effect, which seemed to suggest that there was a way of affecting gravity by electrical means. The report written in 1956 by Gravity-Rand of London (see Deyo) reflected on Townsend Brown's work and described it as 'the brute force approach of concentrating high electrostatic charges along the leading edge of the periphery of a disc which yields propulsive effect'. The report also noted that Brown's work was most applicable to aviation, especially considering the use of disc-shaped condensers in his experiments.

Brown's work suggested that a flying disc might be able to generate an electrogravitational field of its own and that this could be controlled, although the work was shrouded in mystery. Nevertheless, there is a possibility that by varying the charge on a disc its direction could be controlled and that the initial experiments might eventually lead to a new and different method of propulsion involving the creation of a 'local gravitational field'. Efforts were made to try to validate Brown's work. Project Winterhaven in 1952 was such an effort. According to the 1956 Gravity-Rand report, 'Winterhaven recommended that a major effort be concentrated upon electrogravitics based on the principle of his [Brown's] disks.' The report went on to make some remarkable statements. These are often dismissed as 'purely theoretical' or 'irrelevant', although in light of the Manhattan District-like secrecy (levels of secrecy similar to that surrounding the development of the bomb dropped on Japan in 1945) surrounding Area 51 we could conclude that something revolutionary is going on behind closed doors (Cook, 1995).

Already companies are specializing in evolution of particular components of an electrogravitics disk. This implies that no new breakthroughs are needed, only intensive developmental engineering.

The report, entitled *Electrogravitics Systems – An examination of electrostatic motion, dynamic counterbary and barycentric control*, was prepared by the Gravity Research Group of London in February 1956 and declassified by the Wright Aeronautical Laboratories Technical Library (Wright-Patterson Air Force Base) in 1990. The report makes several equally intriguing remarks, especially in light of leaked security video footage made public in 1995 showing a UFO moving erratically through the air at high speed operating near Area 51. *Jane's Defence Weekly* writer Nick Cook commented in an interview that the footage was very interesting indeed.

Electrogravitics Systems notes the existence of electrostatic rigs said to be 'in operation' at the time of writing – 1956. It also said that the rewards of such technology could not be overlooked and that patents relating to electrostatic devices had been taken out in Europe and America. Townsend Brown's work is duly noted in the report and it is suggested that:

> using a number of assumptions as to the nature of gravity, **the report postulated a saucer as the basis of a possible interceptor with Mach 3 capability** [TM's emphasis].

Creation of a local gravitational system would confer on the fighter 'the sharp-edged changes of direction typical of motion in space'. And they were typical of recent UFOs captured on film, often in the vicinity of military facilities.

It appeared that an electrogravitics saucer would be able to fulfil the function of a classic lifting surface without the need for a flow of air, hence conventional propulsion systems, by producing a 'pushing effect on the under surface and a suction effect on the upper'. Under these circumstance an electrostatic VTOL vehicle was not beyond the bounds of possibility although, as noted in the similar Gravity-Rand study, such a development lay many years in the future.

It is not surprising that electrogravitics received a guarded welcome from the powers that be, who had only comparatively recently come to terms with advances in jet propulsion, and that this more advanced system would need to be hidden for economic reasons. Remember that the Glenn Martin Company said that gravity control could be achieved within the medium term but 'that it would entail a Manhattan District type of effort to bring it about'. The unparalleled security inside Area 51 would be perfect for such work from the late 1950s until the present day. You will recall that some researchers have claimed that saucers arrived at Groom Lake in 1958 or 1959.

According to the Gravity Research Group study, Clarke Electronics had an electrostatic rig in operation and General Electric was attempting to use electronic rigs to 'make adjustments' to gravity. Interest in this type of research had, according to the authors of the report, been shown by the major companies within the military/industrial complex: Lockheed, MIT, Princeton University, Boeing, North American, Curtis-Wright and Convair.

A couple of interesting names emerge as a result of the investigation into this work – Edward Teller and William P. Lear of Learjet, whose son John was to take such an interest in saucers later on. Teller was quoted in the *Proceedings of the National Academy of Sciences* (Vol. 74 No. 4) (Stirniman) as having postulated a relationship between electromagnetism and gravitation – just like Townsend Brown.

In the first part of his paper Teller describes how an electric field due to polarization can be induced in a dielectric material which is subject to angular or linear acceleration, or if subject to a gravitational field. In the second part of the paper Teller describes... how a magnetic field might be produced by a spinning mass.

Perhaps Bob Lazar's role was to try to obscure as much of this work as possible. After all, as 'evidence' that he had worked at S4, an Office of Naval Intelligence (ONI) payslip was produced appearing to show that a Robert Lazar of Las Vegas had worked consecutive days at a facility. Oddly enough the letters 'MAJ' appear at the top of the payslip, supposedly referring to 'Majestic 12', the name of an alleged secret group of 12 scientific experts set up to examine the alien craft that crashed at Roswell in July 1947 (Good, 1992). Of course, who knows what an ONI payslip looks like? Lazar was no fool and, given his close relationship with John Lear, it could be argued that both men were involved in a programme of on-going active disinformation relating to Area 51. If this is the case, then the programme has been tremendously successful, with Lazar appearing on numerous TV documentaries and in several books. Mention Area 51 and you hear about Bob Lazar. People want to know about secret bases and aliens. Things like electrogravitics systems are far too complicated – maybe even for the scientists.

Defence experts claim to know the true meaning of the Groom Lake riddle, while Glenn Campbell of the Area 51 Research Center describes Area 51 as a 'state of mind'. He has done more to further the understanding of the Area 51 phenomenon than anyone else. A state of mind? Maybe, and yet the more secrecy put in place by the controllers, the more paranoia and disinformation emerges. Still, Sandra Grundy, a colleague of mine, got near Area 51 in September 1997 via the Little Ale'Inn in Rachel and managed to get chased by Wackenhut Security personnel – the infamous 'cammodudes' who guard the borders of this most secret place. If Area 51 has closed down, as a recent *Popular Mechanics* article would have us believe, then why are workers still being transported to Groom Lake via 'Janet Airways' and why are English tourists a focus for attention?

It seems to me that Groom Lake has been a convenient place to develop a range of amazing technologies, and, quite rightly, new technologies need to be tested. One wonders whether the stealth aircraft enthusiasts and alien believers, who used to jostle for position on Freedom Ridge to gain a last look at the distant mirage of Groom Lake before them, really want to know what is going on. Where would the mystery be then? What would they all do? Maybe this is an overly cynical point of view, and as a result it seems sensible to leave the last words to Nick Cook of *Jane's Defence Weekly*:

> Groom Lake is the epicentre of classified USAF research into Stealth and other exotic aerospace technologies. Several years after the collapse of the Soviet threat, activity and investment at this remote, highly secret air base...is still on the increase.
>
> While research into less sensitive technologies such as two-dimensional thrust-vectoring and Advanced-Short-Take-Off and Vertical Landing (ASTOVL) is pursued in the open at nearby Edwards AFB, Groom Lake is set to hang onto its secrets. The USAF's recent confiscation of 1,600 acres [648 ha] of public land bordering the facility is consistent with the Pentagon's desire to maintain its lead in quantum-leap technologies – some of which,

according to well-qualified observers in and around the Nevada area, defy current thinking regarding the predicted direction of aerospace engineering.

Before he died, Ben Rich, who headed Lockheed's Skunk Works from 1975 to 1991, was quoted as saying: 'We have some new things. We are not stagnating. What we are doing is updating ourselves, without advertising. There are some new programmes, and there are certain things…some of them 20 to 30 years old – that are still breakthroughs and appropriate to keep quiet about. Other people don't have them yet.'

One day the truth will emerge from Groom Lake. The signal will emerge from the background noise. Let us hope that we are still alive to hear about it. I hold on to the hope that I will go on a grand tour of the site one day!

TWENTY

AURORA,
GODDESS OF DAWN

URORA, REAL OR IMAGINED, has niggled at the UFO community for years. The idea of a hypersonic aircraft (one that can achieve a velocity in excess of Mach 5) streaking through the night certainly captures the imagination. Unfortunately, nobody seems to be able to agree on the aircraft responsible for the ear-splitting noise created by the ultimate mystery aircraft.

The main and most credible source on 'Aurora', Bill Sweetman (1993), believes that it is an aircraft of approximately 100 feet (30 m) in length, while Philip Handleman claims that it is a huge aircraft approaching 300 feet (90 m) in length (1994). Others seem to think that it is much smaller, perhaps 75 feet (23 m) in length.

Active Disinformation

Unsurprisingly, Ben Rich in his official history of the Lockheed Skunk Works (Rich and Janos) has claimed that Aurora is not a hypersonic aircraft and reports that:

> *A young colonel working in the Air Force 'black program' office at the Pentagon named Buz Carpenter, arbitrarily assigned the funding [for the B-2] the code name 'Aurora'. Somehow...the rumor surfaced that this was a top secret project assigned to the Skunk Works – to build America's first hypersonic airplane...there is no code word for the hypersonic plane; because it simply does not exist.*

Rich also neglects to mention Groom Lake in his 1994 book. His is possibly the best example of the official line relating to secret military aircraft. Nevertheless, it is widely believed that one of the only reasons to develop a hypersonic manned aircraft would be as a replacement the Mach 3 Blackbird (Rose, 1997). From the point of view of UFO reports, any object moving through the skies at high speeds deemed by both aviation 'authorities' and debunkers to be beyond the cutting edge of technology should be of great interest to us all.

All the evidence suggests that hypersonics has been achieved, at least in the sense that certain black-project aircraft have the ability to fly at hypersonic speeds for a limited time. At the outset it should be pointed out that the problem of fuel capacity for such an aircraft is thought to be a major stumbling block, but not an impossible hurdle (Windle, 1997).

Evidence in the Detail

The evidence for the reality of a hypersonic aircraft is complicated to grasp. The main sources on the subject are Bill Sweetman (1993) and the Federation of American Scientists (FAS); much of the information here is taken from these sources. Curtis Peebles has an on-going disagreement with Bill Sweetman; his counter position on Aurora is detailed in his 1995 book *Dark Eagles*. These three draw on a variety of primary material including information made available relating to other black-project aircraft (the U-2, SR-71, F-117 and B-2) on witness statements (UFO reports, to all intents and purposes), reports from the aviation press and occasionally artists' impressions of future aircraft. Quality aviation journals occasionally carry articles on hypersonic aircraft.

In 1985 researchers perusing the latest batch of Air Force procurement documents for evidence of funding for secret projects came across the name 'Aurora' in relation to P-1 budget requests for aircraft production (not Research and Development). A total of $455 million was to be made available for this black project in Federal Year 1987.

In early 1988, *The New York Times* reported that a stealthy reconnaissance aircraft capable of Mach 6 was being built to replace the SR-71.

Just a year later Chris Gibson, to whom I have spoken about this, a 12-year Royal Observer Corps veteran and aircraft identification expert, chanced on a remarkable sight in the North Sea as he was working on the Galveston Key rig. He saw a KC-135 refuelling aircraft and two F-111s keep station to the port side of the tanker. An unidentified triangular aircraft was refuelling as Gibson watched in amazement. The craft appeared to be somewhat larger than the accompanying F-111s. Subsequently Gibson kept quiet about his sighting because he had signed the Official Secrets Act. Nevertheless, he contacted Bill Sweetman (1993) to break the story. Although it was assumed by most commentators that this was the Aurora aircraft, Gibson has an open mind on his sighting. He would certainly be intrigued to know which aircraft he saw.

In an important development, I have spoken to the relative of a man who regularly works on North Sea oil rigs. He stated that on several occasions in 1996 and 1997 both this man and a few of his co-workers saw an unidentified diamond-shaped aircraft flying out to sea. The aircraft had always been accompanied by F-15s. It looks remarkably similar to stealth expert Bill Sweetman's conceptual diagram of 'Aurora' (*see* illustration no. 21) (Sweetman, 1993). The UK–US special relationship obviously extends to the flight of advanced aircraft in coastal waters. This much is confirmed by history (Bissell; Graham).

In 1971 a team working for the ATV programme *Farming Today* were on location when they heard a strange sound and looked up at the sky (Barlow). They saw a dart-shaped object accelerating at incredibly high speed, leaving a large contrail behind it. The film has become particularly popular with Ufologists, who like using it to support their claim that our skies are full of such aircraft: if they are supposedly flying faster than any known aircraft, they 'must be' of extraterrestrial origin. On the other hand, sceptics have rather meekly argued that the film shows an airborne fuel dump in progress. I have shown the film to several former RAF personnel and aviation enthusiasts, and it appears that this is not a fuel dump. I have seen several photographs of a fuel dump which is totally dissimilar.

An Explanation – In Part

Maybe now there is a partial explanation of events. It has emerged, through conversations with aviation experts, that as early as 1962 staff at English Electric Aircraft were working on designs for a hypersonic aircraft. This was almost 30 years before the flurry of media interest in 'Aurora' (Ransom and Fairclough).

I cannot help thinking that the aircraft recovered by the 71st MU (Maintenance Unit) personnel in 1967 was in some way related to this programme. Of course, it will be denied. One of the biggest problems is the cynicism and lack of imagination of the British aviation enthusiast – perhaps encouraged by the publication of Derek Wood's influential *Project Cancelled* in 1986. The book explains how numerous radical proposals were begun and cancelled or not funded at all. In the background one gets the impression that the Americans were hovering – ready to take the best UK ideas and use their political muscle to keep their lead in terms of advanced aircraft. (They had done so in the late 1940s by applying pressure to the Miles Aircraft Company to cancel their work. Subsequently the US Bell X-1 officially broke the sound barrier. This story was featured in a 1997 TV programme shown on Channel 4 entitled *Secret History*.)

As an aside, the UK did take a great deal of interest in delta-wing aircraft for transonic research in the 1950s and 1960s (Vicary). The two aircraft involved were the Fairey Delta and the Handley Page 115. Built during 1960, the HP-115 was flown as early as 1961 in trials at RAE Bedford (Royal Aeronautical Establishment) to examine the handling characteristics of a delta at high speeds. It was hoped that the research data might specifically lead to a supersonic airliner able to travel at Mach 2.2. The HP-115 was 50 feet (16 m) long with a sweepback of 75 degrees, and it handled well at a minimum speed of 60 knots. Coincidentally, during the late 1960s, the aircraft flew to the three airfields most closely associated with UFO activity in Britain: Warton, West Freugh and Boscombe.

Nevertheless, the programme was completed in summer 1972 and the aircraft now lives in the museum at RAF Cosford. There are several possibilities relating to the HP-115, including the belief that the initial tests were undertaken to test the radical triangular shape in order that similar and more radical designs could be developed. Certainly English Electric thought so. Unfortunately, as Wood (1986) shows, successive UK governments failed to support home industry adequately – perhaps as a result of pressure from the USA, which no doubt took all the fruits of the research. All that was left for the UK to do was to hang on to the coat-tails of the Americans and become involved in secret joint programmes. This could explain the footage recorded by the ATV team and also a sighting reported in 1977. On this occasion a witness heard a sonic boom and looked up to see an arrowhead-shaped craft moving across the sky near Weymouth, Dorset. It left an unusual contrail, something typical of many of the supposed Aurora sightings. The witness, Brian James, saw a similar craft in 1976.

Until very recently the English Electric work was known to only a tiny number of researchers but now the spotlight is firmly on it. As early as 1959–60 the company was studying aircraft in the high-supersonic regime (the P.30), while the P.42 is described in Ransom and Fairclough's *English Electric Aircraft* as a 'hypersonic research aircraft'. I suggest that among the reasons that the aircraft was seen in public so infrequently were not only its obvious high speed, but also the fact that there are tremendous problems associated with hypersonic technologies.

At Mach 5.4, over 3,600 mph (5,800 kmph), the temperature at the front of an aircraft increases because the air stagnates. At these speeds fuel is used at a tremendous rate. Nevertheless, hypersonic technologies have been applied for at least 35 years. Several strands of technological development are apparent in terms of high-speed technologies. One came, yet again, via German rocket science. Walter Dornberger worked upon the 'Dyna-Soar' hypersonic glide vehicle (HGV), which was similar to the X-15 project in that it favoured a rocket-powered solution for high-speed flight (Sweetman, 1993). Unknown to many Ufologists are several unpalatable facts:

- The X-15 flew at Mach 6.7 at an altitude of 354,200 feet (100,000 m) for several seconds.

- Nearly all studies related to high-speed flight involved delta-shaped aircraft.

- Many of the delta-shaped aircraft were similar to the 'UFOs' reported in recent years.

There were numerous delta-wing aircraft involved in a series of US studies stretching from the early 1960s through the 1970s and into the 1980s (Rose, 1997).

The best-known triangular craft was the X-24B, thought to be based upon a collection of hypersonic study designs undertaken by Lockheed and the US Air Force Flight Dynamics Laboratory (FDL) during the 1960s. The X-24A and X-24B were tested at Dryden Dry Lake Bed by NASA in the 1970s; the last test took place in 1975. They were developed for testing the possibilities of a reusable re-entry vehicle (Bullard). Some observers have suggested that an X-24C, thought to have existed only in model form, was actually flown in 1978 (Rose, 1997). One of the FDL designs, FDL-5, is remarkably similar to the aircraft spotted by Chris Gibson. It would seem that in terms of hypersonics at least, the various attempts at permanent manned flight have been problematic – more of a stop, start, stop, start process.

'LoFlyte'

The work of British scientist Terrence Nonweiler hit the headlines in 1996, but only briefly (Windle, 1997). The response to Nonweiler's work was a ripple when compared to the excitement generated by official NASA statements that it had been working in conjunction with the Accurate Automation Company of Chattanooga, Tennessee to develop an unmanned hypersonic reconnaissance vehicle called 'LoFlyte' (Low Observable Flight Test Experiment).

As early as the 1950s Nonweiler had proposed that a 'waverider' system might solve the problems of dead air in high-speed flight (Osborne). Those involved with LoFlyte were clearly aware of Nonweiler's work, begun in 1951. At that time he published his first paper on waveriders for atmospheric re-entry vehicles.

By the end of the decade he was working at Queen's University, Belfast on the theoretical aspects of 'wedge flow' for a manned re-entry vehicle. We know that the UK was heavily involved in early high-speed research – Nonweiler worked in conjunction with Armstrong-Whitworth Limited. The reason that most reported high-speed delta-wing 'UFOs' are of similar shape is entirely the result of aerodynamic principles and nothing to do with alien technology!

Richard Osborne of STAAR Research notes the engagement of the waverider principle to use shockwaves built up in high-speed flight to increase lift. The waverider 'surfs' on a stream of air because of the wedge-shaped design of the aircraft. The sharp leading edges of an aircraft shaped like the LoFlyte tend to wrap the shockwaves around the fuselage. A cushion of air is trapped below it. Osborne states:

Waveriders have sharp noses and wing leading-edges, which the underside shock-surface attaches to, therefore air flowing in through the shock-surface is trapped between the shock and the fuselage, and can only escape at the rear of the fuselage. Shocks are one-way, the second law of thermodynamics prevents air flowing back through a shock the way it came in.

Given that a great deal of theoretical work has been undertaken in relation to waveriders, the announcement that small-scale prototypes of the LoFlyte aircraft were to be tested from 1996 makes one wonder what else is hidden in the black world. We must be suspicious that LoFlyte is but the tip of an iceberg. It is not just Ufologists and stealthchasers who are making noises about the continued secrecy. Dr John Pike of the Federation of American Scientists said in a 1996 *Sunday Times* interview (Windle, 1997):

I continue to be puzzled by the vast number of theoretical studies into the waverider configuration that apparently have no basis in existing hardware. The public showing of the LoFlyte vehicle is very odd. It leads me to the conclusion that there may be classified work going on in which this hardware exists.

Given that the ultimate shape of a waverider is said to a delta with sharp edges, then we might have an answer to the many UFO sightings stretching back to the late 1960s to early 1970s. It is likely that such sightings would be accompanied by a sonic boom or that the craft seen would not seem silent unless at very high speeds. Seen near a military facility, a triangular craft is most likely to be slowing down upon approach. One problem with such an aircraft would be that it requires a long runway from which to operate. This limits the number of facilities from which such a craft can operate. One of these may well have been RAF Macrahanish in Scotland, a very remote base on the Mull of Kintyre conveniently situated for incoming flights from the USA (Bruce; Sutton).

Scottish Hideaway

Scotland has been linked with Aurora for a number of reasons: the base at Macrahanish, the sightings of the UFO under escort by F-111s and F-15s off the coast, and also reports from Scottish air traffic controllers that an unidentified aircraft has been shooting through their airspace at high speed. These have been accompanied by ground witness reports of sonic booms and strange pulsing sounds.

A report by Jim Rogers for *Inside the Air Force* magazine (24 April 1992, pp. 10–11) noted that:

> *RAF radars have acquired the hypersonic target travelling at speeds ranging from about Mach 6 to Mach 3 over a NATO–RAF base at Macrahanish, Scotland, near the top of the Kintyre peninsula, last November and again this January.*

Although nominally under UK control, Macrahanish was really under US control. The base grew as a result of Cold War realities which required an out-of-the-way base from which to operate both the U-2 and SR-71 spyplanes. It was also a convenient spot to drop off US personnel before flying back home.

The base has a 10,000-foot (3,000-m) runway, the longest in Europe; in the event of hostilities breaking out it would have seen a great deal of activity. It also functioned as a staging post for various covert activities involving US Navy Seals from 1976, who brought with them some serious hardware including nuclear demolition charges for behind-the-lines sorties. Just over 50 RAF personnel were always on-site, but far more US personnel, a true indication of US dominance (Bruce).

There are, as with all bases associated with military UFOs, several rumours. In this case, I have heard the following: that various 'unmarked convoys' were seen entering the base; that massive 'underground facilities' were constructed; and that there is or was a 'UFO base' underwater off the Kintyre coast. These stories always serve to distract our attention from the real issue.

More realistic perhaps are the stories of RAF personnel painting the runway at the base before it officially 'closed' a few years ago. Richard Sutton suggested that this might be something to do with the need to match the infra-red (IR) signature of the runway to an incoming 'Top Secret' stealth aircraft. Given the tremendous heat generated in hypersonic flight this might not be so far-fetched.

Sutton photographed a particularly anomalous event at midday (not midnight as stated in *UFO Magazine*, May/June 1996) during a trip to Kintyre on 7 September 1995. Looking south-west from Gigha Island, and using Kodak 400 ASA infra-red mono 35mm film, he took some photographs of a contrail with no aircraft in front of it (*see* illustrations nos. 22 and 23)!

The film was developed on Ilford ID11 and printed on to multigrade paper through an APO Rodogon high-quality enlarging lens. Manipulation of the exposure did not reveal any trace of an aircraft; it is likely that we have a photograph of an aircraft without an IR signature.

If Sutton's analysis is right, this means that an advanced stealth aircraft may have been operating at the time over RAF Macrahanish. The camera does not seem to have been at fault given that numerous other IR photos showing a variety of aircraft and taken at about the same time came out perfectly. Sutton also reports having experienced an unusual prickly electrostatic sensation while driving close to Macrahanish on the A83 road.

In more recent years Macrahanish has continued to defy common sense. The hangars were used in 1997 to film an advertisement for a then new Saab car, and just days later hundreds of US troops arrived at the base during a combined military exercise. I spoke with Brian Ashby of the *Campbeltown Courier* newspaper, who told me that, although he had heard various rumours, he could not help me in terms of UFO sightings. Nevertheless, Stephen Stratton, a colleague of mine, visited the area in 1995 and spoke to a number of locals who had seen US Special Forces personnel at the base as well as having heard innumerable sonic booms. In one case, a man Stratton spoke to claimed that an unidentified aircraft almost shook the windows in his house to pieces.

Now Macrahanish is in mothballs and is described as a stand-by airfield for NATO. It is still used by the local Air Ambulance service, and aircraft have been heard flying into and out of the base on regular occasions by military monitors in 1998. Brian Ashby has heard a rumour that the base may be re-opened. Perhaps its remoteness is too tempting for the operators of secret military aircraft. After all, who is going to see an aircraft coming in to land at night? Even if they do see something at night, how can they be sure that it is not a run-of-the-mill military jet?

Denial by an 'Expert'

At one point in the unfolding tale of government denial, Britain's very own supposed UFO 'expert', former Sec Air Staff 2a man Nick Pope, claimed that he had been given categorical denials that any such plane as Aurora existed (Pope, 1996). This has been taken to heart by several researchers who appear to be unaware of the questions of secrecy surrounding US black programmes. There is no way that Pope would ever have been 'in the loop' regarding flights of a 'Top Secret' reconnaissance aircraft to the UK. In fact his efforts to engage in the debate are almost laughable. In his best-selling book entitled *Open Skies, Closed Minds,* we learn very little about UFOs and only a limited amount about the activities of Sec AS2a. Nevertheless, there is an interesting exchange on pp. 175–80 of the paperback edition.

Firstly, Pope appears to argue against the need for a reconnaissance aircraft given the capabilities of the modern satellite, although he admits to satellites' limitations. This argument is incorrect, as demonstrated by the many military commanders eager to employ both UAVs and other reconnaissance aircraft to provide real-time data relay. Satellites are a far from perfect method of gaining timely information, as we have seen (Burrows).

Secondly, Pope omits to mention the Chris Gibson sighting. He does provide us with an intriguing report about two RAF Tornados overtaken by a much faster 'aircraft'. One wonders how Pope, given either the panic engendered by the Peter Wright 'Spycatcher' affair or the David Shayler MI5 debacle of the late 1990s, is able to tell us this. Perhaps it is an example of 'if you ask the wrong questions you get the wrong answers'. Defence spokesman Nicholas Soames stated in Parliamentary replies to Llew Smith, MP, that:

> There are no United States Air Force prototype aircraft based at RAF Macrahanish...no authorization has been given by Her Majesty's Government to the United States Air Force...to operate such aircraft within or from the United Kingdom.

For a start, who says that this is a prototype aircraft? Who says that they are 'based' in the United Kingdom? Soames also stated that 'No new types of high-altitude, long-range reconnaissance aircraft have been based or are being considered for basing in the UK.' But who says that this is a purely reconnaissance craft, and who says that this is/was a 'new type' of aircraft? Given the possible existence of such an aircraft since the late 1980s, this would not have been a new type at the time the questions were asked in the House of Commons. Given the 'Most Secret' nature of the UK–US relationship, Pope's formal enquiries made through the American Embassy 'and all relevant American military branches' were almost laughable. I wonder if the US Embassy has the number for Air Force Flight Detachment 3 at Groom Lake?

In a conversation I had with Nick Pope in October 1996, he claimed that his enquiries had 'almost caused a diplomatic incident'. That's more like it – the heavy-handed approach works well, no doubt, as does active disinformation, of which there seems to be plenty in Pope's book.

Much of Pope's argument is predicated on the acceptance that one of the aircraft in question is called 'Aurora'. If the release of the original 1985 procurement document by the Pentagon was a mistake that escaped the censor's pen, then undoubtedly the name would have changed. In any case there is something too convenient about giving an aircraft a name that conjures up images of the 'goddess of dawn'. Readers might like to reflect on the fact that in several interviews Nick Pope denied knowing about the existence or function of RAF Rudloe Manor – a possible centre for the covert evaluation of UFO reports in the UK (Williams). It emerged through a series of letters sent between Welsh researcher Chris Fowler and Pope's successor at Sec AS2a, Kerry Philpott, that during his tenure Pope had regularly and routinely sent documents from his Whitehall office to Rudloe Manor.

Pope ends his engagement in the Aurora debate by strongly suggesting that an alien intelligence could be using black programmes as a cover or that there is on-going research into 'genuine alien vehicles'. Given this sort of propaganda we might conclude that as long as Nick pumps out similar pro-extraterrestrial hypothesis material and continues to be taken seriously by the general public as a genuine 'expert', then certain elements with the defence intelligence community will see him as a vital asset. Who knows? The mystery continues, and although we strongly suspect that a mystery hypersonic waverider has been flown around the Scottish coast, the USA has been the focal point for sightings of, and research into, these aircraft (Sweetman, 1993; Rose, 'The Hidden Aurora', 1996; 1997).

Hypersonic Craft in the USA

California has been the site of some most unusual UFO events during the 1990s – perhaps not surprising given that Groom Lake is just a few minutes' flying time away.

The evidence that a craft approaching hypersonic speeds was flying came in 1992 when some of the 220 sensors employed by the US Geological Survey (USGS) in the western USA picked up sonic booms. The equipment used suggested that the aircraft were travelling at between Mach 3 and 4 – possibly slowing down for approach to Groom. Dr Jim Mori of the USGS said that the waveforms detected by his equipment indicated that the aircraft in question was less than 122 feet (37 m) in length: the size of the Space Shuttle. He had recorded sonic booms during previous Space Shuttle launches. Most importantly from the point of view of corroboration, neither the SR-71 nor the shuttle were flying on the days when the booms were recorded.

The distinct 'donuts-on-a-rope' contrail, said to be associated with exotic propulsion systems and hypersonic flight, has been reported across the USA. Steve Douglass was again in the thick of things when he snapped a similar contrail from his house in Amarillo, Texas on 23 March 1992. He also managed on a subsequent occasion to record a stereo 'skyquake' typical of the sort associated with sightings of the mystery black aircraft. Steve described the engine noise from the mysterious dark eagle as a 'strange, loud pulsating roar...unique...a deep pulsating rumble that vibrated the house and made the windows shake...similar to rocket engine noise, but deeper, with evenly timed pulses'.

It was believed that Lockheed Martin was the company responsible for the development and construction of this hypersonic aircraft. One way of tracking such developments and the huge sums of money associated with them is, as we have seen, through an examination of the amounts of money flowing into a company's coffers. A team of financial analysts, Kemper Securities, looked at Lockheed Skunk Works (Advanced Development Company) funding and notice a huge rise in black-budget funding from 1987. In fact, it appeared that the budget allocation for 'Project Aurora' was $2.7 billion – more than enough to fund a black aircraft of the type reported.

More Than One Are Out There

Although reports suggested several kinds of 'Aurora' aircraft, there is a distinct possibility that witnesses are reporting several black aircraft under development. One supposed 'Aurora' was said to have a large planform, not unlike the 1960s XB-70 Valkyrie. This was seen in Georgia and over the Mojave Desert in California.

An *Aviation Week and Space Technology* report (24 August 1992) by Bill Scott claimed that five separate reports came in of this large light-coloured delta-shaped UFO during the summer of 1990 when observers reported seeing an unusual lighting configuration on the underside of the craft. The reports also mentioned a low-pitched rumble.

Sightings of the large UFO came in from Atlanta, Georgia on 10 May 1992. The twin-engine noise was typically described as a deep-pitched regular pulsing sound. Two months later, on 12 July, an intriguing report was made by a man who had apparently seen the same aircraft descending from high altitude towards the Lockheed Radar Cross Section range at Helendale, California. The observer reported the UFO in some detail. It was very large, perhaps 200 feet (60 m) in length.

A report from Edwards Air Force Base said the UFO 'dwarfed' accompanying F-16s. This was a delta-planform craft with a blended fuselage. It had light-coloured top and bottom surfaces with darker leading edges. Although the report is fascinating, especially given the location – a restricted Lockheed facility – it is unlikely that this was Aurora (McGinnis). It may be associated with the hypersonic aircraft as a launch platform. Many studies suggest that a manned hypersonic aircraft or unmanned variant could be flown to a certain altitude and then released from the host. It is very possible that this was the function of the XB-70 'UFO' (FAS; Rose, 1997).

Future (Present) Technologies

With this in mind it may be worthwhile to examine a study produced as part of the *Air Force 2025* survey by the Air University of America. Several proposals related to the 'Global Reach, Global Power' concept of US domination through superior technologies are put forward. *Air Force 2025* is an on-going study into 'future' (that is, present) technologies. The voluminous reports are taken very seriously and the research involves influential scientists within the military/industrial complex. Technically speaking the authors of the report seek to distance themselves from actual developments, by claiming that the study does not reflect the official policy or position of the sponsors, the US Air Force. Nevertheless, a quick look at the list of those asked to brief the authors makes for interesting reading. The authors thank the 'leaders of the aerospace community' for their assistance and these include personnel from Sandia National Laboratories, Langley Research Centre (Virginia), a member of the USAF Scientific Advisory Board (remember *New World Vistas*?), representatives of the Hi-tech Program Office and Flight Dynamics Directorate at Wright-Patterson Air Force Base and the technical director from Science Applications Corporation in Philadelphia.

A heavyweight cast, indeed, and all the more interesting given their adherence to aircraft systems most likely to be responsible for UFO sightings: UAVs, hybrid airships and hypersonic aircraft. Many of the proposals relate to aircraft that could well be reported as UFOs. Certainly the idea of a zero-stage launch platform is considered.

It has already been pointed out that there are several potential flash-points for future conflict: Bosnia, Korea and the Middle East. Any could involve the United States and the *Air Force 2025* study notes that there must be the military potential to 'deliver an accurate lethal blow' to an enemy. This is to be achieved through an integrated weapons approach involving three main air vehicles: a supersonic/hypersonic attack aircraft (SHAAFT); a standoff hypersonic missile with attack capabilities (SCHMAC); and a space control reusable military aircraft (SCREMAR). SHAAFT would be a dual-stage hypersonic aircraft at Mach 12 using a platform to propel it to Mach 3.5 before launch. The hypersonic attack aircraft would be triangular, use a waverider design and be based in part on the data resulting from the 1980s National Aerospace Plane (NASP) programme. SHAAFT would be used to strike deep into enemy territory, eliminating the 'war-fighting infrastructure' of the enemy.

It has been suggested that the tiny island of Diego Garcia and the Hawaiian islands might be used as staging posts for these long-range missions. Rumours have already linked the former with Aurora, while Kwajelein Atoll in the Pacific is another suspected secret base for this most dangerous aerial asset (Sweetman, 1993).

All Things Are Possible

The tremendous heat generated in hypersonic flight is no longer deemed as problematic as it was in the past. (During flights of the X-15 in the 1960s the high temperatures resulted in serious damage to the wings.)

Today it is believed that advanced lightweight Diboride Ceramic Matrix Composites (CMC) are based on zirconium diboride and hafnium diboride, which are able to withstand temperatures of between 3,500 and 4,000 degrees Fahrenheit (2,000 and 2,200 degrees C).

One of the propulsion systems thought to be involved in the Aurora aircraft is a Pulse Wave Detonation Engine (PWDE). Several witnesses have reported an unusual banging sound at the time of their UFO sightings that could be related to the employment of such an engine. Another method might be the use of an aerospike similar the LASRE (Linear Aerospike Rocket Engine) system tested in 1997 on an SR-71 and destined to power the X-33 Advanced Technology Demonstrator (*Jane's All the World's Aircraft, 1997–8*). Linear aerospike engines are not new, having been around for over 30 years. They were originally designed by the US Air Force's Propulsion Directorate in the early 1960s. The main difference between the new improved aerospike and a traditional rocket is that the engine uses the atmosphere as part of its nozzle, with the surrounding airflow containing the rockets' exhaust plume. In addition, this system is much smaller than normal rocket engines with similar thrust.

Yet again, the technologies capable of powering triangular or dart-shape 'UFOs' are not new. In the black world such developments have probably already been used. Nevertheless, there has been a great deal of speculation about the continued use of a hypersonic aircraft because reports of strange engine sounds have decreased. In addition, the SR-71 was brought back out of retirement in 1995.

The future of hypersonics is guaranteed and proposals by Northrop for a small Mach 8 UCAV raised some eyebrows – especially given that the company claimed that it would be operational within a few years (Lopez). Maybe these types of aircraft are 'alien to our way of thinking'. Does that mean they are of alien origin? It is unlikely.

If we are talking about rockets, ramjets or air-breathing systems, then we are talking about old technologies completely unrelated to the 'anti-gravity' systems said to be used to power UFOs. As long as there are secrets to hide and technologies that it may be unwise to make public, then the claims of some Ufologists about 'extraterrestrial technology' will persist.

TWENTY-ONE

THE BLACK WORLD

NUMEROUS AIRCRAFT ARE still to emerge from the black world. One is the formidable 'Bat' or TR-3A 'Black Manta'. It is thought that this aircraft is one of the older 'black' aircraft and that it has been operational for some time. There is considerable evidence to suggest that it has been used in tandem with the F-117A – more particularly during the Gulf War of 1991. However, this is not a high-speed aircraft, but a stealthy reconnaissance aircraft able to operate in the subsonic regime – between approximately Mach 0.85 and Mach 1.15. TR-3A is thought to refer to 'Tactical Reconnaissance 3A' – the U-2 being 'Tactical Reconnaissance 1' (Douglass).

The 'Black Manta'

During Operation Desert Storm, it is believed that the Manta was used to pinpoint targets for the F-117A 'Nighthawk' through real-time or near-real-time data relay (Rose, 1997; Benningfield). Of interest to UFO researchers is the probability that the TR-3A operates at relatively low level (Zinngrabe); I have spoken to sources who strongly suggest that it has operated out of UK airfields including RAF Mildenhall from 1984. It is thought that the US home for the aircraft is at Holloman Air Force Base. In addition, insiders claim that the use of muffled F-404 powerplants has significantly reduced engine noise. In combination with the latest Low Observable techniques the Manta is a formidable opponent.

The TR-3A appears to have been built as an improved version of the Tactical High Altitude Penetrator (THAP) concept and this is where the idea of a manta-ray shape may have come from. Certainly there are conceptual drawings of THAP, and it is noted in Jones' book on stealth, where the author connects it to the Advanced Tactical Bomber (ATB) – the B-2 (see FAS report on TR-3A).

Dan Zinngrabe suggests that the Manta may have been the product of several strands of advanced aircraft research that came together after the US Air Force started the 'Compass Cope' programme in the late 1970s in the hope of developing a survivable reconnaissance UAV not dissimilar to today's Tier UAV systems. By that time, much work had been done in terms of stealth technology as a result of the Have Blue programme, and it was hoped that this could be applied to a 'natural' wing-shaped aircraft.

Of course, John Cashen and his Northrop team had made a huge commitment to winning the contract for the development of the stealth fighter, and they were mortified when Lockheed beat their design (Sweetman, 'B-2 Spirit', 1997). It is thought that Northrop may have revived Jack Northrop's 'span-loader' flying-wing platform and were able to make significant progress after winning massive funding for the B-2.

Interestingly enough, both Dan Zinngrabe and Paul McGinnis have been able to track down research papers and patents relating to Northrop's span-loader, including a line diagram of the THAP with documents prepared by the USAF Aeronautical Systems Center at Wright-Patterson Air Force Base. Technical drawings indicate the use of a Kevlar/honeycomb sandwich for stealth, as well as a sleek all-wing design supported by shrouded turbo-fan engines.

Note the many designs and concepts put out by the US Air Force which appear very similar to aircraft referred to as 'UFOs'. It has even been suggested to me that in addition to the UAVs flying in the Midlands and Yorkshire in the UK during 1987–8, some of them might have been a THAP/TR-3A aircraft. Also note the similarity between them and the artist's impression of the UFO seen published in IUN reports (Clarke).

Up to 1989 funding for the B-2 was to be found in the Air Force Aircraft Procurement item designated 'other production charges'. Money for Aircraft Support Equipment and Facilities was added to this. Meanwhile Lockheed were the recipients of large sums of money from 1982 to 1892 rising to nearly $800 million in the latter year, despite the fact that the F-117A and TR-1 programmes had been completed. The full car parks at the Lockheed Skunk Works attest to continued work. Approximately 4,000 people work at the plant in California (see McGinnis).

Although it seems as if Northrop were responsible for the Manta, there are other possibilities. A look at the US Patent Server might indicate an alternative solution to sightings of a rounded-edge triangular aircraft. Patent number 4,019,699, filed on 21 July 1975 and issued on 26 April 1977, like other similar patents tends to throw new light on the accepted wisdom of black aircraft sightings.

This was a Teledyne-Ryan design and the company has often been seen as a minor player in terms of stealth aircraft, despite its work on advanced Low-Observable UAV systems (Munson, 1988). The particular concept in question is quite radical and indicates an understanding of the finer principles of stealth, including the selective use of Radar Absorbent Materials (RAM) in combination with a delta-wing and electrically conductive surfaces in order to minimize the Radar Cross Section.

The message is clear: the delta-wing is in no way an 'alien' concept; it is fundamental to modern-day stealth. Although the F-117A and B-2 are seen as the main examples of stealth, numerous other and less well-known designs were also under development. It is estimated that between 10 and 20 different black-aircraft projects have been initiated since the 1970s (J. Jones).

Other snippets of information derived from the Teledyne-Ryan patent are that, as early as 1971–2, it was known that RAM, and other methods including 'energy absorption by a radioisotope produced plasma', could have a radical effect upon future aircraft design. The key to success was in perfecting the balance between low-aspect-ratio design and RAM treatments.

An examination of the funding for the B-2 indicates, as we have seen, that huge sums of money were appropriated by Northrop, almost certainly to be pumped into the development of other aircraft. As usual in this kind of research we need to look at the financial position as indicated through funding for compartmented or 'Special Access Required' programmes (FAS).

Much of the talk about the Black Manta remained talk until Steve Douglass was able to capture several seconds of video footage during the Operation Roving Sands exercises in May 1993 (Patton, 1997). This was the ultimate tantalizing image of a UFO: fuzzy, filmed at dawn – but something structured blending into the skies above is seen. It does not look like the F-117A, and it is reported to have sounded different and flown rather more slowly.

Interestingly enough, Greenpeace activists, protesting at the underground nuclear testing within the Nevada test site in 1986, saw a similar craft as they hiked into Dreamland/Area 51. If this credible sighting was in any way connected to the B-2 design, then we can finally lay to rest the disinformation that no large-scale prototypes existed for the Advanced Tactical Bomber. If another aircraft was seen then we know that black aircraft exist for sure – this was certainly not the F-117A!

The 'Flying Artichoke'

Bill Sweetman, in an article for *International Defence Review* in 1994, noted the existence of a smaller version of the B-2 with a span of around 66 feet (20 m), possibly to be used in an attack mode. This may be a follow-on to the F-117A, itself the subject of upgrading. Importantly, the author notes that new stealth technologies allow for all-weather operation.

We also suspect that rather more came out of the US Navy A-12 Avenger programme. Various sources associated with the aerospace industry claim that a new aircraft has been developed specifically to attack high-value targets in raids not dissimilar to that launched from the UK against the Libyan regime in 1986. The craft has been dubbed 'Omega' or the 'Flying Artichoke'. It has a serrated tail, thought to significantly reduce engine noise, and has been spotted in the south-western United States in the company of F-111s. The home for this recent addition to the secret weapons inventory is reportedly Cannon Air Force Base in New Mexico, the site of numerous improvements and the recipient of several million dollars of funding, including an unusually large hangar, new hospital and additional housing facilities. Some researchers claim that this is a swing-wing aircraft like the F-111 built for attack and used in wings-forward mode to enhance lift and improve range through reduced fuel consumption. The forward-wing mode reduced observability and the craft may have been mistaken for a UFO as a result (Brown and Douglass).

Swing-wing aircraft have been both popular and successful in the post-war period, although it has been suggested that video footage taken by Steve Douglass near Holloman Air Force Base showing two triangular aircraft operating in formation might in fact be two German Tornados or maybe even 'Tomcats' seen from a distance. The problems of identification never diminish! The reader can access the twin triangles pictures at Douglass's web site.

Germany and Elsewhere

Triangular aircraft are not only a UK–US phenomenon. Since 1996, a little more information has emerged about the German stealth aircraft programme of the late 1970s–early 1980s sponsored by the Luftwaffe, known as 'Firefly' or Lampyridae (Cook, *Interavia*, 1995). Firefly was built in complete secrecy – nobody but those involved knew about it; it used similar calculations and the use of faceting to scatter incoming radar waves to reduce observability.

Prototypes were built, and it is said that the Americans found out about the aircraft only through a chance sighting by US officials in 1981. They were shocked by the knowledge that the Germans had the capability to build a more effective rival to the F-117A – through the use of a multi-faceted polyhedral design under the leadership of Dr Gerhard Lobert – and it is thought that American muscle was applied and the programme scrapped. Deutsche Aerospace also put forward several designs for a Mach 6 two-stage turbo-ramjet-powered triangular aircraft (Sweetman, 1993).

We can expect other countries to acquire stealth (Sweetman, 1994). Given the rather open market in arms and the fact that the secrets of stealth are better known and understood, it is thought that countries like Russia, China and even Iran have been working on stealth.

One wonders what people in those countries will make of secret military aircraft. Will UFO sightings increase with the same secrecy measures having been put into place to protect the various projects? Given the nature of proliferation, the arms trade, the critical importance of stealth and the fact that some people would sell anything for the right price, we can expect to see these technologies become more freely available (Burrows and Windrem). The result will be that Western allies will be required to upgrade existing stealth systems and to develop a whole new range of stealth aircraft with active countermeasures. These will undoubtedly be triangular in shape and will incorporate as standard smart skins, non-lethal weapons and new propulsion systems in order to maintain the advantage.

As an example of the growth in advanced aircraft programmes, it is now said that a new and secretive stealth-testing facility, not unlike Groom Lake in terms of its location, is situated at Overberg in South Africa (Douglass). Several German stealth aircraft have supposedly been tested there including the revolutionary Daimler-Benz AT-2000, which takes the best features of the F-22, the joint DASA/Rockwell aircraft and classified UK work relating to the first HALO stealth programme of the late 1980s. According to Steve Douglass, Overberg is open to all-comers as long as the price is right, and numerous countries have taken the opportunity to use the facilities there including Russia, China and the UK.

Maybe this is the next focal point for UFO sightings? As small bands of stealthchasers and military monitors home in upon secret aircraft and sweep discreet frequencies on their scanning rigs, small pieces of the larger puzzle will no doubt fall into place.

TWENTY-TWO

CONCLUSION: STRUCTURED, TERRESTRIAL CRAFT

T HE ONLY SENSIBLE conclusion we can reach is that many UFO reports relate to man-made objects. Despite this, several attempts to mislead or disinform the worldwide UFO community have taken place.

The Bennewitz Affair

The best and most obvious example of this is the Paul Bennewitz case of 1979–80, when UFO researcher William Moore was approached by the notorious Air Force Office of Special Investigations (AFOSI) hack Richard Doty (Clark; CUFON; Brookesmith, 1996; Hesemann and Mantle).

In return for access to supposed sensitive and classified information about UFOs, Moore seems to have acted as a conduit between Doty and Paul Bennewitz, an Albuquerque-based UFO investigator who had been picking up strange low-frequency signals from a variety of local hi-tech military/industrial facilities including Kirtland Air Force Base and Sandia National Laboratories. He had also photographed several anomalous light phenomena emanating from an area close to the Manzano nuclear storage facility situated nearby. In the dissemination of disinformation laced with hard fact, Bennewitz was encouraged to believe that aliens were conducting a variety of shocking experiments at underground facilities throughout the USA with their focal point at a facility located beneath Dulce, New Mexico.

As a result of this tortuous process, in which Moore tried to white-wash his personal involvement, Bennewitz was driven to the point of suicide and ended up with a number of serious medical complaints from which he has never fully recovered (CUFON). Obviously he had got too near some programme or other, and his technical background, by which he was able to make his initial determination concerning the strange goings on, made him a possible source of trouble as far as the intelligence community was concerned.

Given that Doty was involved with UFO researcher Linda Moulton-Howe, who has done so much to promote the idea of animal mutila-tions, one might conclude that a deliberate policy was being carried through at the highest level. UFO researchers have suggested that Doty acted alone and that his handlers had little or no idea what he was up to, although according to Peter Brookesmith (1996) AFOSI acted delib-erately and with clear intent:

> AFOSI then decided that they would feed Bennewitz a mass of misleading information about aliens, subterranean bases and anything else they could think of – so that, should he leak any technical details of their work, he could and would be discredited as a crank by all and sundry.

More Myths and Fantasies

Given the amounts of quite frankly ludicrous material to emerge in recent years, I think it is fair to conclude that the seeds of disinforma-tion might be sown by the placement of a couple of wild stories in the UFO research community, perhaps by 'government agents'. The Bennewitz affair does seem to be a little unusual and the people involved or associated with it seem to have spawned many of the myths and fantasies so prevalent in modern Ufology today. Among them are Linda Moulton-Howe, who claims animal mutilations by aliens, and William Moore, who has been accused of having been involved in the production of the Majestic-12 documents, the source of a long-standing debate with Philip Klass. This has been reflected in several issues of the scurrilous *Saucer Smear*, an informative though occasionally discon-certing bi-monthly scandal sheet edited by Jim Moseley that exposes the petty personal politics so prevalent in Ufology. It appears (Vol. 44, Nos 8 and 9) that Doty was demoted and subsequently removed from his AFOSI job in 1986 and now works as a policeman in New Mexico. He is said to have adopted the somewhat untenable position that the

MJ-12 documents were faked, although an MJ-12-type group did exist.

It is difficult to believe that Doty could get involved in such scandalous activity while working in a middle-ranking intelligence role in the US Air Force without his employers knowing about it or seeking to control it in some way. I suspect Doty was given the boot precisely because he had outlived his usefulness. The fact is that his work, undertaken in the full knowledge of certain prominent UFO researchers, influenced UFO research from the mid-1980s onwards and set the scene for more extreme material to emerge in the form of the John Lear document and William Milton Cooper's *The Secret Government*, published in 1989 (Brookesmith, 1996). This culminated in the Lazar revelations of 1989–90 which have featured prominently in best-selling books on UFOs by authors like Timothy Good (1992; 1996) and also documentaries. These have tied into pre-existing beliefs about aliens and the extraterrestrial origin of both flying saucers and flying triangles. Any research which has sought to counter this barrage of alien-oriented propaganda has been largely ineffective, although it is hoped, within the more objective elements of the UFO research community, that people want more than just tales of abductions and spaceships.

Psycho-social or geo-psychical explanations do not adequately explain sightings of large structured aircraft moving slowly across the countryside. They explain neither why similar aircraft are seen in and around military facilities, nor why so many expert aviation researchers and journals have concluded that many black-project aircraft exist and are hidden from us through a variety of means.

The alien material is often confusing and entirely anecdotal, whereas we can find studies relating to advanced aircraft, artists' impressions of such aircraft having been released by companies like Lockheed-Martin, McDonnell-Douglas or even British Aerospace.

The idea that everything relates to the crash retrieval of an 'alien flying disc' at Roswell has not only been disproved, but is a clear example of the reductive thinking so prevalent within modern Ufology. No evidence for 'alien flying saucers' makes any sense. We are largely expected to believe people like Wendelle Stevens, William Cooper, Bob Lazar and Michael Wolf, although there is no reason why we should, given much better evidence that flying discs and triangles are of terrestrial origin. All too often the researchers' information sounds like a modern-day episode of *The Invaders*. Perhaps now that the Soviet threat has diminished we need a new focus for fear and paranoia?

I have appeared on many radio and TV programmes on the subject of UFOs, and I believe that the public are not particularly taken with stories about aliens and close encounters. It is just that they have had this standard fare rammed down their throats for so long. There is a definite misconception at the heart of many people's understanding of UFOs, allowed to go unchecked by well-known UFO personalities. It is simply this: there may well be aliens 'out there'; in fact I hope there are. That does not mean that they are here interacting with us on any level. There must be a distinction between Search for Extra Terrestrial Intelligence (SETI) programmes now under way and reports of UFOs. SETI is scientific and UFO reports are largely anecdotal. There is little or no evidence to suggest a link between UFOs and 'aliens'.

It seems to me that reports of close encounters might relate to some sort of natural intelligence that exists on the fringes of scientific understanding or which can only be researched unscientifically (because it is not reproducible) within the paranormal field of study.

I think we can say with a certain assurance that flying triangles, flying discs and the more unusual aircraft associated with UAV programmes are of terrestrial origin. Even if 'ET' landed tomorrow outside Whitehall and brought humanity tidings of joy this would not alter my conclusion.

The 1997 airing of *The Best Ever UFO Evidence* programme on Sky TV gave Admiral Bobby Ray Inman, former Director of the NSA and former Director of Naval Intelligence, the opportunity to make an intriguing suggestion: 'When we see these observations over military installations then instantly my perception is that we are probably observing some test of some new technology.'

I think Inman is being honest. It is interesting that in the last few years we have seen the release of very significant documents from Wright-Patterson Air Force Base including 'Electrogravitics Systems' and 'Project Silver Bug'. However, I doubt that this is the beginning of a flood of information. Nevertheless, when one starts to look at UFOs in terms of military technology in action, a whole new world of opportunity and understanding is opened up before one's eyes.

This book is largely aimed at people who are interested in UFOs, but who may suspect that the military have been using stories of aliens as a cover behind which to fly their advanced technology aircraft. Hopefully I have been able to introduce enough evidence to indicate that this is the case. I suspect that information on black projects will continue to trickle out, although we must realize that many of the projects will not be made public until well into the next century. As a result classified aircraft researchers will have a difficult job, but I am sure that the growing number of military UFO researchers will make good progress in their search for the truth behind reports of unusual craft in our skies.

We know that 'the truth is out there' and we have a pretty good idea where to look!

BIBLIOGRAPHY

Air Force 2025, Air University of America, 1996–7.

Aldrich, Jan L., '1947 – Beginning of the UFO Era', in *UFO 1947–1997, Fifty Years of Flying Saucers*, John Brown Publishing, 1997, pp. 19–28.

Angelucci, Enzo, and Bowers, Tom, *The American Fighter*, Orion, 1987.

Arnold, Kenneth, 'What Happened on June 24th 1947', in *UFO 1947–1997, Fifty Years of Flying Saucers*, John Brown Publishing, 1997, pp. 28–35.

Barlow, Bruce, *Aliens or Illusions – Penetrating the Web*, video documentary, Artsmagic Ltd, 1996.

Barnaby, Wendy, *The Plague Wars*, Vision, 1997.

Barrie, D., 'UK Funds Tornado Replacement Study', *Flight International*, 1–7 January 1997.

Basiago, Andrew D., 'Dreamland and the CIA', *MUFON UFO Journal*, No. 291, July 1992, pp. 10–12.

Beaver, Paul, 'RAF 2006', *Air International*, September 1996, pp. 165–7.

Beaver, Paul, 'Blacking Britain', in *X-Planes* (*Air Forces Monthly Special*), February 1998, pp. 69–71.

Bellamy, Christopher, 'Don't worry. If you see a flying saucer it's probably one of ours', *Independent*, 17 December 1996.

Benningfield, Damond, 'Deep Black – Probing America's most secret airbase', *Focus*, May 1995.

Beveridge, John, and Ollier, Kevin, 'The Glastonbury Triangle Enigma: Update', *UFO Reality*, June/July 1996, pp. 34–7, 57.

Birdsall, Graham W., 'Stealth', *Twenty Twenty Vision*, YUFOS, 1988, pp. 41–3.

Birdsall, Graham W., 'Area 51 – America's Dreamland', *UFO Magazine* (UK), March/April 1995.

Birdsall, Graham W., 'Welcome to the Real World – Tony Gonsalves and the B-2', *UFO Magazine* (UK), May/June 1995, pp. 26–9.

Birdsall, Graham W., 'The Flying Triangle Mystery – A genuine security threat?', *UFO Magazine* (UK), July/August 1996, pp. 42–7, 49, 64.

Bissell, Richard M., *Reflections of a Cold Warrior*, Yale University Press, 1996.

Botting, Douglas, *In the Ruins of the Reich*, George Allen & Unwin, 1985.

Bowyer, Michael, *Force for Freedom: The USAF in the UK since 1948*, Patrick Stevens, 1994.

Brookesmith, Peter, 'UFOs: A Federal case', *The Unexplained*, Vol. 5, Issue 56, 1981, pp. 1118–20.

Brookesmith, Peter, *UFOs: The Complete Sightings Catalogue*, Blandford, 1995.

Brookesmith, Peter, *UFO: The Government Files*, Blandford, 1996.

Brown, Mark, and Hall, Graham, 'The Case of the Silent Vulcan', *UFORM Report*, November 1982.

Brown, Stuart, and Douglass, Steve, 'Swing Wing Attack Plane', *Popular Science*, January 1995, pp. 54–6.

Bruce, Ian, 'The top secret springboard', *Glasgow Herald*, 18 February 1996, p. 14.

Bryan, C. E. D., *Close Encounters of the Fourth Kind*, Orion, 1995.

Bullard, Douglas. Nurflugel Flying Wings Internet site (1997) is one of the few resources with information on Horten, Lippisch and Northrop flying wings. Rare documents and photographs, section on NASA's X-Planes (X-15, X-24A and X-24B) at www.nurflugel.com

Burrows, William E., *Deep Black*, Berkley Publishing Group, 1988.

Burrows, William E., and Windrem, Robert, *Critical Mass – The Dangerous Race for Superweapons in a Fragmenting World*, Pocket Books/Simon & Schuster Ltd, 1995.

Butcher, Tim, '3,000 mph Jet Would "Surf" the Airways', *Electronic Telegraph*, Issue 448, 12 August 1996.

Butler, Phil, *War Prizes*, Midland Counties Publishers, 1994.

Campagna, Palmiro, *The UFO Files: The Canadian Connection Exposed*, Stoddart, 1997.

Campbell, Glenn, 'Lazar as a Fictional Character', *MUFON UFO Journal*, February 1994.

Campbell, Glenn, 'Tales of the Test, Part 2', *Groom Lake Desert Rat*, 17 March 1995.

Campbell, Glenn, Area 51 Research Center, and UFOMIND web site is an invaluable resource for information on Area 51, its history, its role as a secret test facility, the claims of Bob Lazar, issues of his *Groom Lake Desert Rat* newsletter and the various characters involved in the plot at www.ufomind.com

Chittenden, Maurice, 'Is it a bird? Is it a UFO? No, it's a waverider....', *The Sunday Times*, 11 August 1996.

Chomsky, Noam, *Deterring Democracy*, Vintage Books, 1992.

Chomsky, Noam, *Media Control – The Spectacular Achievements of Propaganda*, Seven Stories Press, 1997.

Clark, Jerome, *The UFO Book – Encyclopedia of the Extraterrestrial*, Omnigraphics, 1998.

Clark, Jerome, and Farish, Lucius, 'The Mysterious Foo Fighters of WW2', *UFO Report*, Spring 1975, at www.ufomind.com/ufo/updates.1997/may/m-19-004.shtml

Clarke, David, *UFO Sightings in South Yorkshire*, Vols 1–3, IUN/Enigma 1988. (Copies available from LUFOS at P.O. Box 73, Lancaster LA1 1GZ.)

Colombo, John Robert, *Mysterious Canada*, Doubleday Canada Ltd, 1988.

Cook, Nick, 'Anti-Gravity for Real', *Jane's Defence Weekly*, 10 June 1995.

Cook, Nick, 'Europe Competes with US Black Programmes', *Interavia Business and Technology*, Vol. 50, No. 592, July/August 1995, pp. 41–4.

Cook, Nick, 'Special Projects Come Out of the Black', *Jane's Defence Weekly*, 29 May 1996, pp. 18–24.

Cook, Nick, and Campbell, Christy, 'Secret US Spyplane "Crashed at Stonehenge"', *Electronic Telegraph*, 19 December 1994.

Cooper, Peter J., 'Appendages and Protrusions', *Air International*, August 1997, pp. 86–92.

Crystal, Ellen, with Cornet, Bruce, *New Revelations about UFOs at Pine Bush*, Omega Publications, 1997.

Cubitt, Duncan, with Ellis, Ken, *Vulcan – Last of the V-bombers*, Chancellor Press, 1996.

CUFON, Computer UFO Network archives. Two big files of CIA documents available at www.cufon.org. The CIA's online Popular Documents Section now includes a wealth of UFO-related material, thus the original texts can be checked: www.foia.ucia.gov

Dabrowski, Hans-Peter, *The Horton Flying Wing in World War II*, Schiffer Publishing Ltd, 1991.

Dabrowski, Hans-Peter, *Flying Wings of the Horten Brothers*, Schiffer Publishing Ltd, 1995.

Darlington, David, *Area 51 – The Dreamland Chronicles*, Henry Holt, 1997.

Devereux, Paul, and Brookesmith, Peter, *UFOs and Ufology – The First 50 Years*, Blandford, 1997.

Deyo, Stan, *The Cosmic Conspiracy*, Adventures Unlimited Press, 1992.

Douglass, Steve, 'Monitoring the Airwaves for Secret Aircraft' (an especially important site for readers seeking information about military monitoring and secret military aircraft) at www.perseids.com/projectblack

Douglass, Steve, and Brown, Stuart F., 'Flying Artichoke', *Popular Science*, December 1994, p. 16.

Douglass, Steve, and Sweetman, Bill, 'Hiding in Plane Sight', *Popular Science*, May 1997, pp. 54–9.

Durant, F. C., *Report of Meetings of Scientific Advisory Panel on UFOs Convened by Office of Scientific Intelligence*, Central Intelligence Agency, January 1953.

Ebert, Hans, and Meier, Hans, 'Prototypen – Einselschicksale deutscher Flugzeuge, der Kreisflügler AS6 V1', *Luftfahrt International*, 1980.

Ecker, Don, 'The Human Mutilation Factor', at www.netizen.org/Arc-Hive/UFO_MUT.TXT

FAS (Federation of American Scientists) This organization, set up after the Second World War, has been concerned to ensure that scientists are not just used as 'military brains', either in the USA or abroad. FAS has developed an interest in secret aircraft technologies, matters of intelligence, US government secrecy and oversight. The federation operates a very useful web site where a great deal of detailed information on mystery aircraft can be found; for example, the report on the TR-3A, at www.fas.org

Fawcett, Larry, and Greenwood, Barry, *Clear Intent*, Prentice-Hall, 1984.

Fortean Times, edited by Evans, Hilary, and Stacy, Dennis, *UFO 1947–1997, Fifty Years of Flying Saucers*, John Brown Publishing, 1997.

Fowler, Omar, *The Flying Triangle Mystery*, Phenomenon Research Association 1996, updated 1997.

Friedman, Stanton T., *Top Secret/Majic*, Marlowe & Company, 1996.

Gehrs-Paul, Andreas, *Tier Drones Summary* at www.umcc.u-mich.edu/~schars/texte.tier.htm

Gilligan, Andrew, 'Defence team gives weapons invisible cloak', *Daily Telegraph*, 22 July 1996.

Godwin, Joscelyn, *Arktos: The Polar Myth in Science, Symbolism, and Nazi Survival*, Thames & Hudson, 1993.

Gonsalves, Tony, *Stealth B-2 Bomber – The American-made UFO*, self-published, 1990.

Good, Timothy, *Above Top Secret – The Worldwide UFO Cover-Up*, Sidgwick & Jackson, 1987.

Good, Timothy, *Alien Liaison – The Ultimate Secret*, Arrow Books Ltd, 1992.

Good, Timothy, *Beyond Top Secret*, Sidgwick & Jackson, 1996.

Gourley, Scott R., 'Battlefield of the Future', *Popular Science*, August 1997, pp. 78-81.

Graham, Richard H., *SR-71 Revealed – The Inside Story*, Motorbooks International, 1996.

Gravity Research Group, *Electrogravitics Systems – An Examination of Electrostatic Motion, Dynamic Counterbary and Barycentric Control*, Gravity Research Group, Knightsbridge, 1956.

Green, William, *Warplanes of the Third Reich*, Doubleday, 1970.

Gunston, Bill, *Jane's Aerospace Dictionary*, Jane's Publications, 1986.

Gunston, Bill (ed.), *Jane's Fighting Aircraft of World War 2*, Studio, 1989 (reprinted 1997).

Gunston, Bill, *World Encyclopedia of Aircraft Manufacturers*, Patrick Stephens, 1993.

Gunston, Bill, *Warplanes of the Future*, Salamander Books, 1995.

Haines, Gerald K., 'A Die-Hard Issue, CIA's Role in the Study of UFOs, 1947–90', *Studies in Intelligence*, Vol. 01, No. 1, 1997 at www.odci.gov/csi/studies.97un-clas/ufo.html

Hall, Richard, *The UFO Evidence*, Barnes & Noble, 1964, reprinted 1997.

Hamilton, William F., III, *Alien Magic: UFO Crashes – Abductions – Underground Bases*, Global Communications, 1996.

Handleman, Philip, *Beyond the Horizon: Combat Aircraft of the 21st Century*, Airlife Publishing Ltd, 1994.

Harbinson, W. A., *Inception*, Hodder & Stoughton, 1994.

Harbinson, W. A., *Millennium*, Hodder & Stoughton, 1995.

Harbinson, W. A., *Phoenix*, Hodder & Stoughton, 1995.

Harbinson, W. A., *Projekt UFO*, Boxtree Ltd, 1995.

Heber, Charles E. Jr (DARPA), *Statement on UAV High Altitude Endurance (HAE) program, Subcommittee on AirLand Forces of the Senate Armed Services Committee on UAV Programs*, 9 April 1997 at www.darpa.mil/documents.heber_04_09-96.html

Henshall, Philip, *Hitler's Rocket Sites*, Robert Hale, 1985.

Henshall, Philip, *Vengeance: Hitler's Nuclear Weapon, Fact or Fiction?*, Motorbooks, 1995.

Hesemann, Michael, *Secrets of the Black World*, video documentary, 1993.

Hesemann, Michael, and Mantle, Philip, *Beyond Roswell*, Michael O'Mara Books Ltd, 1997.

Hill, Mike, 'This is proof of our own stealth say UFO experts', *Lancashire Evening Post*, 11 December 1996.

Horten, Reimar, 'The Idea', at www.nurflugel.com

Horten, Reimar, 'Towards the Theory of Flying Wings', at www.nurflugel.com

Hynek, Allen J., *The UFO Experience: A Scientific Enquiry*, Ballantine, 1972.

Hynek, Allen J., *The Hynek UFO Report*, Dell, 1977.

Imbrogno, Philip J., 'Government Cover-up of a Classic UFO Case', 1990 (?), at www.members.aol.com/asmorrison/hudson.txt

Imbrogno. Philip J., 'Incident at Indian Point', at www.iufog.com/spotlight.incident.html

Imbrogno, Philip J., and Horrigan, Marianne, *Contact of the 5th Kind*, Llewellyn Publications, 1997.

Imbrogno, Philip J., Pratt, Bob, and Hynek, J. Allen, *Night Siege: The Hudson Valley UFO Sightings*, Ballantine, 1987.

IUFOG (Internet UFO Group) declassified US intelligence documents archive (see list below).

> Air Force investigation into Muroc Field sightings, 8 July 1947:
>
> Final report File No. 1208-1
>
> Date 18 August 1947
>
> Controlling Office – Air Defense Command, Mitchel Field (report written in response to Air Defense Command request entitled 'Investigation of Flying Disc', file D333.5 ID.)
>
> (includes submissions from 1st Lieutenant Joseph C. McHenry)

> Letter from prospector Fred Johnson to Headquarters, Fourth Air Force, dated 20 August 1947 reporting a flying disc sighting on the same day as Kenneth Arnold.
>
> File reference 4AFDA
>
> Date 25 August 1947
>
> Headquarters Fourth Air Force, Office of the Assistant Chief of Staff, A-2 Intelligence, Hamilton Field, California.
>
> Author – Lieutenant-Colonel Donald Springer
>
> Enclosed – true copy of letter from Fred M. Johnson

> Subject – 'Air Material Command Opinion Concerning Flying Discs'
>
> File reference TSDIN/HMM/ig/6-4100
>
> Date 23 September 1947
>
> Headquarters – Air Material Command, Wright Field, Dayton, Ohio.
>
> Author – Lieutenant-General Nathan Twining.
>
> Sent to – Brigadier-General George F. Schulgen (Commanding General, Army Air Force, Washington 25, D.C) AC/AS2.

'Schulgen Memo'
Subject – 'Intelligence Requirements of Flying Saucer Type Aircraft'.
Date – 28 October 1947
Air Intelligence Requirements Division, Office of Assistant Chief of Air
   Staff (AS) 2.
Author – Brigadier-General George F. Schulgen.
(Includes 'Inclosure' headed 'Research and Development' which goes into
   detail about intelligence requirements related to German flying-wing
   aircraft.)

Subject – Flying Saucers
File reference – APO 159
Date – 10 November 1947
Headquarters – Air Material Command, Wright Field, Dayton, Ohio.
To – Commanding Officer Bayreuth Sub Region – Counter Intelligence Corps
   (CIC) Europe, Region Vl (970th Counter Intelligence Corps Detachment).
(Requests information on German aircraft specialists and test-pilots with
   knowledge of flying wing/flying saucer aircraft.)

'Horten Letter'
Subject – Horten Brothers (Flying Saucers)
File reference – APO 742, US ARMY
Date – 16 December 1947
From – US Army Intelligence HQ, Berlin.
To – Deputy Director of Intelligence, European Command, Frankfurt, APO
   757, US Army.

Subject – 'Flying Object Incidents in the United States'
File reference – T-73017
Date 3 November 1948
From – Major C. P. Cabell, Major-General USAF, Director of Intelligence,
   Office of Deputy Chief of Staff, Operations.
To – Commanding General, Air Material Command, Wright-Patterson Air
   Force Base, Dayton, Ohio.
Subject – 'US Air Intelligence Division Study No. 203, 10 December 1948'.
Date: 10 December 1948
File reference: 100-203-70 (reference no. on facing page. Refer to as Air
   Intelligence Report or (AIR) 100-203-79

Subject – 'Headquarters USAF Air Intelligence Report' (referred to as AIR 100-
   203-79).
'Analysis of Flying Object Incidents in the U.S.'
File reference – 100-203-79
Date – 28 April 1949

From – Headquarters United States Air Force Directorate of Intelligence,
Washington, DC
(Goes into some detail about important UFO sightings and the possible
technologies behind them. Lists detailed information about Flying Wing
and Flying Saucer aircraft. Includes famous Rhoads photographs of UFO
taken on 7 July 1947.)

These documents and others can be read and downloaded from the
following web site at http://www.iufog.org/project1947

Jacobs, David M., *The UFO Controversy in America*, IUP, 1975.
Jane's All the World's Aircraft, 1995–6, Jane's Information Group.
Jane's All the World's Aircraft, 1997–8, Jane's Information Group.
Jeffrey, Kent, 'Roswell, Anatomy of a Myth', *UFO Magazine* (UK),
September/October 1997, pp. 4–11, 62–5.
Jones, J., *Stealth Technology – The Art of Black Magic*, Airlife Publishing Ltd, 1989
Jones, R. V., *Reflections on Intelligence*, William Heinemann Ltd, 1989.
Jung, Carl Gustav, *Flying Saucers: A Modern Myth of Things Seen in the Skies*,
Princeton University Press, 1991.
Jungk, Robert, *Brighter Than a Thousand Suns*, Harcourt Brace, 1970.
Keel, John, *Operation Trojan Horse*, Putnam, 1970.
Keyhoe, Donald E., *Flying Saucers from Outer Space*, Wingate–Baker, 1953,
reprinted 1969.
King, Jon, 'Nightmare on Salisbury Plain', *UFO Reality*, December 1996/January
1997, pp. 9–12.
Klee, E., and Merk, O., *The Birth of the Missile: The Secrets of Peenemunde*, Harrap, 1965.
Lake, John, 'Secret Missions of the Stealth – The F117A stealth fighter's Tonopah
years', *Combat Aircraft*, February/March 1998, pp. 368–76.
Lindemann, Michael, 'Witness says US had flying saucer in 1946', CNI News,
1997 (based on a story featured in the *Lancaster New Era* newspaper,
Lancaster, Pennsylvania, 12 July 1997).
Lockheed Horizons , 'We Own the Night!', Lockheed Corporation, May 1992.
Loewy, Robert G., 'Recent Developments in Smart Structures with Aeronautical
Applications', *Smart Materials and Structures* , Vol. 6, No. 5, Institute of
Physics Publishing, October 1997, pp. R11–R35.
Long, Roger, and Ruffle, Robert, 'More Truth Is Out', *Air Forces Monthly*, June
1997, pp. 17, 22.
Lopez, Ramon, 'USN Considers Future UCAV...as Northrop Grumman Reveals
Stealth Design', *Flight International*, 2–8 July 1997, p. 20.
Lusar, Rudolph, *German Secret Weapons of World War II*, Neville Spearman, 1959.
Maccabee, Bruce, 'The McMinnville Photos, in The Spectrum of UFO Research',
Proceedings of the 2nd CUFOS Conference, September 1981, Centre for UFO
Studies, 1988.

McCall, Ken, 'Stealth Search for History', July 1997, at www.lasvegassun.com

McClure, Kevin, 'Recovered Memory and Hypnosis Special', *Abduction Watch*, self-published newsletter, February 1998.

McClure, Kevin, 'Yesterday Belongs to Me', *Abduction Watch*, self-published newsletter, March/April 1998.

McClure, Kevin, *Secrets or Lies*, self-published essay, 1998.

McDaid, Hugh, and Oliver, David, *Robot Warriors*, Orion Media, 1997.

McGinnis, Paul, Freedom Ridge Oversight Group Incorporated: an international web site which has a good deal of information on US military intelligence matters and secret military aircraft. McGinnis is very concerned about issues of secrecy and oversight at www.frogie.org

McGovern, James, *Crossbow and Overcast*, Hutchinson & Co., 1965.

McManners, Hugh, 'Plastic Tanks for Stealth Warfare', *The Times*, 29 September 1996.

Maher, John, and Groves, Judy, *Chomsky for Beginners*, Icon Books, 1996.

Mahood, Tom, Blue Fire web site. This web site contains detailed information about Bob Lazar and his claims relating to Area 51 and 'S4', where he claims to have worked (Mahood is very critical of Lazar's position) at www.serve.com/mahood/bluefire.htm

Marchetti, Victor and Marks, John D., *The CIA and the Cult of Intelligence*, Cape, 1974.

Masters, David, *German Jet Genesis*, Jane's Publishing Company, 1982.

Matthews, Tim, *Stealth, Lies and Videotapes*, self-published, Southport, 1996.

Matthews, Tim, 'Military UFO Programme Exposed', *UFO Reality*, February/March 1997, pp. 25–7.

Matthews, Tim, 'The New Ufology', *Sightings*, November 1997.

Miele, Frank, 'Giving the Devil His Due', at www.skeptic.com/02.4.miele.holocaust.html

Miller, Jay, *Northrop B-2 Spirit*, Midland Publishing Ltd, 1995.

Miller, Jay, *Lockheed's Skunk Works*, Aerofax/Midland Publishing Ltd, 1995.

Miranda, J., and Mercado P., 'German Circular Planes', 'Reichdreams', Dossier No. 10, self-published.

Moseley, Jim, *Saucer Smear*, Vol. 44, Nos 8, 9.

Moulton-Howe, Linda, *An Alien Harvest: Further Evidence Linking Animal Mutilations and Human Abductions to Alien Life Forms*, Linda Moulton-Howe Publications, 1989.

Munson, Kenneth, *World Unmanned Aircraft*, Jane's Publishing Company Ltd, 1988.

Munson, Kenneth, UAV Directory Parts 1 and 2, *Air International*, July 1997, pp. 40–6.

New World Vistas: Air and Space Power for the 21st Century, USAF Scientific Advisory Board, December 1995–6.

Northrop, Jack, 'The Development of All-wing Aircraft', transcript of the 25th Wilbur Wright Memorial Lecture to the members of the Royal Aeronautical Society, 29 May 1947 at www.nurflugel.com

Oliver, D., 'The Next Fifty Years: USAF – Celebrating Fifty Years of the US Air Force', *Air Forces Monthly Special*, April 1997, pp. 76–80.

Oliver, D., *Sky Robots, in X-Planes* (Air Forces Monthly Special), February 1998, pp. 72–5.

Osborne, Richard, 'An Introduction to Waveriders'; 'An Historical Overview of Waverider Evolution' (Staar Research) at www.gbnet/orgs.staar/wavehist.html

Patton, Phil, 'Stealth Watchers', *Wired*, 2 February 1994.

Patton, Phil, *Travels in Dreamland*, Orion Media, 1997.

Peebles, Curtis, *Dark Eagles: A History of Top Secret U.S. Aircraft Programmes*, Presidio Press, 1995.

Pflock, Karl, *Roswell in Perspective*, Fund for UFO Research, 1994.

Pike, Dr John, 'Security and Classification', at www.awpi.com/Intel-web/US/misc/classification.html

Pocock, Chris, 'Groom Lake – The top secret base that officially doesn't exist', *USAF Yearbook*, 1997, pp. 22–6.

Pocock, R. F., *German Guided Missiles*, Ian Allan, 1966.

Pope, Nick, *Open Skies, Closed Minds*, Simon & Schuster, 1996.

Potter, Clive, 'Silent Vulcan Makes a Reappearance', *IUN/Enigma*, Ref. UF 24, April 1985.

Potter, Clive, 'Encounter with Silent Vulcan at Uttoxeter', IUN, 1989.

Powers, Max, 'Area 51, Behind the Black Curtain', *High Times*, Vol. 240, August 1995.

Randle, Kevin, and Schmitt, Don, *The Truth about the UFO Crash at Roswell*, Evans, 1995.

Randles, Jenny, *UFO Retrievals*, Blandford, 1995.

Randles, Jenny, *MIB – The Men In Black Phenomenon*, Judy Piatkus Publishers Ltd, 1997.

Ranelagh, *The Agency: The Rise and Decline of the CIA*, Sceptre, 1988.

Ransom, Stephen, and Fairclough, Robert, *English Electric Aircraft*, Putnam/ Conway Maritime Press, 1987.

Redfern, Nicholas, *A Covert Agenda*, Simon & Schuster, 1997.

Redfern, Nicholas, and Bott, Irene, 'Flying Triangles and Historical Perspective', *Alien Encounters* magazine, Christmas 1997.

Rich, Ben R., and Janos, Leo, *Skunk Works*, Warner Books, 1995.

Roberts, Andy, and Clarke, David, *Phantoms of the Sky*, Robert Hale, 1990.

Rodeghier, Mark, *UFO Reports Involving Vehicle Interference: A Catalogue and Data Analysis*, Centre for UFO Studies, 1981.

Rogers, Jim, 'RAF Radar Tracked "Aurora" over Scotland at Speeds from Mach 3 to Mach 6', *Inside the Air Force*, 24 April 1992, pp. 1, 10–11.

Rose, Bill, 'Forces of Darkness', *The Unopened Files*, No. 1, 1996, pp. 75–80.

Rose, Bill, 'The Hidden Aurora', *UFO Magazine* (UK), March/April 1996, pp. 4–7.

Rose, Bill, 'America's Secret Spaceship', *UFO Magazine*, September/October 1997, pp. 51–3, 72–3.

Ruppelt, Edward J., *The Report on Unidentified Flying Objects*, Doubleday, 1956.

Sauder, Richard, *Underground Bases and Tunnels*, Adventures Unlimited Press, 1995.

Sayer, Ian, and Botting, Douglas, *America's Secret Army*, Grafton, 1989.

Schick, Walter, and Meyer, Ingolf, *Luftwaffe Secret Projects*, Midland Publishing Ltd, 1997.

Scott, Bill, 'Recent Sightings of XB-70-like Aircraft Reinforce 1990 Reports from Edwards Area', *Aviation Week and Space Technology*, 24 August 1992, pp. 23–4.

Scully, Frank, *Behind the Flying Saucers*, Henry Holt & Company, 1950.

Sheffield, Derek, *UFO – A Deadly Concealment*, Blandford, 1996.

Simpson, Christopher, *Blowback – America's Recruitment of Nazis and Its Effects on the Cold War*, Weidenfeld & Nicolson, 1988.

Sivier, David, 'Heart of Darkness – Notes towards the deconstruction of a myth', *Strange Daze*, No. 15, February 1998.

Späte, Wolfgang, *Top Secret Bird – The Luftwaffe's Me-163 Comet*, Pictorial Histories Publishing Co. and Bookcraft, 1989.

Spaulding, William H., 'UFOs – The case for a cover-up', *The Unexplained*, Vol. 5, No. 53, 1981, pp. 1041–6.

Spaulding, William, H., 'Agents of Confusion', *The Unexplained*, Vol. 5, No. 55, 1981, pp. 1086–9.

Spencer, John, *Gifts of the Gods? Are UFOs Alien Visitors or Psychic Phenomena?*, Virgin Books, 1994.

Steinman, Williams with Stevens, Wendelle C., *UFO Crash at Aztec*, self-published (Boulder, Colorado), 1986–7.

Stirniman, Robert, *Electrogravitic Reference List*, at www.padrak.com/ine.RS_REFS.html

Strieber, Ann, 'How Disinformation Agents Spread Fear about the UFOs', *Communion Newsletter*, Vol. 1, No. 3, Autumn 1989, pp. 1–3, 13.

Sutton, Richard, 'Scotland's Invisible Flying Objects', *UFO Magazine* (UK), May/June 1996, pp. 50–3.

Sweetman, Bill, *Stealth Aircraft – Secrets of Future Airpower*, Airlife Publishing, 1986.

Sweetman, Bill, *Stealth Bomber: Invisible Warplane, Black Budget*, Motorbooks International, 1989.

Sweetman, Bill, 'Mystery Contact May Be Aurora', *Jane's Defence Weekly*, 28 February 1992, p. 333.

Sweetman, Bill, 'Hypersonic Aurora – A Secret Drawing?', *Jane's Defence Weekly*, 12 December 1992.

Sweetman, Bill, *Aurora – The Pentagon's Secret Hypersonic Spyplane*, Motorbooks International, 1993.

Sweetman, Bill, 'The Future of Airborne Stealth', *International Defence Review*, March 1994, pp. 31–8.

Sweetman, Bill, 'The Invisible Men', *Air and Space*, April/May 1997, pp. 18–27.

Sweetman, Bill, 'B-2 Spirit – The "Stealth Bomber"', *World Air Power Journal*, Vol. 31, Winter 1997, pp. 46–95.

Sweetman, Bill, 'Area 51 – No Past – No Future', *X-Planes*, February 1998.

Sweetman, Bill, and Goodall, James C., *Lockheed F-117A: Operation and Development of the Stealth Fighter*, Foulis/Haynes, 1990.

UK (L)2 – En Route Low Altitude Chart, No. 1 AIDU, RAF Flight Information Publication, August 1997.

Urban, Mark, *UK Eyes Alpha: The Inside Story of British Intelligence*, Faber & Faber, 1996.

Vallee, Jacques, *Passport to Magonia*, Spearman, 1970.

Van Utrecht, Wim, 'The Belgian 1989–1990 UFO Wave', in *Fortean Times*, ed. Evans, Hilary, and Stacy, Dennis, *UFO: Fifty Years of Flying Saucers*, John Brown Publishing, 1997.

Van Utrecht, Wim, 'The Belgium Wave, A Three-cornered Affair', *The New Ufologist*, No. 6, 1997, pp. 4–13.

Verga, Maurizio, UFO Online Internet web site, includes sections on possible German flying saucer and secret weapons developments, at www.ufo.it

Vesco, Renate, *Intercettateli senza Sparare*, Mursia, 1968 (translated into English and re-published by Grove Press in 1971 as *Intercept but Don't Shoot*, and again in 1974 by Zebra as *Intercept UFO*).

Vesco, Renate, and Childress, David Hatcher, *Man-Made UFOs 1944–1994*, Adventures Unlimited Press, 1994.

Vicary, Adrian, *British Jet Aircraft*, Patrick Stephens, 1982.

Walden, Michael. Information on his airships and other material are available at www.nevada.edu/home/8/walden/ltas01.html

White, William J., *Airships for the Future*, Sterling Publishing Co., Inc., 1978.

Williams, Matthews, 'MOD Bundle', *Truthseekers Review Special*, 1997.

Windle, David, 'Hypersonic waveriders take off', *The Sunday Times*, 23 March 1997.

Windle, David, 'X-Flyers', *Tomorrow's World* magazine, pp. 30–1, April 1998.

Wood, Derek, *Project Cancelled: The Story of Britain's Abandoned Aircraft Projects*, Jane's Publishing Inc., 1986.

Zinngrabe, Dan, Black Dawn Internet web site. Important information about secret military aircraft including the Tier 3, Aurora, Brilliant Buzzard, declassified documents and more at www.macconnect.com/~quellish

Note: An Explanation of 'AIR'

In the UK, AIR refers to Air Ministry, the precursor of the combined services Ministry of Defence. The files relating to investigations of 'UFOs' at the Public Record Office (PRO), Kew, are located via the PRO Eureka Database. The file AIR 14/2800 is therefore an Air Ministry file from 1943. This file relates to UFO reports, known at the time as 'foo fighter' sightings, made during RAF bomber raids in 1943. Researchers can visit the PRO and request files released by the government.

In the USA, AIR 100-203-79, for example, is the correct designation for: 'Headquarters US Air Intelligence Report
Date 28 April 1949, No. 100-203-79
Headquarters United States Air Force Directorate of Intelligence Washington D.C.
Top Secret'.

This document was actually completed in 1948, hence the information relates to sightings up to and including 1 August 1948. It should always be described as: AIR 100-203-79.

INDEX